How to Grow as a
Musician

How to Grow as a
Musician

What All Musicians
Must Know to Succeed

SHEILA E. ANDERSON

ALLWORTH PRESS
NEW YORK

© 2005 Sheila E. Anderson

09 08 07 06 05   5 4 3 2 1

Published by Allworth Press
An imprint of Allworth Communications, Inc.
10 East 23rd Street, New York, NY 10010

Cover design by Derek Bacchus
Interior design by Mary Belibasakis
Page composition/typography by Integra Software Services
Author cover photograph by Vince Diga

ISBN:1-58115-416-X

LIBRARY OF CONGRESS CATALOGING-IN-PUBLICATION DATA

Anderson, Sheila E.
   How to grow as a musician: what all musicians must know to succeed/Sheila E. Anderson.
   p.   cm.
   Includes index.
1. Music–Vocational guidance.   I. Title.

ML3795.A827 2005
780'.23–dc22

2005010278

Printed in Canada

Dedication

In loving memory of my friend, Harvey S. Wise, who passed away on November 15, 2003, one year to the day that I turned in my manuscript.

Contents

Acknowledgments

I have Tad Crawford to thank for suggesting that I take on this book. He is to me what an executive producer is to a musician! I thank my editor, Nicole Potter, as always, for her guidance. Thanks to the rest of the Allworth Press staff: Monica P. Lugo; Derek Bacchus for the cover; and Michael Madole, Nana Greller, and Cynthia Rivelli for marketing.

I must thank all of the musicians who allowed me to peek into their minds and hearts. A special thanks to Eric Reed who came to my rescue, providing me with books, a link to some musicians, and copies of their music. As always, he has gone above and beyond the call of duty. Thanks to Jeff Clayton, who continues to keep me amused and on point and is always full of good advice. Jeff and Eric are my anchors. And, thanks to Gary Walker, Howard Nashel, Carl Griffin, James Browne, Laura Hartmann, and my dear friend David Alexander who returned my call even though we had not spoken in months.

The transcribing of the interviews was, at times, a bit taxing, so I thank Awilda Rivera for her assistance. Thanks to Gerald Cannon, Sandrine Stoffalani, and Vince Diga for graciously submitting art and ideas for the cover. Thanks also to all of the staff at The Newark Museum, specifically Lucy Brotman, Linda Nettleton, and Kim Robelda-Diga. I must thank them for their patience and understanding when I functioned with little sleep, especially Linda who reminded me that "I could."

Thank you to all my friends and family who still love me after my disappearing act for months. This book kept me up many late nights into the wee hours of the morning. It was Brian Delp, the overnight weekday host on WBGO, Jazz 88.3FM, who kept me company by playing such great music. Thanks, Brian!

Introduction

This is a book about growth, success, and personal discovery. It is designed for musicians who want more out of their careers—although you do not have to be a musician to benefit from the wisdom of the people interviewed. Most of the interviews are from musicians, but I have included non-musicians in the music industry in Part Five, "On the Business."

In my ten years working in the jazz community as a radio announcer and as a TV talk-show host/producer, I have met many musicians. Often our conversations turn to musicianship. I have discovered that, for the most part, musicians are divided into two groups: the A-team and the B-team. I once asked Jeff Clayton his definition of these teams, and he said, "The A-team is made up of those who are always working, and the B-team is made up of those who are barely working." Upon further investigation, I found the team concept to be much more complex than that, although the A-team does tend to work more often and get the best work. Throughout this book, I use actual examples of the situations, behavior, and characteristics of musicians in each group to help you to understand the differences. At the end of the book a self-evaluation has been provided for you to determine which team you are on and where you fit.

Success is defined in many ways, and it is subjective. You might judge your success by your monetary status, your social standing, your celebrity—or all three. Chick Corea wrote an article entitled "The Function of an Artist" in the October 28, 1971 issue of *downbeat* magazine in which he restated what saxophonist Jeff Clayton once told me about what an artist needs to have in order to succeed. Jeff said that each musician/artist must have 100 percent of three things to be successful: ability, business acumen, and drive. It did not matter what percent of each was present, but together, the three parts had to equal 100 percent:

❁ ❁ ❁ ❁

*A composer who has developed his artform very far (technology) and
has the best intentions with it (ethics) but who makes no attempt to have*

his music performed (administration) will not be successful. Or, a painter who has good intentions (ethics) and promotes his work a lot (admin) but whose paintings are lacking in quality (tech) won't be successful. Or a film-maker who has a quality product (tech) and promotes it well (admin) but whose intentions are to enslave others for personal gain (ethics) will, in the long run, fail. So an artist is and does all these things well when he is functioning successfully.

❄ ❄ ❄ ❄

The musicians interviewed in this book are from varied genres, but all have integrated those elements that have led to their success. Many of the musicians I interviewed are people I have listened to over the years: Edwin Hawkins, Al Jarreau, Ron Carter, Oscar Brown Jr., and Ruth Brown. When I watched *The Arsenio Hall Show* years ago, it never occurred to me that I would one day meet Arsenio's musical director, Michael Wolff. Michael was extremely candid about everything, especially when I asked him about some of his pet peeves:

"Most people are mediocre, librarians, doctors, musicians ... They don't listen; they don't play great. I hate when you go to a gig and some musician onstage says, 'Thanks for supporting live music' ... I feel [like saying] F-you! I say if you are not getting much out of the music, don't come support this shit. If it needs to die, let it die. That's bullshit! What is this, a charity? When I'm giving new music, I am giving you a gift! If you don't want it, don't take it; if you want it, I'm going to open up my heart and give it everything I have to give ... that's my approach to the music. I want you to love it! If you don't feel it, you don't feel it. It's not intellectual."

Though I had known Dorothy Lawson for many years, we had never had an extensive conversation about music. We had met when my friend Nancy Cristy introduced me to the late Florence Joffe, who, at the age of eighty, had been quite taken with the young Dorothy. I had attended several of her performances, and so I was shocked to see Dorothy as part of Ron Carter's "Nonet." Not so surprising was her insight into who she is and how she keeps the different parts of her life together.

I found the musicians to be generous, introspective, and, most of all, humorous. The oldest person was John Levy, who at the age of ninety-two continues to look to the future. Though he has not been a working musician for many years, he has evolved into a manager. He had much to share about the business of music and the success of those whom he has managed. He has no plans to retire; he says he has "half-eimer's not Alzheimer's."

Ruth Brown has been able to keep a positive spin on life, too; her life seems to be about perspective. She told many amusing stories but each taught a lesson. On her experience in the movie *Hairspray*: "I was doing a play called *Stagolee* with Adam Wade. An agent came in and asked if I would read for a movie. The woman was to have been a disc jockey. When I went to try out, I had no idea who Jon Waters was. I did not meet him until I went to Allentown, Pennsylvania, to film. When they brought in that white wig, I said, '*No way!*' It was the first day of shooting, and I met Divine, too. He said, 'Put that wig on your head, child, and let's make some money.' I think about him every time I get a check for *Hairspray*."

Ms. Brown was sheer inspiration. At the age of seventy-six, after losing everything in an earthquake, as well as enduring colon cancer and a stroke, she has come back with a vengeance and continues to thrill audiences with her singing. Her life has had its challenges, yet she holds no bitterness.

The youngest person interviewed is pianist Eric Reed, who, at thirty-four, is mature beyond his years. I have always been impressed with his ability to grow and adapt to the world around him. Oscar Brown Jr. had me in stitches, not only when I interviewed him, but also when I transcribed the interview. I was curious to hear his reaction to hip hop. Although it has done little to further his career (which spans over fifty years in the business), "it helps my morale," said Oscar. If there is anyone who can turn lemons into lemonade, it is Oscar Brown.

At the time of our interview, David Randolph was ninety years old and showed no sign of slowing down. Our two hours together were fascinating. When I asked David if music is mathematical, his answer surprised me:

"*Emphatic . . . no!* It is an absolute canard, a falsehood. The idea has gotten so much currency. When a chef does cooking, it's a matter of how much ingredients, that's mathematics. The man who made your chair, which you are sitting on, knows more about mathematics than a musician, an artist, or a painter. You can quote me on this . . . *Remove it from your lexicon.* Music and math are no more related. You count one, two, three, four; that is simple arithmetic."

Then there is Bobby Sanabria, one of the most enthusiastic people I know. He is a man high on life and music. He is kinetic and mercurial, perhaps because he is a Gemini. Our interview took place at 2:00 A.M. in "his office"—which is his car. What was supposed to be one hour turned into more than two. Bobby has had a colorful life; he "grew up in the glory days of radio and in what was to become the hot bed of new music, hip hop. It was an amazing time period that will never be duplicated. In 1973 hip hop was beginning. I knew about it but did not really listen. That was happening in the North Bronx; I grew up in Fort Apache—the South Bronx, the example of urban decay. The only thing that kept us alive was the music. It gave us joy and hope, and salsa was born, and Fania Records was born. They signed up groups and got the music heard. Lou Donaldson, George Benson, Cannonball Addereley, Nancy Wilson, and others lived in the Bronx. By 1977 that was it. The blackout did it."

I enjoyed interviewing musicians who were eager to talk about their connections to other musicians. Edwin Hawkins had a great influence on Gospel music, and one person touched by Edwin was Richard Smallwood.

"Edwin Hawkins was a great influence on me. He set the foundation, taking Gospel music to the masses as opposed to just being in church. He and those after him, like Kirk Franklin, got flak from traditional church folks. Now it seems tame, but in 1969, it was very new and different. He set the precedence in spite of the church's narrow-minded, self-righteous opinions. Jesus Christ was out talking to the masses, and that is what we are supposed to do. Before 'Oh, Happy Day,' there were no [Gospel] artists playing on secular stations. The only exception was, maybe, Mahalia Jackson."

I was curious to find out how my interviewees defined Gospel music, given how much of what I hear sounds like any other popular music, including hip hop. Both Richard Smallwood and Edwin Hawkins agree that it is about the message, the lyrics. Says Richard: "Gospel means 'the Good News of Jesus Christ,' so the message is what makes Gospel music. It is not a particular style that can say this is Gospel music; it does not have to have certain chord changes. I believe that Gospel can have any kind of playing. It's black music, and in terms of feel, you can't escape what black music is. All black music is related, and all [of it] comes from the same roots. Now God is using a lot of young artists to reach a crowd that 'Amazing Grace' will not reach. When they hear the sound, the message will go forth."

Edwin elaborated, "The first part, my definition of music, the root of music is Gospel, the Gospel is Jesus Christ. I had a serious encounter with secular musicians. It is strange how when it is time for them to do something that they think is spiritual or Gospel, their mentality changes. They think that the music itself has to change, but that is not the case necessarily. It's easier for one who has lived the life of Gospel music to write Gospel than it is for those in secular [life]. You can't just all of a sudden give a proper delivery of music if you have not lived in that."

As you will see, my quest to find out how a musician grows lead me down all sorts of spiritual and secular byways.

Like Corea and Clayton said, to succeed as a musician, you have to have a handle on all aspects of the business, not just the artist part. That is the reason I interviewed a lawyer, a club owner, a radio person, a manager, and a record-label executive. Carl Griffin has had an extensive career as a producer, an A&R (artist-and-repertoire) guy, and as the head of a label. He expressed dismay concerning what has become of some of his peers:

"Myself, who signed Diana Krall and Jane Monheit; Brian Bacchas, who, while at Blue Note Records signed Norah Jones; and Jerry Griffith, who, when at Arista Records, signed Whitney Houston. Three black guys who got no credit for this, three of the main talents, signed by black men, who never got the recognition they deserved. All are out of the business except for me. We should be at the height of our careers for what we've done, especially Brian. Norah is selling *beaucoup* records! My idols were George Butler, Tim Tyrell at Epic; those are the black men in the business that I looked up to. From the rap side, you have Russell Simmons and P. Diddy, but on the jazz side, where are the black guys? On the business side of it, this needs to be addressed; executives should be hired."

The importance of radio is a frequent topic of discussion. Carl said, "Radio has always been a partner to the record label. Even in the old days of payola, it was the program director or a jock who knew what the market called for; no consultant in Arizona can determine that. You need a record being played to effect sales. In jazz radio, like public radio, the audience wants to hear classics, but you have to assign special programs for new artists so that they can be heard, tour, and sell CDs."

Several jazz musicians, especially members of the younger generation, believe that it is the responsibility of the radio stations to create "hits." Gary Walker, music director and weekday morning host on WBGO, Jazz 88.3FM, stated, "the possibility of a hit being made always exists. I don't think that we need to take one tune of, let's say, Stefon Harris, and just play that and eliminate all other tunes of his catalog. I think that if musicians understood that making a hit would mean that only one song of theirs would be played, they wouldn't like it. That would defeat any purpose that they have in mind."

This book is not a book of back-to-back interviews, but a book of themes. There are six sections: on development as an artist; on composing; on personal growth; on putting on a performance; on the business; and self-evaluation, in which you, the reader, get to determine your own place in the music world, whether on the A-team or the B-team.

You may ask what gives *me* the authority, or the nerve, to address this subject of success, as Al Jarreau said to me when I called him for the interview: "*You've got balls!*" He pointed out that the topics of this book are actually a lot like semesters in college. I have a bachelor of arts degree from Bernard M. Baruch College, but I say that I got my advanced degrees by immersing myself in the music community and from my quest to succeed. Michael Bourne, on-air announcer on WBGO, Jazz 88.3FM, gave me the moniker "The Queen of Hang." When I decided to get involved in the jazz community, I went to every jam session, club, and jazz festival that I could attend. I made a point to meet everyone, and I was happy to be accepted so quickly.

I observed a vast difference in conversation, mindset, and approach to career as I moved up the musical food chain. One of the differences between the groups of musicians was how they saw themselves and their art. The more successful the musician, the more interesting the conversation became. They spent time telling funny stories, talking about ideas. Most times, members of the A-team were constantly working, and they never complained about anyone taking their gigs, or *not* getting gigs.

The path that lead me to write this book is really a part of my life path, which has been a journey of self-discovery. As far back as I can remember, I asked the question, "What was I born to do?" In my search for the perfect career path, my road has taken many twists and turns. As a child, I read several self-help books (and I continue to do so), such as *The Magic of Believing*, *The Power of Positive Thinking*, and *In Search of the Meaning of Life*. In addition, I have been consumed with biographies, autobiographies, and books of interviews. My interests have always been in music, art, literature, and especially in the people who created it. My siblings and I had to take music lessons. Of the many instruments I studied, I played the piano, the recorder, and lastly the flute. I abandoned my aspirations to be a jazz flutist when I got involved in civil rights and I realized that I did not want to do the necessary work to be a full-time musician.

As I looked for the perfect arena in which to work, I delved deep inside myself to understand and learn what I am good at. It was and still is my belief that if I found the right field, I would find a way to be successful. I worked in publishing, considered getting a degree in social work, went to bartending school, attended modeling school (on the suggestion of my mother), but nothing came out of any of these things. What did happen, however, was that I got hired, temporarily, to host

Sunday Morning Harmony on WBGO, Jazz 88.3FM. My temporary job turned into nine years as the show host, and I now host *Late Night Jazz* on Saturday nights on the same station.

I used to wish that I had been alive during the Harlem Renaissance, living as a wealthy patron of the arts who hosted Sunday brunches for the intelligentsia of the day. Reading and hearing about those who lived at that time gave me goose bumps. In a way, I have been able to create for myself a life that resembles the experience I imagined. I am surrounded by artists who continue to have a positive effect on me.

I have learned so much from all of the people that I interviewed. All have taken different roads to reach their goals and to continue in the game. I am forever enriched from hearing their knowledge and experiencing their wisdom. The interviews were their gift to me; this book is my gift to you.

Who's Who

David Alexander

David Alexander is a previous National Black Music marketing director at PolyGram/Universal Distributors and a previous regional vice president of sales at Motown Records. He is currently in special markets with Viacom.

Kenny Barron

Kenny Barron moved to New York in 1961 where he worked briefly with James Moody, Lee Morgan, Roy Haynes, and Lou Donaldson. Most significant were his four years playing and recording with Dizzy Gillespie (1962–66). Barron followed that important association with periods in the groups of Freddie Hubbard (1966–70), Yusef Lateef (1970–75), and Ron Carter's two-bass quartet (1976–80). Barron was a co-leader of the group Sphere in the 1980s, and went on to be the leader of his own trios. He was the pianist on Stan Getz's final session (a series of brilliant duets) and has recorded many dates as a leader. In the 1990s, Barron received long overdue recognition. Since 1992, he has received nine Grammy nominations for only a few of his recordings, including *People Time*, *Freefall* (2002), and *Wanton Spirit*. His latest recording is *Canta Brasil*. His Web site is *www.kennybarron.com*.

D. Channsin Berry

A native of Maplewood, New Jersey, "Chann," as his friends refer to him, is a graduate of Rutgers University with a bachelor of arts in journalism/film. He moved to the Bay Area in 1984 to work as a disc jockey, and then he moved to Los Angeles in 1993 to work for Disney Studios in the area of development finance for feature films. Currently he is working on his documentary; directing/producing *The New York Turntable* and the video documentary, *The Black-Line*, a profile of the African-American male over sixty-five. His third project in the works is the much-anticipated film, *Hand over Heart*, directed and produced by Berry, starring Richard Roundtree, Beverly Todd, and Clifton Powell. Berry directed the Chaka Khan music video for "Never Miss the Water," which received a Grammy Award nomination in 1997 for Best R&B Performance by a Duo or Group with Vocal.

Andy Bey

One of the great unsung heroes of jazz singing, Andy Bey is a commanding interpreter of lyrics who has a wide vocal range and a rich, full voice. *Ballads, Blues, & Bey*, released in 1996, was considered his "comeback" album. Subsequent releases, *Shades of Bey*, *Tuesdays in Chinatown*, and *American Song* (2004) have met with great acclaim. *American Song* received a Grammy Award nomination for Best Jazz Vocal.

Oscar Brown Jr.

At the age of seventy-eight, Oscar Brown Jr. lives like a man with not much time, yet also like a man with all of the time in the world. The Chicago-born composer, singer, actor, playwright, and director, who spent more than half a century in the entertainment industry, earned a reputation for being a major artist, both as writer and a performer. At age fifteen, Oscar made his professional debut acting in a national network radio series, *Secret City*. At twenty-one, he was the first to broadcast news about America's largest minority with his *Negro Newsfront* radio program. Brown's album *Sin and Soul*, the first of four on Columbia Records, was produced early in 1960. Oscar Brown Jr. has composed several hundred songs and over a dozen full-length theater pieces, including *Journey Through Forever*, which deals with aging, and *Great Nitty Gritty*, which depicts the plight of youth in Chicago's low-income housing developments (from which its 1983 cast was largely recruited). Oscar put words to songs like "Dat Dere," "Afro Blue," and "Work Song," and he also penned songs such as "The Snake," "Rags and Old Iron," and "Somebody Buy Me a Drink." Hailed as a genius and the high priest of hip, he continues to record and perform. His Web site is *www.oscarbrownjr.com*.

Ruth Brown

Ruth Brown's autobiography, *Miss Rhythm: The Autobiography of Ruth Brown, Rhythm & Blues Legend*—written by Ruth Brown and Andrew Yule and published by Donald I. Fine Books—reads like a novel. Brown's well-known moniker is "Miss Rhythm." As the first rhythm-and-blues singer, she remains a living legend. Brown starred in Allen Toussaint's Off-Broadway musical

Staggerlee, made a spectacular splash in the film *Hairspray* as Motormouth Mabel, hosted the *Harlem Hit Parade* series on national public radio, and won a Tony Award for her role in the Broadway play *Black and Blue* after appearing in the original Paris production. In 1989, she received her first Grammy Award for the album *Blues on Broadway*.

James Browne

James Browne, a twenty-five-year veteran of the music industry, is a former radio announcer, artist manager, and festival producer. He was manager of Sweet Basil—the legendary jazz club located in the heart of Greenwich Village in New York City—from 1994 until 2000, when it was reopened in as Sweet Rhythm. He now owns and operates the club with Martha Baratz.

Gerald Cannon

Gerald Cannon came to my attention not just as a solid-grooving, hard-driving powerhouse on the bass, but also as a songwriter. I had heard his composition "Peri" on a Ralph Peterson recording and then again on a Roy Hargrove recording, and I thought it was just beautiful. A native of Milwaukee, Wisconsin, he came to New York City to test his metal. After five years with Roy Hargrove, he went to play with Elvin Jones's "Jazzmachine" until Mr. Jones's death in 2004. Gerald has produced his self-titled CD on his own Woodneck label and continues to make waves. His Web site is *www.geraldcannon.com*.

Ron Carter

Ron Carter has been a world-class bassist and cellist since the 1960s. He's among the greatest accompanists of all time, but he has also done many albums exhibiting his prodigious technique. Carter is nearly as accomplished in classical music as he is in jazz, and he has performed with symphony orchestras all over the world. He played in the Eastman School's Philharmonic Orchestra, and gained his degree in 1959. He joined Art Farmer's group for a short time in 1963, before he was tapped to become a member of Miles Davis's band. Carter remained with Davis until 1968. He is possibly the most recorded bassist in jazz history. He has led his own bands at various intervals since 1972. As a leader, he has recorded over fifty albums. Carter also contributed many arrangements and compositions to both his own groups and to other bands. He even invented his own instrument, a piccolo bass. His recordings have encompassed an unusually imaginative range of ideas—from cello ensembles to reexaminations of Bach. His Web site is *www.roncarter.net*.

Jeff Clayton

Born in Venice, California, Clayton's musical education began at a local Baptist church, where his mother was the pianist and conductor of the choir. He began playing various reed instruments, including the clarinet, but he concentrated on alto saxophone. He later added the soprano saxophone and the flute, extending his studies during his high school and university education, in which his principal instrument was the oboe. He dropped out of the university before graduating in order to go on the road with Stevie Wonder. Later, he mixed studio work with touring, playing with artists as diverse as Gladys Knight, Kenny Rogers, Patti Labelle, and Michael Jackson. He gradually shifted toward a more jazz-oriented repertoire, and although he continued to work in orchestras backing popular singers such as Frank Sinatra, Mel Tormé, Lena Horne, and Sammy Davis Jr., it was in the jazz world that he established his reputation during the 1980s. He played in the Tommy Dorsey Orchestra under the direction of Murray McEachern; with Count Basie, the continuing Basie band under Thad Jones, and with Alphonse Mouzon, Juggernaut, Woody Herman, Lionel Hampton, Ella Fitzgerald, the Phillip Morris Superband led by Gene Harris, Monty Alexander, Ray Brown, and many others. Clayton continued to work with pop stars, playing saxophone solos on the *Dick Tracy* (1990) soundtrack album and on *I'm Breathless*, Madonna's companion album to the film. Clayton has worked extensively in partnership with his brother, John Clayton; and the Claytons are also active in the big band they co-lead, the Clayton-Hamilton Jazz Orchestra, with drummer Jeff Hamilton, as well as The Clayton Brothers Quintet. His Web site is *www.jeffclaytonjazz.com*.

Olu Dara

Although he didn't record under his own name until 1998, Olu Dara enjoyed a reputation as one of the jazz avant-garde's leading trumpeters from the mid-1970s on. Early-1980s' records and performances with the David Murray Octet and the Henry Threadgill Sextet revealed Dara to be a daring, roots-bound soloist, with a modern imagination and a big, burnished tone in the style of Louis Armstrong and Roy Eldridge.

Dara was born Charles Jones. He moved to New York in 1963, but he did not perform publicly until the early 1970s, when he became a part of the city's loft jazz culture. By that time, he had changed his name to Yoruba Olu Dara. Besides his work with Murray and Threadgill, Dara also played with Hamiet Bluiett, James "Blood" Ulmer, and Don Pullen, among others. Dara was an intermittent presence on the jazz scene in the 1980s and 1990s occasionally leading his Okra Orchestra and Natchezsippi Dance Band. In 1985, he recorded with Pullen and in 1987, with saxophonist Charles Brackeen. In the 1990s, he worked with vocalist Cassandra Wilson, playing on her Blue Note album, *Blue Light 'Til Dawn*. Not much else was heard from him—from a jazz perspective, anyway—until 1998, when Atlantic released *In the World: From Natchez to New York*, the first album released under Dara's name. The record was only tangentially related to his free jazz work. The music drew upon country-blues and African-American folk traditions. In addition to playing trumpet and cornet, Dara composed all of the tunes, sung, and accompanied himself on guitar. Atlantic released Dara's follow-up, entitled *Neighborhoods*, in early 2001.

Brenda Feliciano

Brenda Feliciano is widely known as a leading bilingual performer of both popular, jazz and classical music, and also as an actress. Born in Puerto Rico and raised in Brooklyn, New York, Feliciano has performed as a soloist with many important symphony orchestras, including the National Symphony Orchestra at the Kennedy Center under the baton of Maestro Leonard Slatkin, the Milwaukee Symphony, the Simon Bolivar Orchestra in Venezuela, the Costa Rica Symphony, and the America Youth Philharmonic Orchestra, among others. Most recently, Feliciano premiered a chamber piece for eight instruments and soprano for the New Jersey Chamber Music Society's Twenty-fifth Anniversary Concert, composed by Paquito D'Rivera, and another premiere at Alice Tully Hall for the Jazz @ Lincoln "As of Now" series. She has also performed "El Amor Brujo," by Manuel DeFalla, with the New Philharmonic of New Jersey and with the New York Virtuosi Orchestra at the Kay Playhouse under the baton of Maestro Kenneth Klein. A regular soloist with the Bronx Arts Ensemble Orchestra, she has performed *Bachianas*. Feliciano received a Grammy Award nomination in 2000 for Best Classical Album for her recording *Music of Two Worlds* on the Acqua Records label. She is married to Paquito D'Rivera.

Carl Griffin

In 1970, at Motown Records, Carl Griffin worked with Stevie Wonder and Marvin Gaye. He found the song "Until You Come Back to Me" for Aretha Franklin, and discovered "Tell Me Something Good" for Rufus. In 1990, he became the director of A&R at GRP Records. While there, he signed Diana Krall and won Grammy Awards for Arturo Sandoval's *Hot House* and B. B. King's *Live at the Apollo*. He went to N2K where he handled Ramsey Lewis and Jonathan Butler and signed Jane Monheit.

Joe Grushecky (and the House Rockers)

Joe Grushecky is a native of Pittsburgh, Pennsylvania, where he continues to live. His life has been quite a roller coaster. He is a songwriter, has recorded and toured with Bruce Springsteen, has been a trailblazer in pushing the limits of rock music, and he still hasn't stopped. Married with children, Joe spends much of his time on the road. Joe celebrated his twenty-fifth anniversary as a recording artist with the release of a new album, *True Companion*, which took twenty-three years to make. The album is a sequel to the 1980 Iron City House Rockers classic *Have a Good Time, but Get Out Alive*. *HAGTBGOA* was the second Iron City House Rockers album. The first, *Love's So Tough*, was released in 1979. Two other Iron City House Rockers albums were released before the band split in 1983. *Blood on the Bricks* was released in 1981, and *Cracking under Pressure* in 1983.

In 1995, Bruce Springsteen produced the House Rockers' album *American Babylon*, which included tracks co-written by Grushecky and Springsteen. Springsteen also plays and sings on the album and even did a one-week stint as the House Rockers' lead guitarist on a tour to celebrate the album's release. Since then, Springsteen has debuted three of the co-written songs at his concerts. "Code of Silence" and "Another Thin Line" were debuted during Springsteen's tour that ended at Madison Square Garden in 2000. A recording of "Code of Silence" from these shows was released on the *Essential Bruce Springsteen* in 2003. Grushecky's Web site is *www.grushecky.com*.

Allan Harris

Born in Brooklyn, New York, Allan Harris was surrounded by music throughout his childhood. His mother was a classical pianist, and his aunt was an opera singer who later turned to the blues. Because his Aunt Theodosia attracted the attention of famed music producer Clarence Williams (you know, the one who made Bessie Smith famous), he became a regular dinner guest and often brought along other performers such as Louis Armstrong. Armstrong once baby-sat young Harris and terrified him with his "frog-like voice."

Harris has thrilled audiences all over the world. He has performed for sold-out venues in Germany, at the Komische Opera House in Berlin and with the New York Voices in Nuremberg. He has also performed with James Morrison for the television show *Swing It*; in a ten-day, standing-room-only tour of Israel; in the Espoo Jazz Festival in Finland; in Lugano, Switzerland, with Jon Faddis and the Big Band de Lausanne singing the lead in Duke Ellington's "Sacred Mass"; and at Lincoln Center's new Rose Theater. The DVD recording of the performance in Lugano, Switzerland, has aired all over the country on public television and is available on both CD and DVD formats. His Web site is *www.allanharris.com*.

Laura Hartmann

Laura Hartmann established LVanHart Artist Productions in 1997—a company devoted to developing the talent of rising jazz artists. This organization encompasses all aspects of its client's business, from personal management to producing tours and special projects that further enhance their careers. Hartmann is formally educated as a classical flutist, educator, and recording engineer. After receiving a bachelor's degree in music education and studio music from the College of St. Rose and a master's degree in music performance from the Brooklyn Conservatory at Brooklyn College, she went on to work as an administrative assistant at the Aspen Music Festival and School. She later became operations director at Herbert Barrett Management. In addition to working with classical artists such as Sherrill Milnes, the Guarneri String Quartet, the Hanover Band, Marietta Simpson, and the Australian Chamber Orchestra, she had the opportunity to work closely with pianist Dr. Billy Taylor, who introduced her to the world of jazz. Her Web site is *www.lvanhart.com*.

Edwin Hawkins

"Brevity" is the word I would use to describe Edwin Hawkins. His surprise Gospel hit, "Oh, Happy Day," in 1968, propelled Gospel music into the secular psyche and reached far and wide. He continues to make music with the Hawkins Singers, and his influence continues to impact music. Just as no one thought that four boys from Liverpool could dominate the world of popular music, who could have predicted that a group of young people from Northern California would record a contemporary arrangement of a nineteenth-century hymn called "Oh, Happy Day"? Taking Negro spirituals and combining them with European hymns was not uncommon, but Edwin did more than that—he turned them inside out!

Al Jarreau

Al Jarreau's unique vocal style is one of the world's most precious treasures. His innovative musical expressions have made him one of the most exciting and critically acclaimed performers of our time, with five Grammy Awards, scores of international music awards, and popular accolades worldwide. He has been singing since the age of four, harmonizing with his brothers and performing solo at a variety of local events in his hometown of Milwaukee, Wisconsin.

Enrolling at the respected Ripon College in Wisconsin, Jarreau continued singing for fun, performing locally with a group called the Indigos during weekends and holidays, and graduated with a bachelor of science degree in psychology. After moving on to the University of Iowa to earn his master's degree in vocational rehabilitation, Jarreau subsequently relocated to San Francisco to begin a career in rehabilitation counseling. His current CD, *Accentuate the Positive*, released in 2004, was also nominated for a Grammy. His Web site is *www.aljarreau.com*.

Paula Kimper

A graduate of the Eastman School of Music in 1979, Kimper is active in New York City as a composer for opera, theater, film, and dance. Her first opera, a libretto by Wende Persons, *Patience and Sarah*, had its world premiere at the Lincoln Center Festival in 1998. Kimper's new opera, *The Bridge of San Luis Rey*, based on Thornton Wilder's classic novel, was presented by American Opera Projects in March 2002. Kimper has created a score for dancer/choreographer Richard Daniels' Bonus Round, with text by Aaron Shurin. "Flight of the Harmonic Messenger," a one-hour meditation on *Sacred Sites of the Earth*, Kimper's 1993 CD release, has aired on New Age radio programs worldwide. She was commissioned by Pocumtuck Valley Memorial Association, of Deerfield, Massachusetts, to compose the opera *The Captivation of Eunice Williams* for the three-hundredth anniversary of the Deerfield massacre of 1704, with librettist Harley Erdman. Her Web site is *www.patienceandsarah.com*.

Dorothy Lawson

Canadian-born cellist Dorothy Lawson comes from the world of classical orchestral and chamber music, with a doctorate from Juilliard, a career in Vienna, and performing experiences with such well-known musical organizations as the New York Philharmonic, the American Symphony, and the Orpheus Chamber Orchestra. In contrast, she performs regularly with modern-dance companies and figures such as Mikhail Baryshnikov and the White Oak Dance Project, as well as new music groups such as the Bang-on-a-Can All-Stars. Lawson is a founding member of New York's premier new music string quartet, Ethel.

John Levy

John Levy is a fountain of youth, and in his nineties, he is sill looking forward. He has had a full life, as his autobiography, *Men, Women, and Girl Singers: My Life as a Musician Turned Talent Manager* illustrates. Levy is currently working on his next book of photographs. He managed George Shearing, Cannonball Adderely, Dakota Staton, Ahmad Jamal, and others. More than fifty years ago, he was a respected jazz bassist. Today he is one of the most respected personal managers in the world of jazz. He put down his bass to become a full-time personal manager—the first black personal manager in pop or jazz music. John Levy Enterprises, Inc. is open for business.

Howard M. Nashel, Esq.

Howard M. Nashel graduated from the New York University School of Law in 1960 and was admitted to the New Jersey Bar in 1961. His practice areas include corporate law, litigation, mental-health law, and entertainment law. He is general counsel to the New Jersey Psychological Association and represents various artists in the entertainment field, including the jazz artists Eric Reed and Mark Murphy, and the father of modern Gospel, Edwin Hawkins.

David Randolph

David Randolph has been the conductor of the St. Cecilia Chorus and Orchestra since 1965. Born in New York City, he received his bachelor of science from the City College of New York, where he planned to be a physicist until meeting up with higher mathematics. Having scored in the 98th percentile on a musical aptitude test, he changed his major to music, which had always been one of his loves. He proceeded to get his master of arts degree at Teachers' College, Columbia University. From 1943 to 1947, he was a music specialist for the United States Office of War Information. In 1947, he became the music annotator for the Columbia Broadcasting System, writing the broadcast scripts for concerts by the New York Philharmonic, the Philadelphia Orchestra, and all other classical music presentations on the network. In 1946, he began a series of weekly broadcasts called *Music for the Connoisseur*, later known as *The David Randolph Concerts*, on New York City's radio station WNYC. For his fourth broadcast, on July 23, 1946, he surveyed the subject of "Humor in Music," thus "inventing" the type of radio broadcast devoted to a single musical subject with commentary. The broadcasts were later heard nationwide on the seventy-two-station network of the National Association of Educational Broadcasters. These broadcasts, which won four Ohio State University Awards as "the best programs of music and commentary in the nation," continued for thirty-three years and resulted in invitations from twenty-three separate publishers to write a book. His book, *This Is Music*, was described by *The New York Times* as "one of the best of the year." He has hosted the *Lincoln Center Spotlight* (heard weekly on radio station WQXR) and *Young Audiences*, a series of thirty-nine programs on the CBS television network. He has also appeared as a guest on the Metropolitan Opera Intermission broadcasts. He has been a regular guest critic on WQXR's *First Hearing*. Although, for all his accolades and contributions to the dissemination of music to the masses, he is perhaps best known for saying, "*Parasifal* is the kind of opera that starts at six o'clock, and after it has been going three hours, you look at your watch and it says 6:20." His Web site is *www.stceciliachorus.org*.

Eric Reed

Eric Reed began his career in the Marsalis's Septet (1990–91; 1992–95) and in the bands of Freddie Hubbard and Joe Henderson (1996–98). He also spent two years with the Lincoln Center Jazz Orchestra, making countless recordings and television appearances with them. Reed continues to perform and record with an assorted multitude of masters, including Wayne Shorter, Ron Carter, Cassandra Wilson, Jimmy Heath, Clark Terry,

Dianne Reeves, and a host of other diverse performers including Natalie Cole, Patti Labelle, Oleta Adams, Edwin Hawkins, Jessye Norman, and Quincy Jones. Since 1995, Reed has been touring the world with his own ensembles, making serious waves in the jazz community. His Web site is *www.ericreed.net*.

Bobby Sanabria

Bobby Sanabria has performed and recorded with a veritable "Who's Who" in the world of jazz and latin music, as well as his own critically acclaimed ensemble, Ascension. His diverse recording and performance experience includes work with such legendary figures as Dizzy Gillespie, Tito Puente, Paquito D'Rivera, Charles McPherson, Mongo Santamaria, Ray Barretto, Larry Harlow, Candido Camero, Marco Rizo, Luis "Perico" Ortiz, Chico O'Farrill, Henry Threadgill, and the pioneering godfather of Afro-Cuban jazz, Mario Bauza. His Web site is *www.bobbysanabria.com*.

Richard Smallwood

Richard Smallwood is currently working on a huge project called "Journey," in which he traces his musical inspirations since he was a child. These sources of inspiration include Roberta Flack (his teacher), Aretha Franklin, the Hawkins Family, and Kathleen Battle, to name a few. World-class composer, pianist, and arranger, Smallwood has clearly and solidly changed the face of Gospel music. He can impeccably blend classical movements with traditional Gospel, and arrive at a mix that is invariably Smallwood's alone. A diverse and innovative artist, Smallwood has achieved many honors; Dove Awards and a Grammy also attest to his talents. Richard's music has never been confined to any one artistic genre. His song "I Love the Lord" crossed onto the big screen when Whitney Houston sang it in the film *The Preacher's Wife*. R&B artists BoyzIIMen used the same song in the tune "Dear God" on their CD *Evolution*.

Dr. Billy Taylor

An educator, radio and television host, curator, leader, writer, and composer, there is nothing Dr. Billy Taylor has not done. He has hosted and programmed such radio stations as WLIB and WNEW in New York, and award-winning series for National Public Radio. In the early 1980s, Taylor became the arts correspondent for *CBS Sunday Morning*. With over twenty-two honorary doctoral degrees, Dr. Billy Taylor is also the recipient of two Peabody Awards, an Emmy, a Grammy nomination, and a host of prestigious and highly coveted prizes, such as the National Medal of Arts, the Tiffany Award, a Lifetime Achievement Award from *downbeat* magazine, and election to the Hall of Fame for the International Association of Jazz Educators. His Web site is *www.billytaylor.com.*

Gary Walker

Gary Walker is the morning edition jazz host and music director of WBGO, Jazz 88.3FM. In jazz radio, great announcers are distinguished by their ability to convey the spontaneity and passion of the music. Gary Walker is such an announcer, and his enthusiasm for this music greets WBGO listeners every morning. For the past thirteen years, this winner of the 1996 Gavin Magazine Jazz Radio Personality of the Year award has hosted the morning show each weekday from 6:00 to 10:00. And by his own admission, he's truly having a great time. You can find more on Walker at *www.wbgo.org.*

Kenny Washington

Kenny Washington is one of the most sought-after jazz drummers today. He was playing with the greats long before there was a "youth movement" in jazz when the "young lions" were heralded in during the 1990s. A virtual walking encyclopedia of jazz, Kenny has worked with performers from Betty Carter to Benny Carter, Lee Konitz, Johnny Griffin, Tommy Flanagan, to name a few. Currently he is keeping time with the Bill Charlap Trio, featuring Peter Washington (no relation), and he sounds better than ever. For ten years, he was an on-air host on WBGO, Jazz 88.3FM, and he has spent five years at Sirius Satellite Radio as one of its first program directors.

Michael Wolff

A pianist and composer who is perhaps best known as Arsenio Hall's music director, Michael Wolff is a brilliant and innovative pianist/composer with a wealth of straight-ahead jazz credentials (Sonny Rollins, Nancy Wilson, Airto, Cal Tjader, Cannonball Adderley, the Thad Jones/Mel Lewis Orchestra, Jean Luc Ponty) as well as an impressive body of movie soundtrack work (*Dark Angel, The Tic Code*).

Wolff addresses his own musical roots while incorporating a fresh, world-beat sensibility as leader of his inventive band Impure Thoughts (with John B. Williams on bass, Victor Jones on drums, and Badal Roy on tablas). After his tenure in television ended, Wolff jumped back into the jazz scene with a string of highly regarded recordings including *Michael Wolff*, *Portraiture—The Blues Period*, and two piano trio outings, *Jumpstart* and *2AM*. The band's chemistry was first documented on *Impure Thoughts* (2000), and subsequently on *Intoxicate* (2002). The band's third album, *Dangerous Vision*, was released in 2004. His Web site is *www.michaelwolff.com*.

Part One On Development as an Artist

The mastership in music, and in life, in fact, is not something that can't be taught—it can only be caught.

— RODNEY JONES

1 Getting Started

Despite the diversity of the musicians I interviewed, they all have one thing in common: drive and determination. Once music became a focus in their lives, they all worked hard to make it in the business. Each had what is called an "Ah-Ha" moment—or moments—when things just clicked. Those moments came at different periods of their lives, some later than others.

Music in the Home

Al Jarreau knew by the time he had sung a few gigs as a kid, around the age of fifteen, that he loved to sing.

"I was hired by the dance band led by a guy in Milwaukee who had been a horn player with Duke Ellington. By the time I had worked in an organized band and a trio beyond church music—which was there for me before all of my growing-up life, and before that were the show tunes I learned in the high-school choir—I was beginning to get the sense that I would sing, even if I had to do it for free the rest of my life. If I could earn a little bit of money, that would be great. Then I began to dream at about eighteen or nineteen, when I was in college, that it would be a wonderful way to go through life. I began to look for opportunities."

It took Al some years before he would completely focus his energy on being a singer. Al chose to go to college. He enrolled at Ripon College in Wisconsin, graduated with a bachelor of science degree in psychology, and then moved on to get his master's degree in vocational rehabilitation from the University of Iowa. He moved to San Francisco, California, in 1964 to take his state board exams. Al chose San Francisco because it was "a hotbed of the new music at the time. It has an active jazz community . . . I had the best of both worlds." Although he tried to make a go of the career for which his education had prepared him, he found himself looking to music more and more:

"When I worked as a rehabilitation counselor, [I said] *maybe* I'd make some contacts and find myself with a recording career. It took some lack of success on the job for me to realize that I had to leave it at the state level and go to a small agency. I could not handle the case load that was expected of a counselor; I'm too slow. I was on my way to a smaller agency or I had to decide to give this music a real chance . . . I worked all day, every day on the music and on finding myself a record deal. It did not happen until seven years later. I left the job in 1968, and in 1975 the *I Got By* album came out."

Like Al Jarreau, **Joe Grushecky** also graduated from college, but with a teaching degree. "I have a teaching degree, so I took a special-education job in a mental institution with total-care kids, and that is what I used to finance my musical ambitions." He was influenced by his father who played professionally: "I grew up in a musician family, and there were always instruments in the house. My father had played professionally, but he gave it up when I was a teenager. There was always a germ, an idea in my head, like a lot of guys of my generation. The Beatles [were dominant]; we watched them on Ed Sullivan, and that was a pivotal moment that led me to buy a guitar."

Allan Harris was born in Brooklyn, New York, but later moved to Pittsburgh, Pennsylvania, where he got to know Joe Grushecky and play with several bands. Although he grew up with "music in my family; my mother was a classical pianist, my aunt an opera singer," it was not until he got to college that the "musician" seeds began to germinate within Allan. Not sure which genre on which to concentrate, he simply started going to clubs. When Allan sang in coffee shops, he started making money playing music.

"I played guitar first. I started to sing along when I started to play in bands. It was an ego thing. I could do singing a lot better than the leader. I noted the reaction of audiences to me versus him. Through that, I developed my voice and said, 'I could do *this*!' I started making money playing music, so I knew that I could be good at this and have a voice in this where I could support myself. As I progressed in school, I went to jam sessions doing R&B and a few [jazz] standards."

Newark, New Jersey, native **Andy Bey** came from a musical family. "I started so young. I was born in 1939 and was considered child prodigy, but I don't know how much talent one has at that age. I played by ear; music was always in our home. I was destined to be a musician even if I was not conscious of it. Around the age of two, I was banging on the piano. By three years of age, I was making some musical sense, so they told me I had a good ear. By five years of age, I was doing gigs, playing boogie-woogie, like Louis Jordan's 'Caldonia.' I was the last child out of nine; there were seven girls, two boys. My father played piano, and he sang and played tuba. There was always an upright piano in our home. My sister Salome studied piano. I had an older sister who sang music like

Ella Fitzgerald, and a sister who loved the blues. We loved Buddy Johnson, who we got into before we got into Count Basie.

"My sister Geraldine loved classical music. There was a woman who lived in the neighborhood, Betty Glover, who sang like Jane Powell. That was not common to see a neighbor sing opera. We had Gospel music in the neighborhood. I was not raised in the church but around the church. There were a lot of Baptist and Sanctified churches and a lot of storefront churches. They would have performances in the churches with neighborhood folks. They used to come to my house and sing because there was a piano in the house. Sometimes they would bring soundies [videos] of Nat King Cole, Hazel Scott, people of the late 1940s and the 1950s, so I saw a lot of black music. A lot of records were called 'race records,' such as Dinah Washington and Eddie Cleanhead Vinson."

Andy worked constantly throughout his youth. It was an audition that led him further toward being a full-fledged musician. He and his sisters auditioned for *Spotlight in Harlem*. Ralph Cooper was the hit. I happened to be on the show at the same time as Dinah Washington, and I still remember what she wore. Dinah was flashy. At that time I was trying to sing like Billy Ecsktine. My sisters were on the show also, but for some reason I went back [without them]. A guy named Ted Gotleib was in the audience; he liked my performance and took me to a kids' show on channel four. Connie Francis was on as well. I did popular tunes and one that Doris Day had sung. I was making money when I was eight years old. I was always encouraged, never forced. At one time I backed away from it; when I was a teenager, my tonsils had been removed. I came back strong, and my voice was better. I made three records with my sister. In 1951, I was around nineteen years old, and we lived in Europe for about eighteen months. We had no manager then but had close encounters with folks. It was tough on young black singers."

Brenda Feliciano said, "I was born singing. I sang in church. I had a *big* mouth, and I liked it. I got into kids' theater. I studied piano but I did not follow up on it, which was a bad thing to do. Anyone who wants to study music, piano is the key regardless, no matter what you want to do. I grew up in Brooklyn; I had a unique upbringing. I was encouraged; music was in my house. I'm instinctual in a sense and sensitive to singers. I was born with it. At home, my stepfather paid his way through college as a jazz singer. Ella Fitzgerald freaked me out. Al Jolson, [Latino] singers, I listened to a lot of music, but jazz and classical impacted me very early. I was able to imitate that somewhat. At the Presbyterian church, I sang Handel, oratorios, things like that, and I was the youngest person with a prominent role; I did solo work. I tried out for the High School of Music and Arts as a vocalist.

"Somehow, with my varied background, I had become removed from my Puerto Rican self, so my uncle suggested that I go to college in Puerto Rico where I, too, had a scholarship. I hardly spoke Spanish but it was good for me."

Life was difficult for some Puerto Ricans. **Bobby Sanabria** talked extensively about what life was like for him as a child growing up in the 1960s in the South Bronx, the area called Fort Apache. Born in 1957, the son of a father who had come to the United States during high school, life was not easy for Bobby. Fortunately for him, his father loved music. He had wanted to go to college, but Puerto Ricans at that time were told to learn a trade and not to bother with college. "My father is a cultured man and educated," Bobby says. In spite of not having a formal advanced education, his father is self-taught.

"Growing up, I was exposed to jazz through my father, who was a machinist. He worked in Valley Stream, Long Island, and it was a long commute. We could not bother him while he relaxed after work, so I would do my homework and listen to what he listened to. He listened to big bands, Machito, swing music, Ellington, Basie, Tito Rodriguez, and folk music from Puerto Rico. He even listened to Brazilian music. He gave me a history lesson when I inquired about the language on those records; he told me it was Portuguese. One great thing he gave me was the gift of reading."

Bobby was not encouraged to be a musician; "My family humored me," he says. His first dreams seemed to be even more far-fetched than that of being a musician: "When I was young, my first dream was to be an astronaut, but in the South Bronx, everyone laughs at your dreams. Then I wanted to be a racecar driver. Then I wanted to be a second base man for the Yankees—a more realistic dream.

"I remember as a kid listening to Harry Belafonte, who represented another branch of Caribbean culture. Though I did not know formally what jazz was, it was still a part of popular culture. It was in theme songs on TV, cartoons, Hanna/Barbera, and WB cartoons had jazz music. Other shows such as *Naked City* and *Peter Gunn* had Quincy Jones doing the music. Talk shows like Mike Douglas, Merv Griffin featured jazz-band orchestras, and I was always fascinated by the drummers, Grady Tate, Bobby Rosengarden, and Ed Shaunessey. I read *downbeat* magazine and found out who was playing on what shows. I was playing congo drums. Music was everywhere in the Bronx."

Kenny Washington's father, like Bobby Sanabria's father, loved great music. Kenny was born in Brooklyn and raised in Staten Island, along with a brother and a sister. His father "had a plan for us three; he wanted us to be musicians. He encouraged it. He probably figured that if he kept us blowing an instrument, then we would not want to blow a safe. He was right; it kept *my ass* out of trouble. He never had any problems out of me. My father had the hippest record collection. He would sit around when he was not working and listen to records. I decided to be a musician about the time I was four years old. When I heard a Ahmad Jamal recording, the tune "But Not for Me," and all the other tracks, on *Live @ the Pershing*, and Vernel Fournier playing the brushes, I said, 'I gotta learn how to do this!' I did not have an instrument, but I knew this was what I wanted to do.

"In the summer, I was in the house practicing and listening to records. At the age of six or seven, Remco had a drum set, a blue sparkle set that looked like the Remco preteen sets for kids they have now. The hardware was sad. I broke the foot pedal; my dad would patch that. The cymbals stands were sad. He went to Sears— they sold pieces separately, so we fixed that Remco set with Sears cymbal stands and stuff so the drums lasted longer. Each time I did well in school, he'd add on another piece, another cymbal stand and cymbal. Those drums finally died; then he got me a brand X set of drums. I think it was called Kent, and I used those for a while. They were not high quality, but they were real. I kept listening to records. I had a different hero every month: Charli Persip, Arthur Taylor, Max Roach, Philly Joe Jones . . . I tried to play like them all.

"Speaking of Max, my father bought me a Ludwig floor tom-tom, bottom of the line; then I heard a Max and Clifford Brown record called *Cherokee*. Max tuned his drums real high, the pitch of the tom-tom, and that sound knocked me out, and that drum solo he played was a work of art. It was fantastic. I went to my room to try to figure out how he got that sound. I got my drums to sound like him.

"My father used to inspect the drums every Sunday. He wanted to see if I was taking care of them. If I was not doing what I was supposed to with them, he would take them away. He said, 'If you take care of the drums, they'll take care of you.' He was not a musician; he just played the record player, and he had a good insight as to how the music was supposed to sound. He was amazing. One Saturday I noticed that the floor tom-tom, the shell, was pulling in because I had the drums tuned so high. The drum was not able to hold the pressure of the head on the shell, and I thought he'd kill me. When he inspected them, he asked, 'Boy, what happened to the drums?' When I told him the truth, he fell on the floor laughing. After that he bought me another set of drums because he knew I was serious.

"I took lessons from Dennis Kenny, and also from Rudy Collins, who had played with Dizzy Gillespie. My father knew him. He had told my father that if he had a son who wanted to play the drums to send him to him. Though they had lost contact, my father found him in Brooklyn teaching at a place called Muse—it was like a museum. It was an after-school program. So I took lessons. Rudy was great with me. Each class was one hour; they had beginner, intermediate, and advanced classes. I would hang out with Rudy for the hell of it in the advance class. When he would dismiss the classes, he would set up another set of drums and give me a private lesson."

Gerald Cannon's story is similar, in that his father insisted that he take music seriously if he were to play at all. Initially influenced by his father and uncle, Gerald got bit by the bug very young. "When I was about four years old, my father played guitar; he had a Gospel group. I was fascinated by it. My uncle George sang in my father's group called 'Golden True Lights,' and he would always sing notes other than the root chord. I now know that he sang flat 5s or the 7th of the chord. So I would sneak and practice my uncle's notes. My dad caught me playing with his guitar, so either I had to play something he liked or get my butt kicked. My dad took me to a store, and he told the guy I could play the bass so they gave me a test—I was nine years old. I passed, so I got six months of free lessons. I didn't like the guitar; I played it for two months, but I hated it. There were too many strings, so I changed to the bass, which was huge. My dad made me play in his group."

I asked him how he ended up playing jazz. "That came later. My parents listened to Gospel and jazz, and my father loved Kenny Burrell. My father always told me *that* was good music, not what my brother and I listened to. We listened to all types of music in my day, Earth Wind and Fire, Weather Report . . ."

Gerald saw that "there was something about the upright bass. It was like the next level. I played electric. I got to play the bass in my art class. The teacher brought one in for us to paint, and I knew then what I was going to do, but I did not get a chance to play it again until I got to college.

"I took classical bass as an elective; I was good at it. Milt Hinton had come to school, and my teacher took me to see him and to meet him. He talked to me for about an hour. What I learned from him was that this could be fun. He told me to go to a conservatory. I called my dad, and he flipped out! He told me I could not make any money. At that time, I had planned to be a gym teacher. So after the end of the semester at Racine, Wisconsin, I got a scholarship at the conservatory, and I got in."

Another father who was not happy about his son's ascent into music was **Billy Taylor**'s dad. Billy explained, "I knew when I was about thirteen years old, I wanted to be a musician. I was playing professionally with people older than myself, with more experience, and I wanted to get closer to the music, more involved in the music. Piano was my first instrument, but piano was hard, so I fooled around with guitar. I tried the saxophone and several other instruments, looking for something easier. I found that they were all hard, so I went back to the one I liked the most.

"My father was a dentist and an amateur musician. He played brass instruments, and he conducted his father's choir in church. He was an amateur, and a very fine musician. He grew up in church, surrounded by church music and other kinds of popular music. My father sang, he had a beautiful voice, something I didn't inherit. He did not encourage me to go into music. I grew up in the Depression; it was hard for a black man to earn a living.

"My father said that when I was young, it was all right to like music, but don't consider it seriously. The only guys who couldn't pay to get their teeth fixed were some of the musicians who lived in the neighborhood, but he treated them, anyway. I said, "Yeah, okay," but it didn't take. His whole family was full of musicians. The one reason for my interest in jazz was his middle brother, Robert; my uncle Bob was a great stride pianist. I had never heard many stride musicians except those in Washington, D.C., where I grew up, so I assumed that my uncle Bob played like Fats Waller. Fats sounded most like what I heard my uncle doing.

"When I grew up and got more experience, I found that he was influenced more by Willie 'The Lion' Smith. He gave me my first Fats record and my first Art Tatum record, then I tried to get him to teach me, but he said *no*, and that I should go and listen to an Art Tatum record. It was fantastic, and I wanted to sound like that. Then my dad got me the music teacher in the neighborhood, Elmira Streets; she was very good, but I didn't want to play like that. I didn't want to be playing scales or Mozart and all that stuff, so I wasted a year trying to figure it out myself, then I went back to studying with teachers. I realized that it would get me closer to what I wanted to do.

"My dad sent me to college, but he said that I had to study something that I could earn a living at. He did not think that I could earn a living doing music, so I should pick something that I liked. He sent me to his alma mater, Virginia State University, then called Virginia State College. I was a sociology major for the first two years. In college, I changed my major to music in my junior year, and my dad cut me off. He said, 'If you are going to change your major, you are on your own. So you can pay your own tuition on your own.' I paid for my last two years by playing with local bands."

Michael Wolff seemed to always know that he would be a musician. "I guess the reason why I never even thought about it is because my father was an amateur musician. He grew up in Indianola, Mississippi, so he grew up in the same town as B. B. King, Albert King, and Muddy Waters, those guys. He played as a kid in the band with a saxophone player by the name of Blue Mar. I grew up in New Orleans. My dad, from the time I was growing up, played his favorites, Sinatra, George Shearing, Oscar Peterson, Ray Charles, and folks like that. Count Basie was his favorite big band. He'd sit me down when I was a real little boy, I'd remember listening to a segue and he'd say, 'See what's happening on the music, you got to pay attention,' and he'd try to explain it to me. So I just grew up hearing that kind of music and having that kind of blues underneath. When I started playing music, I had that kind of . . . I grew up in the 1960s and 1970s with The Beatles, the rock 'n' roll, and all that, I played the drums and all that, but when I played the piano, which was my instrument, it seemed like that is what came out, so that's what I was drawn to.

"I knew when I wanted to be a professional musician—when I was in high school, I was fifteen, tenth grade—and that's when I didn't even consider anything else. I always loved it; my parents said, 'You want to play jazz, you have to take classical piano lessons until you are thirteen to fourteen.' So I did that, but I just wanted to do jazz; I always did jazz on the side. When I got to be fifteen, I got out of tenth grade—by then we moved to Berkeley, California, in the late 1960s [sighs]—what a different world. But then I had a great jazz piano teacher, Dick Whittington; It just was like coming home."

Wolff's entry into a pan-global mix of sounds was triggered by a trip that his parents took to Yemen and Ethiopia. As he explains, "They brought me back a bag of cassettes to check out, music that they had gathered from their travels. The tapes were all labeled in Arabic, so I didn't know what they really were. It was a mixture of African sounds and Indian beats that was absolutely amazing. Those countries have somehow absorbed that influence of tablas and tamboura . . . that kind of drone built into their musical culture . . . along with the influence of African percussion. To me, that was really the essence of what Miles was trying to get to with *On the Corner*. All this music, harmonically, is so simple. But the intrigue comes from the groove, the textures and tension in the music. I never really liked the pyrotechnical kind of chops-oriented fusion stuff. That's not what

I want to play. I want the music to flow and breathe more. And I just love the aspect of mixing different elements together in the music."

Love at First Exposure

Ron Carter was hooked from the beginning. "When I was ten years old, I had my first lesson on cello, and I thought this was for me." Though he does not like to talk about his transition to jazz, he did reluctantly and briefly: "I wanted to be a classical cello player. To be a jazz musician didn't come along until much later. . . . Well, when I was in Detroit, my saxophone player neighbor liked Paul Desmond, Dave Brubeck. At the time, they had a big hit, 'Jazz at the College,' in 1954 on Fantasy. There were a lot of sorority/fraternity dances on these big boats, and he knew somebody who did these bookings, and he told the guy to get a band in to play for the dances. So he got together myself, and a piano player and drummer, and had rehearsals and made these boat rides out in Bell-Isle. I was a classical cello player. I went to string bass because I thought all the white guys were getting all the gigs. As a classical bass player, I saw all the auditions were being steered toward the white bass players in school. And then in my senior year in college, I was in the orchestra, and the guest conductor told me he would love to have me in his orchestra, but that the board directors weren't hiring colored musicians. That was 1958–59. I went back to New York. The Philharmonic had no black people, maybe one. So I thought, let me do something else, then. I decided to go to Manhattan School of Music. I had a full scholarship to go to Manhattan in 1960 upon graduation from college. When I got to New York, I met Chico Hamilton in Rochester during a concert, and he told me when I got to New York, if he was working around town, come to say hello. Well, actually, I auditioned for him as a cello player, but the cello player decided to stay in the band. When I got to New York, the bass player quit. So I joined the band as a bass player with Eric Dolphy. I played with Randy Weston for almost a year, a couple of years, and Bobby Timmons, Betty Carter, Herbie Mann, and so on and so forth."

Eric Reed had no question that he would become a musician. "The gift of music was given to me by God. I probably always knew, but it did not manifest itself as a goal until I was a teenager. I think that everybody knows, everybody always knew. My talent was extraordinary for someone five years old; it was clear that this would not be a passing fancy. I played with other kids, but music was always the center. My childhood was typical, but more often than not, I was at the piano or listening to music. One of the earliest recordings of myself was at eleven to twelve years old at a church service. When I listen now, I say, 'That was really good.' If you listen to it, you can tell that it was something that a child would not play. A child sits at the piano and tends to bang out, but I was not doing that, it was by ear. Nobody taught me; that is why I knew it was a God-given talent. I could listen to a recording and hear what I heard, listen to a few bars, and I could play it.

"Our neighbors, Mack and Betty Hall, had a piano. The teacher did not drive, so he would come to their house on the bus, in Philadelphia, Pennsylvania. Mack was a good friend of jazz pianist Bobby Timmons. We did not get a piano until I was seven years old. Septa [the transportation system] went on strike, so that was the end of my lessons. We moved to a suburb in Philly called Vala Kenwood, so I went to a music school there. The piano was a light lime-green-yellow console. There was a mirror on it, the lid, so you could see your hands, and I thought that was kind of cool. Then I enrolled in the settlement music school; Christian McBride went there, Stanley Clarke, and Al DiMeola, too. When I was eleven, we moved to Los Angeles, and there I was able to get wider exposure to jazz. In Philly, I was in church doing Gospel. The idea that there was a 'scene' was unbeknownst to my parents and me. My parents did not listen to much jazz, so they weren't going to jazz clubs. I had heard some records, but most of my exposure was Gospel music. My parents did not mind showing me off, but they were not backstage parents; in fact, they tried to play it down, so I would not get a big head.

"My dad was a blue-collar worker, a pastor and not a working musician. My parents didn't encourage me either way. They wanted me to get good grades and go to college. They wanted me to do my best, but they seemed to have resigned themselves that it was something I was gonna do. They just wanted me to go to college to have something for me to fall back on. They made every effort for me to continue studying; they sacrificed.

"I had to take theory lessons. I *hated* it, but I was good at it. Surprisingly, the basics were a breeze, but when I got to college, at advanced theory—analyzing scores and such—I was a complete failure. My thing was about the ear. I did not care if I could ever read music; I just wanted to play music. I knew automatically when I heard Horace Silver playing with Art Blakey and the Jazz Messengers, *Live at the Bohemian Café, that's* what I wanted to do! I wore the grooves out of the record.

"It was not until 1985, when I met the Clayton Brothers, John and Jeff, Gerald Wilson, Clora Bryant, while I was living in Los Angeles, that I figured could do this for a living. I had no idea what I was going to do. Word began to spread that there was a young kid who could play jazz piano. I went to the R. D. Coburn Community School of Performing Arts, an annex of USC. My theory instructor, Jeff Lavenor, knew that I liked jazz and made me tapes. He went to the dean of the school and urged him to do something for me. There was also another kid, Myron McKinnley, one year older than me, also black; we were the 'two spots.' They were more than happy to take advantage of this interesting opportunity, so they decided to send us out to other schools. This was good exposure for the school, these two kids who played jazz. We would talk about the music we were doing, that was before Wynton Marsalis. I think that Jeff Lavenor did not get the recognition that he should have gotten, and Joe Thayer, of course. Joe knew Wynton when he was a teenager. So he called Wynton and told him that he needed to hear Myron and me. Wynton came out to Los Angeles once or twice a year to play at the now-defunct Wetbrook Playhouse, so he came and gave us a master class. Wynton had won two Grammys, I taped the class, I tape everything, and Wynton was impressed with me. I had played some Tatum stuff. He took more interest in me than Myron; I guess Wynton saw in me my passion."

Richard Smallwood was another child prodigy, a baby in the crib making music. Never one to doubt his calling or his choice of genre, he says, "As far back as I remember, as long as I was aware of being alive, I wanted to be a musician. I showed musical talent before I began to talk. I would hum melodies I had heard at church; it freaked my mother out. My parents put a toy piano in the crib; I'd sit up and bang rhythms on the keyboard. At five years of age, I started singing and playing by ear. By the time I was seven, I was playing in my dad's church. I've never wanted to do anything else. Music has always been one of the most important things in my life. I didn't know that I would be successful." I asked him when he knew he would be a professional musician. "When I was in college at Howard University in D.C., I was part of the first Gospel groups on the Howard campus called 'The Celestials.' Donny Hathaway was one of the organ and keyboard players and singers. When he left, I stepped into his place."

Dorothy Lawson stated it well when she said, "You pick it up [a musical instrument], and sooner or later, you've been doing it all of your life." Her story is not unusual.

"I picked up the cello at age nine, not that young. For me, there was something healthy that it was a choice that I made." She knew right away that she wanted to be a classical musician.

"Classical music was the language in my household. My parents did not listen to popular music on the radio and never bought any. I grew up loving classical music, and then I was offered a chance at school. I was happy, and my parents were very excited. They did not push me. It just became part of my life and part of my sense of myself that I never considered giving it up. It was a very satisfying experience. I got good feedback from people, my teachers, and I was encouraged all the way along."

Being from Canada, Dorothy wanted to try her hand in the United States. "I came to the States to go to Juilliard. Before coming, I had done an undergrad degree at Toronto, at the local university with a good music program. Then I chose to go to Vienna for three years to study with a great cello teacher there. When I came back to North America, I tried working in Toronto for about a year. Then I decided to see what the big deal was about at Juilliard."

Before finding her way to opera, **Paula Kimper** came to New York City for a different musical experience: "I moved to New York City in 1979 and went into the pop-music field, into songwriting, and I had a small band for about five years where I wrote all the songs, but they never connected with a singer who could present them. I'm not a singer; I played piano. That evolved naturally into stuff, using a custom synthesizer in my own studio, and I could do all by myself. That led me into film scoring and doing music for theater. Listen, you say you decide to change genres; I don't think of it as a decision *before* it happens, it is almost like it happens, then you decide to follow it. It feels like you are being shuttled through a process, then you never know where it will lead. While you are doing it, you just know it will lead somewhere, but I never thought I'd write an opera. I liked opera, and I listened to opera broadcasts, and I was in opera in college where they needed stage bands. I played in the orchestra, and I always thought it had too many notes, and I never thought that I could write all those notes, but I'm older. You really can sit longer, and things build up, and you can write all those notes."

On Their Own

Oscar Brown Jr. grew up during the Depression in Chicago, Illinois. His father was a lawyer, so he was solidly middle class. By his own admission at that time, his ambitions were limited. "Before I was political, I was just a bourgeois college student who wanted a new sports coat and a convertible, and I was very interested in girls. So my parents sent me to Lincoln University, which was an all-boys school. It just made it harder to get to the girls. I just kept getting kicked out of college. I went to about five colleges and was still a freshman. I did not get into what they were talking about much; I tried hard to get into math, biology, Spanish, English literature, and stuff they required you to take. They require that you take it, not because life requires it, but because they need it to conduct *their* business. I did not realize that at the time. So flunking out of college was very depressing for me then. I would get over it because I was too conceited to commit suicide."

Writing songs was just something that he did to amuse his friends. Oscar had no training as a musician. "I don't play an instrument. I got into songwriting when a girl broke my heart. I wrote a heartbreaking song. Then I wrote vulgar songs, and I'd regale my friends. I started copyrighting my stuff when I was a teenager and thinking in terms of being a songwriter, but it was a vague thought. I did not get much encouragement other than kids wanting to sit and hear my songs. In those days, they did not encourage a colored boy to be in show biz, at least not a middle-class kid like me. They recommended I be a lawyer, doctor, enlist in the service, or be in religion, things like that. Your loved ones discouraged you when you talked about being in show biz; it was too unstable. About a decade after high school, I was influenced by Harry Belafonte; though we were about the same age, he had a Calypso hit. I saw him sing at a club in Chicago, the Black Orchid, and I had a lullaby called 'Brown Baby.' I wanted him to sing it, and I went to meet him and tried to get him to sing the song. He never did sing any of my songs.

"Harry inspired me by not just being a singer but an actor, producing stuff. He was in the *business* of the business, and that inspired me. He was the captain of the ship, not just a performer."

When I asked Oscar if he considered himself to be a jazz singer, his response was similar to Andy Bey's response, which was, "I'm a musician, but jazz is my main love. Jazz is a great art form. I consider it a privilege to be considered such, but people have negative connotations about jazz."

Oscar Brown said, "I'm not resisting it or trying to be cute. I'm not a jazz musician, but I've made a living as a jazz musician and singing in jazz clubs. But only some of it's jazz. I grew up listening to music a lot, the King Cole trio, Duke, Ella, Louis Jordan, you could see a whole show for ten cents. We could not go to the Regal; that was for white acts.

"Eventually, I decided to go the way of Harry Belafonte, into show biz where you could declare a type of independence that you could not get in politics where you had to follow the party line and do as they said. I always had high aspirations of a genre, to do it big-time like Harry Belafonte. I was working in real estate when *A Raisin in the Sun* came to Chicago. I had known Lorraine Hansberry's family. I went to see Lorraine, and she was interested in my songs, and I told her and her husband, Robert Neimiroff, about my play idea I had. They encouraged me to continue. Her husband was taking my songs around New York City trying to get record people interested in singing them. I was not interested in being a performer myself. Al Ham, an A&R man at Columbia records, liked my performance of the songs, so we talked about that, and I wound up getting a recording contract to do *Sin and Soul*.

"I brought the script of *Kicks* that I had been working on to Bob, his partner, Burt D'Lugoff, the brother of the owner of the Village gate—Art. They liked it and wanted to produce it. They got a budget of $400,000, and we began backers' auditions. If I thought that it would cost that much, I would not have undertaken it, because I would have assumed it was too much to get. Ellen Steinberg, who had come to the rescue of New Orleans when it was in a tight pinch about segregation in schools, said that she would put in $100,000 if we got $300,000, and she did!"

The Great Depression devastated the entire country, regardless of race. **David Randolph**, too, was a child at that time. Music of any kind was limited in his home. He recalls when he was first struck by music: "I remember when I first became aware of music, I was around seven years old. My parents took me to a whist party, and there was an orchestra on the bandstand, but I remember standing there with my mouth open. That was the first time I heard live music. My father brought home a victrolla. He played the famous record of Carusso from *Aida*, and I was so thrilled by it. I was like a kid outside a restaurant window with my nose to the glass. I could read about concerts in New York but could not afford to go to any of them; I went to the free concerts at the public library. I'm a product of the Depression where dreams were not realized. My first job after college was an office boy. I went to college on an allowance of one dollar a week. Carfare was five cents, so I could spend the rest any way I wanted. In graduate school, I copied music in the back of the room, hoping the teacher would not see me. I had to take a loan from the college. Even if I did well, there was nothing to be had [in terms of work]. At college, I was devoted to the scientific method of thinking; I took physics, but higher mathematics was my obstacle. I love the concept of mathematics, the beauty of it; it can be exact, I think. In college, I went through differential and integral calculus. *How?* I don't remember; it was with great difficulty. I moved to music education when I found that I was not going to be a physics major.

"In New York City, WNYC radio, at that time, was run by the city; they had classical music most of the day. My musical education came largely from listening to WNYC. At one point, I conceived of the idea of going to the director on WNYC with my idea of a one-hour show called *Off the Beaten Path*. Instead of playing Beethoven Fifth, I'd play his Fourth. I got a call from the dean of adult division of education and asked if I would teach, which I did. I taught music appreciation for the layman. I spent two years at SUNY New Paltz, and fourteen years at Montclair State College. That job was the river like the Mississippi running through my life. Then I was asked to do commentary at Hunter College at each of their concerts in the hall that seated 2,000 people.

"I had no interest in classical music as a kid—had no connection, even in college. I had been a lifeguard in Peekskill from 1933 to 1940 and got to be assistant lifeguard. I became the examiner for American Red Cross. I'm the most unathletic person. My bunkmate, Jack, was from Philadelphia. He would bring four-hand music. I'd bring four-hand music from the New York Public Library; we'd play concerts of Brahms, Bach. There was also a kindergarten camp counselor there called Mildred. In 1936, Jack and Mildred became [engaged]. Mildred and *I* actually got married in 1938! They called to say that they were joining the New School Chorus and asked if I wanted to join. I did. That was my exposure to classical music. I became hooked. Arthur Leif, who died recently, introduced me to choral music. That call was one of the most fateful things in my life because I developed a love for choral music. I created my own chorus of ten to twelve people; dues were ten cents a week, and that led to my conducting. Another person had a chorus, and we combined the two, renting a studio for one dollar a week. I went to WNYC and asked if they would broadcast it, and they did."

Olu Dara can be described as an unlikely musician, given how long he resisted becoming one. "I did not choose to be a musician; somehow I was forced. Since I was a kid, people put me in the music and kept me there. I tried to escape many times. One time I escaped from 1964 to 1971; that was my longest period without playing. I had to do some things I did not like in music, like playing in marching bands. When I got to college, there was an excellent marching band at Tennessee State College. I enjoyed that band because they did all types of music: jazz, funk, classical. I like the diversity; they were innovators. That school and Florida A&M, there were only two bands that would get away from the John Philip Sousa music at that time. I enrolled in that school to be in that band. I wanted to be a doctor; I was studying premed at Tennessee State. My plan was to go to Meharry Medical School in Nashville. I got into music again some kind

17

of way. I wanted to get away from the school and the band, then I left music again, so I joined the navy to play music, because that was the only thing that interested me at that time. I played music in the navy for four years. When I got out, I was happy not to play music anymore. I used to play with Wynton Kelly in Brooklyn, modal music with Doug and Jean Carne. After I got a call from Art Blakey, I had never really actually played bebop, never studied it, practiced it, or thought about it. I was with him for one year. I was excited about that, I enjoyed listening to bebop. But after that, I quit music again."

2 Learning One's Craft

When I began as an on-air host at WBGO, Jazz 88.3FM, I would fill in for as many shifts as I could. There was a period of time when there was no weekday overnight host, so I would work three of those shifts, take a nap on the couch, and then go to my publishing job. I would work my Sunday morning shift at 6:00 A.M, go home, sleep, then begin again. After six months, I collapsed, but the experience was invaluable. When I began to get requests to emcee, I would host for free, or almost free. To develop my skills, I asked to emcee the summer Jazzmobile Wednesday concerts to get practice. In the beginning, each week, Johnny Garry, the production man, would tell me what I did wrong and explain what I needed to do to get it right. His advice was excellent.

In order to learn your craft, you must find places to work. In addition, I have always sought out the advice of those whom I respect, and I watch what those people do and glean the information that I need. What I have done, and continue to do, is what the musicians have done. Natural ability alone is not enough for one to be a complete musician. It might work for a while if you stay within your musical genre of music but if what you do goes out of style, it will be difficult to work with others. A young jazz musician, a tenor saxophonist, asked a veteran musician why he needed to learn standards, songs that have become the canon of jazz. The veteran musician told him that one day that attitude would get him in trouble. As it turned out, about a year later, the two worked together on a date with Eric Reed. I was in the in the green room when Eric was going over the set. One of the tunes that Eric wanted to play was "Polka Dots and Moonbeams." The gentleman knew the song but only in *one* key, and it was not the key that Eric wanted to play. The young man took a few moments to practice the song, but on the stage, he struggled with it, and the others just played over him. Eric and I discussed his performance, and he replied, "I was shocked! How do you only know a song in one key? That's like only being able to make love in one position. I was pissed off at how he messed up some other tunes on the gig—he couldn't even hear what key we were in on some of the standards!" I asked Eric if he had known ahead of time of this musician's lack of knowledge of standards. Eric said, "Well, I wasn't too concerned because I had charts, but for cryin' out loud . . . I expect A-team players to have it more together."

Michael Wolff learned early on from Cannonball Adderely that he should "learn everything in all keys and to play all over the keyboard." He "listened to the records and learned every tune."

There are several ways to learn one's musical craft. It can be from listening to records, by taking classes, by being mentored, by learning as you go, and/or by working with different types of musicians. Kenny Washington advises that "it is important to tell musicians: Study the music, get a good teacher, listen to the musicians and players that came before you. Never let anyone tell you it's old fashioned. Don't be afraid to copy any of the musicians. You must sound like others before you sound like yourself. In classical music, you have to go back; in jazz, the young people don't know nearly as much as they should about this music, and it's a disgrace. Learn standards; when the record company drops you, you'll have to be a sideman."

Eric, Michael, and Kenny reflect the opinions of the A-team; they are well-versed on their craft and continue to grow. I asked Jeff Clayton if one can transition from the B-team to the A-team and he said, "Yes, you can move, but you have to be open to information. If you know everything, then you shut down. Even at fifty, I try to be open and aware."

When I was in Europe, I watched MTV one day when they were featuring women. I watched the programs on Madonna, Missy Elliot, and Beyonce. Three different artists, three different genres, but all of them worked *hard*! With dogged determination, the support of those already in their fields, and a keen understanding of where they were headed, they all rose to the top. As you go along in this business, it is essential to seek help and surround yourself with musicians more advanced then yourself. David Randolph summed it up: "I work, work, and work! I write until 2 to 3 A.M. to do what it takes to give a concert at Carnegie Hall."

Sometimes it is beneficial to attend workshops. **Edwin Hawkins** has created a place for musicians to learn. I asked him about his workshops. "As the Hawkins Family, we traveled a lot, and we saw a lot of young people who wanted to get into the business. We got Richard Smallwood involved and people like that to be a part of the conference to give a week of instruction and offer resources on how to get started. We wanted to help give direction to those talented in the arts, not just

Gospel, but also sacred dance, drama, and the business of Gospel music, as well as the ministry of Gospel music. We did not have *all* the answers but shared some of the knowledge we have."

Brenda Feliciano remembers, "When I was a kid, there was a show called *Canta Puerto Rico* that was bilingual. My mom said it would help me get into my roots while I was doing classical music; I was schizophrenic," she laughs. "I went to American University in Puerto Rico, but it had people from all over the island. I came back and went to City College in Brooklyn. I did a lot of things; I worked with the 'Salsa Refugees' with Mario Rivera, Hilton Ruiz, Andy Gonzalez, and all of those people. I could have gone straight into opera, but I didn't, I was looking around. I was a Young Lord and doing poetry and a lot of experimental theater; I did vocalese where I utilized the operatic voice and screams, I did weird things."

Allan Harris understood what he needed to do when he was starting out: What helped me grow as an artist was jazz because of the melodies and you had to study your craft. . . . In jazz, because of the caliber of musicians I needed to play with and to accept me, I had to learn my craft, or I would not work with them. In other genres, the door was open. You had to have a certain look, some sort of gimmick, or fill the bill of what they were looking for that evening. In jazz it did not matter how, you had to learn your craft. You had to know the songs that were presented to you, and that was your calling card. I found that my participation was remunerated, not by the pay scale, but by growth. The more I learned the music, the more I grew as an individual."

Bobby Sanabria said, "When I was twelve years old, Tito Puente and Machito and others came to perform, and I watched them from my neighbor's bedroom. I urged him to go down to see it, and we got there when Tito took a solo. I was mesmerized, and it was like an epiphany, and I knew I wanted to do it the rest of my life. I started working when I went to Berklee College of Music. My father was so busy, and he had gotten laid off when the Vietnam War ended, and he could not take the long travel. We were on welfare for a year, and it was embarrassing. When I told my father that he had to sign the papers for me to get a loan for school, and I told him I was going to do music, he said that he thought it was a hobby, and he freaked out. My mother made him sign the papers. In high school, I had started my group, Ascension, but I had no real musical knowledge. In that first incarnation, I was writing arrangements and melded all the aesthetics I was acquiring. Berklee was an incredible experience for me, but it was very difficult. My first year I took applied music, the hardest program at the school. My first year in Boston, I got a rep. No one there was into Latin music at all."

Each genre of music requires different kinds of knowledge. Though his chosen genre has been jazz, Eric Reed pointed out that the demands on a jazz musician can be at least as rigorous as those put upon a classical musician. "It was so bizarre, I'd be competing in jazz against classical [musicians]. There were music competitions; nobody was playing jazz, just me! I was the only one doing jazz. I was better than them; I played my music better than they played their music. I'd have my suit and tie, and I'd play with a lot of personality. Before people heard me play, they'd be intrigued by this thirteen- or fourteen-year-old kid who could articulate a point of view about music so eloquently."

When I asked Eric about jazz musicians who had had a desire to be classical musicians before transitioning to jazz, he said, "Jazz and classical music are different types of music, but they both require a higher level of skill and discipline than most other types of music. Not to say that other music such as pop, R&B, don't require talent. What it takes to play both jazz and classical as a pianist is advance knowledge of all elements of music, melody, rhythm, and harmony, whereas in popular music, that level of skill is not required. That's why it's popular music. In pop music, you don't have to do a whole lot of things in order to appreciate it. It's designed for a certain kind of stimulation, whether it's emotional, mental, or mental de-stimulation. You don't have to know how to play the 'Rock 3'—Rachmaninoff's Third Piano Concerto—to play pop music."

Jeff Clayton straddled genres and continues to do so, although he is primarily considered a jazz musician. "I began in jazz music; it is the art of being a chameleon, it is so special, it prepares you to do any music. You steal solos, jazz, funk, or classical music; you just copy and mimic that. Then you understand the parameters of these styles, and good jazz musicians can copy. I started out on Concord Records as a jazz artist, then I did pop because someone asked me if I could, so I stole some solos, learned some songs of Stevie Wonder from his records until I knew how to play pop. When I did that, I changed the way I played in my mind and body and played pop. When I stopped playing pop, I turned on jazz and classical; they are closely related."

I remember the first time I went to hear Ron Carter's "Nonet" and saw Dorothy Lawson as a member. Though classically trained, she takes her knowledge of that genre and applies it when working in that musical setting, which combines the two elements, jazz and classical. She spent many years studying and understood the importance of surrounding herself with masters. "I spent a long time working with powerful people and being an apprentice and doing what they asked me to do or what they approved of. It never stopped me from feeling I had my own taste somewhere. The process for me to find my own voice was, for me, getting really secure and comfortable with the idea that I was going to say something without the approval of others and take the consequences."

Finding one's voice is something that is much discussed in the jazz community. If you read reviews, you will find that critics tend to focus on "voice" when reviewing young musicians. Just in his thirties, Eric Reed has been playing professionally since his teens. "I'm finding my voice; it's a lifelong thing. I'm still finding my voice though I'm certain that I've found it. It takes so much time because you have to develop a certain kind of rapport with other musicians. I prefer trio settings; I play off other musicians well. It allows me the complete freedom to express myself rhythmically, harmonically, and melodically. Sometimes I'll do work for hire, such as, I'll be asked to do a concert on Gershwin. I'm very meticulous; I do a lot of research. For example, if I'm going to do a concept record based on Gershwin's work, I'll do a certain number of his hits, some things not hits, but people know the songs, and some obscure songs that no one knows about. People need to know that it's Gershwin."

Sometimes the best lessons come in the cruelest ways. **Ruth Brown** learned the hard way from one of her idols, Billie Holiday, that she needed to find her voice. "I did not find my voice immediately. After Billie told me I sounded like her, I found it a few years after that." Ruth had been booked to play in the Cafe Society Club that Billie had made her own. It was a double bill with folk singer Josh White, a close friend of Billie's. As Ruth expected, Billie came into the club to hear them. Upon hearing that Billie was there, Ruth decided to redo her set and play all of Billie's songs. This was her way of paying tribute to her idol. When Ruth finished, Billie got up and walked away in apparent disgust. Backstage, Billie said:

❄ ❄ ❄ ❄

Right now, I know you're hurt . . . Let me tell you something, and
I want you to remember this. Although you may not understand it now,
every time you open your mouth and do what you just did out there,

they're gonna call my *name, not* yours . . . *I appreciate your likin' me so much you want to be like me. But you can't be me, 'cause* I'm *me; there's only one Billie Holiday . . . Don't try to be someone you're not. Be yourself.*

❊ ❊ ❊ ❊

"When Billie told me that, I was considered a rhythm-and-blues singer, not a jazz singer, so I never got to sing her songs. I'm just a stylist; I can sing jazz, Gospel, show tunes, sing standards and do country and western. I just had not done all these things, but I can! That is the only way I have been able to survive. My records were not being played. I've been singing almost sixty years, but I never won a Grammy singing rhythm and blues. The only time I won anything, a Grammy, it was for jazz—*Blues on Broadway*, my record with Thad Jones, Kenny Burrell, and all jazz artists. I never got a gold record, but I've been Miss Rhythm and Blues for years!"

Another Grammy-Award winner—he has won five—is vocalist Al Jarreau, who is known for his scat singing. I asked him to respond to something a famous jazz pianist has told me many times—no one should scat. That musician said to me, "Louis Armstrong, yes, and *maybe* Ella Fitzgerald." He challenged me to find an album of Johnny Hartman scatting and told me that I would not. My reason for asking Jarreau about scatting is that I had heard about singers who teach scat and I was curious as to how one goes about learning to scat. Al said, it is "a long story . . . as long as all the nights I've stood on a stage. In a few words, it is on-the-job training. You have to dare to stand onstage and dare to do it, go home, and study the solo, and dare to do it again. I'm still learning to scat sing and sing jazzy solos. I'm not sure if it can be taught. You get real nervous trying to teach scat.

"On the other hand, you have to let people experiment and try it. Okay, maybe if this is a classroom situation where this gets taught. I'm not sure what gets said in the classroom other than, go get such-and-such record, learn the solo of Johnny Hodges in the record, then go learn the solo of Jon Hendricks and sing it. I think, pound-for-pound, Jon is the best jazz singer. It's all about listening and learning. Something has to be said about the singer who can sing the melody and the lyric and is a good craftsman. That is different than the musician/singer who understands the chord structure, *feeling* underneath, understands, and has a sensibility for the chords that are in any one phrase as he solos. That's what horn players do.

"There are singers who sing the melody, and fit inside that chord structure. Someone who does not grow beyond being a technician does not appreciate what goes on at the other level, and you've got to in order to scat sing. I don't know how easy it is to learn. By singing these songs, I learned my craft. My older brothers brought the music into the house. Songs like 'Straighten Up and Fly Right,' that kind of music [he sings some bars]; they brought Nat Cole, Billy Eckstine, and Sinatra, Ella. Listening to those artists, *feeling*, sensing, learning was *very impor-tant*! My singing took another leap when I heard Jon Hendricks, and Lambert, Hendricks, and Ross signing as a trio, arrangements of Count Basie. I had to rediscover the Basie band because Jon had his trio all singing those great solos where I learned to appreciate the lyrics."

Singers are not the only musicians who learn much of their craft from records. Drummer Kenny Washington listened endlessly to records. Kenny's father had a great record collection, and he charged him with the importance of listening. "He always listened to the best music, and I heard it all. He did not say a lot about it; he'd just tell me to listen to it, and I wanted to play high quality music, too. Not to be Philly Joe Jones, but high musicianship when I got out there. I'd practice my backside off, and I said if I was not great, I'd never make it. It's good to be around guys who are better than you. I tell folks to go see the 'Holy Four'—Jimmy Cobb, Roy Haynes, Ben Riley, Louis Hayes. If Mickey Roker comes to New York City, then the 'Holy Five.' I learned by watching for things you can't learn on records."

Around 1990, Kenny ended up on the radio, on WBGO, Jazz 88.3FM. He was asked to do a newly created program called *The Big Band Dance Party*. Begrudgingly he did it. "First, it was not my idea; I did not want to do it, but I wanted to be on the radio. I liked big bands, but I did not want to play bands I *thought* I did not like, such as Glenn Miller, Harry James, and a lot of those white big bands—Claude Barnett, Claude Thornhill, and Woody Herman. What I did was to go through the WBGO library, and I saw the complete boxed set of Glenn Miller, and I said to myself, *I hate Glenn Miller*, but I checked it out. Much was commercial, but the next track was hitting, and I could not believe it! It sounded like a different band. From that point on, I went through every white band I could think of, and I did my research at the Institute of Jazz Studies at Rutgers University in Newark. I found all the white bands to be the same, with the pop side and good side. On the positive side of things, going through all those records made me a better musician. I knew a lot about big bands before radio, but I checked out bands I might never have checked out.

Clark Terry told me about Harry James and told me not to sleep on him. At that time, I was doing Lincoln Center concerts and repertory concerts and such, so it helped me."

Dr. Billy Taylor had the good fortune of starting out when many jazz legends were still living. He, too, used radio hosting to further his education, and he also did a lot to keep jazz in the public eye. Always one to strive and grow, he knew how necessary it was to seek the guidance of others. "Two things [made me continue]; when I came to New York I was lucky to meet people who were kind to me. One person was Teddy Wilson. I loved his touch, and I wanted to study with him and to sound like that, but he was real busy and had no time to teach me. Instead, he took me to his teacher—Rich McClanahan—he changed the way I touched the piano. I was playing hard, and my fingers hurt, and I figured that there was a better way to do it. He worked with me on that. When I play a ballad, they can tell it's me playing."

Having had no formal training, Oscar Brown Jr. learned from being around great musicians. "I had to depend on others. I got the benefit of people who knew music, and I didn't. I used to be embarrassed going among musicians. They all read music and talked about changes, and I didn't know anything. I didn't even know what key I was in for the most part, but little by little, I learned as you experience things. I still don't know music."

You must recognize where you are and what you need to do to get where you want to go. You must take responsibility for what you must do to get the knowledge. As Paula Kimper says, "Discipline . . . you gotta love it. You can't force yourself to be disciplined." Says Andy Bey: "I don't want to sabotage what I'm trying to get good at, or better at. So if I have to sing, I'm not gonna do things that might sabotage that. We all do that, but the more I learn about business, the more my relationship to what I try to do, or I'm trying to do, the more I enhance what I do. I'm still learning to live life. Becoming positive helped me through challenges. I've always had discipline. You may be mad at things and people, and you might have reasons, but it's a choice on how you deal with it. One has to be focused; you want to make the best music by being focused and the choices that you make."

Honesty is the key. Be honest with yourself about your talents. Conversely, the sought-after givers of advice must be honest with those who come to them for help. When I asked Richard Smallwood about how honest he was with people, he did say that he tries not to be cruel with his assessments, as he has witnessed others being. He shared an experience that he had with a young woman: "People come to me all of the time with demos. Some time ago, a singer with bad pitch gave me her demo, but she could not carry a tune in a bucket. She had a problem with her intonation, so I suggested that she get some voice lessons and ear training. She came back to me, and said she had done what I had told her to do, but she was worse than before. Can't people hear themselves? She told me that people said that she was no good, but until *I said* that she was no good, she would not listen to them. I told her that she was not up to par; she got mad and did not speak to me again, but I had to be honest."

3 Formal Education Versus Learning on the Bandstand

A few years ago, I was asked to work for the producer of BET's Harlem Block Party as they were opening an office in New York City. The celebration was an evening of stars from all genres of black music: Stevie Wonder, Mary J. Blige, Wyclef Jean, and many others. During a rehearsal, one of the featured artists, a singer, came late, and she had not learned the song that she was supposed to sing. I was sent to purchase the CD that contained the song, by its original artist, so that she and the other musicians could learn it. After several tries, she gave up and left the studio in disgust. Two of the other musicians in the backup group could not "hear" their parts, either. During a break, I was talking to the one "trained" musician whom I had met years earlier when he was playing jazz. He left jazz to go to work with pop artists, including Madonna. We talked about how the day had progressed and how difficult it was for him to work with those musicians. He was so frustrated that he had told them they needed to get some formal training. Because of his education (he had graduated from Berklee College), he was able to play in any key, he could hear the music, he was able to arrange on the spot, and he could play anything that was put in front of him. In the end, the artist convinced the producer to let her sing *her* hit song. He agreed, and the program was altered. The next day during the dress rehearsal where all musicians were required to show up, Stevie Wonder came out. I had heard that when Stevie warmed up, he would play John Coltrane's "Giant Steps." In fact, he did that. Stevie was magnificent.

A schism has developed in the music industry as rap and hip hop have grown in stature. While rappers may have natural musical ability, they often do not have the formal musical education others may deem necessary. Much criticism has come down upon the rappers for not being musical, or for not even being musicians. Some question whether what they do is even music. Over the last twenty years or so, pop music has also been under attack, with the rise of megastars who are criticized for not knowing anything about music. Singers tend to be blasted for not playing an instrument (other than their voice) and sneered at for having no knowledge about the notes that they sing. Music and music education has almost been eliminated from public-school curriculums. Rap and hip hop was born in the streets. Hip-hop historian Kevin Powell talked about this on my TV show, *The Art of Jazz*. His contention is that when music was eliminated from the schools, young people used what they had at their disposal, the turntable and bottles, cans, or any other item that could be turned into an instrument.

When I was growing up, almost everyone I knew had to take music lessons on an instrument. We had music in our schools, diverse music was played on the radio, there were free concerts in the park, and many of my friends played in a band. My first boyfriend, Dallas, played guitar, and I used to love to see his band perform, even if all they played were covers of Earth, Wind, and Fire. I can't recall if any of them became working musicians, although they worked often in Buffalo, New York.

Some of the greatest jazz musicians could not read a lick of music, but their musicianship was, and is, beyond reproach. As in any art form, exceptions find their way to the top. It is rare in classical music for someone to be successful without formal education, but Dorothy Lawson has known of this happening: "That is much more difficult. I have only seen that where people got that from the family, where there is a lot of music and they got a lot of training inside the family." Every few years, I will read or hear about a virtuoso in either classical music or jazz music, so I asked Dorothy to explain what one is. "A virtuoso is a person who has control of her instrument and is so fluent and so smooth between her brain and her hands, there is no perceived block when you are listening to her playing. You are not observing a lot of work, but a lot of thought. It can be simple; it does not have to be technically showing off."

Talent with Education

On the topic of formal education versus learning on the bandstand—that is, learning as you are doing—the answers of the interviewees were very interesting. Basically, they stressed that learning formally was important, but some cautioned that musicians should not get too hung up on it, instead using education as a tool. Billy Taylor offered two examples of musicians who excelled without education: Ruth Brown and Erroll Garner. He said, "Ruth Brown was one of those people who had so much talent, that like many self-taught people, she could learn from having good people around her. There were many people who were able to do that, instrumentalist or vocalists, but it was a handicap because you were forced to depend on someone else. Aretha Franklin could read; she grew up in the church.

She could read and play music, sit at the piano, and say, 'No, it sounds like this.' Carmen McRae and Sarah Vaughan were funny; they would challenge each other. The fact that Erroll Garner did not read music did not lessen the fact that he was a great musician. He grew up in Pittsburgh, Pennsylvania, he had a brother and sister who studied music, and he looked over their shoulders and figured out things on his own. He was quick, and his ears were good, and he could get everything he needed by ear. Not many people have that kind of discipline because what he did was not just learning to play in one or two keys, he played in all twelve keys. He played in *hard keys*—B and E, keys like that. Later I found Art Tatum—he was legally blind, and other guys who had that experience whether they read or not; it was fascinating to me, and it was one of my lessons. I was there when Don Byas taught Erroll the tune 'Laura' from that movie. Don learned the music, and Erroll wanted to learn that tune; he got the music and taught it to Erroll, and it was Erroll's first big hit."

Although he lacks the benefit of being formally trained, Al Jarreau commented, "They are both important. I have no formal music education. My mother taught piano, but I was too stupid to take the baseball glove off of my hand. Formal training is not the only way to get there, but it is important. If you have the time, get some, but I'm not sure when I would introduce it. If a person had some native talent, I'd like to see them explore that before I'd dump them into a formal situation. But how do you discover that when you pick up a sax? You have to have someone show you how to put the mouthpiece in your mouth. I suppose you can get it on your own. But for most musicians, it is the formal situation where they get exposed to an instrument. For the singer, I'd like to have heard him singing in Sunday school for a few years before you take him to a teacher to cultivate that voice."

Edwin Hawkins echoed the same thought: "It is if you can marry the two. Instructors, back in the day when I was a kid, believed that once you started to receive formal education, you should never do it by ear, which I think is the greatest mistake. I think it siphons your ability to create on your own. I've seen musicians who adhere to that kind of suggestion and wouldn't do anything by ear. As a result, they were very limited, too, in terms of being creative on their own. A good example of doing both is Richard Smallwood. He was able to study formally and then continue to create on his own. I *wish* that I had been encouraged to do that in a bigger way. Richard can write or chart his own music; I cannot. I would depend on him or someone else to score a piece for me."

Richard Smallwood had addressed that in our discussion before I interviewed Edwin. A graduate of Howard University who holds a master's degree,

Smallwood said, "I think that it [formal education] is very important. If God has given us a gift, we are charged to develop it, and to be the best we can be. A lot of things that you know by ear, or that you do naturally, you get to understand why they are, or how they are put together. You learn about the history of music and why you do what you do. Knowing who the pioneers are helps you to be the best when you get there. I started formal classes at age seven and continued through until I graduated from Howard."

Allan Harris said, "I had both. I had many teachers. Formal education is necessary so you can express what you want to express to a select few people, jazz especially. Other artists don't have time to teach you via trial and error. They need people who can read. There are exceptions to the rule, those who are just prodigies and geniuses. But they are exceptions. I wasn't; I'm good, but not a genius. Formal education is good to have to give you an understanding of what you need to do. But a lot of time is wasted. If you read, with formal education, you can cut to the quick. I found that jazz people were more into mentoring because their music was a lifestyle and a love, whereas R&B music meant to have fun with it, to make money and garner wealth. When you go into anything with that feeling of, this is what I love to do because this makes me feel better as an individual, then you want to share with your fellow man, especially when someone sits at your feet, you can impart some of your knowledge."

Brenda Feliciano feels, "You need both. You need to learn your vocabulary, then put your hands on it, learn your ABCs—technique—then go hang out. To get a degree and think that you are a professional is not enough. I am learning all of the time, and you gotta *practice*." When I interviewed her, she was working on a difficult piece of music. She said, "I am working on a piece by Baia, and I've done his work, such as *La Vida Breve*, which was his opera. He is a brilliant composer. My first impression was, 'Oh, my God, what a boring piece,' and I did not like it. For the last two weeks, I sat down with the piece, and I studied the tempos and the meaning of how he wrote it, and what it means in terms of the text, and what is happening, and I found it to be a brilliant piece. You gotta study a piece before you dismiss it; you really have to study when you stand in front of an orchestra; you have to be prepared."

Andy Bey was encouraged to build on his talent, although most of his education came from doing. "I had formal lessons much later; my parents did not want to destroy my natural talent. I could accompany because I could hear things. My sisters would take me to high school to play with them. I wanted to grow [as a musician], so once I got to high school, I went to Music and Art School. I learned theory and harmony, but learning was limited due to the number of students in the classrooms. I learned to read simple stuff. Later I took private lessons. Most of what I learned was from musicians. I didn't go to a music college. I had this gift that kept developing, and I taught myself. In my mid-twenties, I had classical training. If you have natural talent, it does not hurt to develop what you have naturally."

Bobby Sanabria did not have an instrument on which to learn. "I had talent, and I could imitate with my hands what the players were doing. I practiced in the shower on the wall, on car bumpers; we did not need drums. But then Mayor Abe Beame stopped the music in the streets and in the park with those 'quality-of-life' laws.

"My second epiphany came when I saw Buddy Rich on the TV. I saw Louis Bellson and Gene Krupa, too. It made me want to play more. There was also jazz radio. From sixth to eight grade, I got more into jazz. I was at the Monsignor William R. Kelly, a progressive school, where I got a scholarship; it was experimental. The teachers turned me on to records to listen to like John Coltrane. At night, I would secretly listen to WNEW-FM, and I heard John McLaughlin, Mahavishnu Orchestra, Procal Harem, Emerson, Lake, and Palmer, and progressive rock. I liked the arrangements, and I heard the blues. All those elements are in my music now. I did not take formal lessons at first, but I listened to records and used what I heard in the streets.

"Both [formal and practical] are important. You can only go so far with street knowledge. I saw the drummers reading music. In order to get to the next level, you need it. I wanted to be like those guys; so to be a total musician, you have to study. I was on a mission to go to Berklee or any music school; I just wanted to study music."

Where Formal Education Ends and Work Begins

What happens often with musicians happened to Gerald Cannon. He studied at the conservatory, but he did not finish because work took precedence. "I think school is very important because you get some structure. I was fortunate: I studied in Milwaukee, and there were great teachers. There were old-school teachers. Hattish Alexander was a great teacher in Milwaukee. They told us to learn some standards and learn harmony and melody. I was put in combos, but I could not read, but I learned as I practiced and in theory class. I went berserk listening to records. Once I got hooked on jazz, I spent all my money on jazz records. My buddies and I would listen and talk about the music. I started working as a professional with a singer named Penny Goodwin—my first big gig. After one month, Penny heard me talking about having an upright bass. She threatened to fire me if I did not bring it on the gig that night. It was hell on me. The bass was out of tune, and it was hard to play."

To appease his parents, Eric Reed went to college for one year. He, like Michael Wolff and Kenny Washington, weighs in most heavily on the side of learning on the bandstand: "Not to put down the idea of formal education— I believe in education, under any circumstances—but I think we've gotten to a place where we have placed so much emphasis on formal education from an institution that we have kind of done away with the whole middle ground of skilled workers, done away with the whole idea of apprenticeship, people who make things, the carpenters, steel workers, blacksmiths, etc.—a whole level of our economy that almost does not exist, so only a handful of those people can do those things. I've heard it said, I think an attorney once told me—a guy who went to Yale University—anything worth knowing/learning, can't be learned in a classroom. I thought that was interesting coming from him. He was not casting aspersions at education, university, or college, but making the point that information can be attained through a variety of sources and places. To place so much emphasis on a college education, you have already limited your options for learning.

"The experiences [I had] were priceless; you can't buy experience and can't get it in a classroom. Playing night after night with top-notch musicians, playing complex music, playing in front of different audiences, you can't get it in school." I asked Eric if he, at any point, found having *no* degree a hindrance. "Not at all," he replied. "Because I work hard, and I knew early that if I was not going to pursue a degree, I'd have to work harder to be successful. Just to show my parents if nothing else. I wanted my folks to be proud of me. In my immature way, I wanted to show them."

Kenny Washington began working steadily in his teens. As he often said, when he came along there was *no* youth movement; he was it. When Wynton Marsalis hit the scene, he was able to focus attention on the young jazz musicians. They were hailed as the "Young Lions." Most had their own groups and were getting recording contracts from major labels. There has been an increase over the last twenty years in jazz education in the institutions of higher learning, but Kenny is wary of them: "To be honest, I hate to put those schools down; they are trying to do something, but it's my opinion that at most of those schools, the teachers need to be taught. It's my opinion, but I've been to some of the schools; what they are teaching the kids is absolutely wrong. Most of these kids in Berklee, New School, etc., they really want to play, and they want to play jazz.

They are not being taught properly from a musician's point of view. I'm not say-ing all the teachers, some don't know how to teach. Most of them are not that great. A lot don't know how to teach; they weren't great to begin with, and they are not good teachers. Many students go for years and don't come out playing much better than when they started.

"The basics should be taught, the rudiments. Many students come to me and say, 'I want to play brushes. I want to sound like Philly Joe Jones. Can you show me?' I'll ask them to play me some swing time, or some tempos, or a five-stroke roll, and it will sound like an egg roll—they don't have the basics together. I tell them that no matter what kind of music they play, they have to get those basics together. You don't necessarily learn on the drums, but on the practice pad to get your hand together first. Those teachers don't insist that they get that together. I would have failed them if they didn't. Many of those students are working, but they are not getting what they should get. I ask them if they have certain records, and I make them get records like Miles Davis's *Walkin'* with Philly Joe Jones."

Michael Wolff said, "I was in college; I was at UCLA to study music, and they had on an okay jazz band, really nice guys . . . down in San Fernando Valley State College, which is called something else now, I can't recall. Gerald Wilson had a jazz history class. I immediately found he was from Shelby, Mississippi, so we immediately fell in love. I love him. He's the nicest guy and a great musician, and I just audited his class, and I just dug being around him, and at the end of the class, he'd have a jam session. He'd let people sit in, and I remember . . . when I sat in and played, they played their ass off one night when magic struck, and I felt myself out of myself just watching the beautiful music come out. That was the first time that ever happened—where I just was like surfing, when you stood up, got the wave . . . that was like an 'Ah-Ha' moment."

Regarding getting a formal education, he says, "It depends on the instrument. I think for piano, it's good if you have both. Also, the great people that I admire have both. I don't know if Thelonious Monk had formal training, but nowadays the guys that were my idols, like Herbie Hancock, Chick Corea, and Keith Jarett, they're all classically trained. I am not a classical pianist, but I studied that stuff, and it really helped me out as a composer to study music. But I think that you know you can't just learn that in college, either. I think the way jazz is now, it's all just about education in college, which is sterile! Great musicians stand out, no matter whether they're in college or not, they're always going to be great. But I think, seeing that I got so much from hanging out with the guys, the vibe . . . why do you get into music? When I was a teenager, a girl would sit next to me on the piano bench, and I'd go, 'Ooh, this is hip!' I was just obsessed with this jazz music. I had to listen to every person who I could get my hands on."

Ron Carter broke it down in percentages: "Probably 60/40. Forty meaning formal education, and sixty learning on the bandstand. You can't have one successfully, completely, without the other. I mean, you need discipline to know how prepare a lesson, how to prepare an arrangement. Discipline to learn how to arrange, how to compose. Bandstand: how to put two sides [sets] together and see what level your talent is. Yes, I worked as a musician while going to school."

No Choice—Institution Is a Must

Classical musicians have no choice in getting a formal education. David Randolph agrees, "Formal education is very important. Nobody whom you ever heard of got there without ability. You have to have the ability! They all have ability. They all have their craft, in varying degrees. After that, it is being in the right place at the right time, contacts, and whom you know.

"I can assure you that there is competition. Like at school, like Juilliard. Everybody who gets in goes with the idea of being a big star. No one has the idea of being the second violin in the Houston Symphony Orchestra. They all want to be Itzhak Perlman. A person who studied at Juilliard told me, 'It's a jungle; they are after each other; they claw over each other. How can they *not* claw at each other? When you get a bunch of virtuosos, how can they not? It's human nature."

In response to David's indictment of schools like Juilliard, Dorothy Lawson said, "Juilliard was a great experience. I loved parts of it. It was all-encompassing. It's a great school. They are as good as any music school, in my opinion. I was lucky that when I went, I had done so much other work, and especially that I was not an undergraduate. I noticed among the undergrads a distinct anxiety, a higher level of anxiety-driven competitiveness. They were worried that if they did not cut it and make it big at Juilliard, they would never succeed. My perspective from my travels was that they were on a very good level, and they'd probably do nicely whether or not they were on the top of the heap in Juilliard. I didn't feel as vulnerable to that kind of pressure. The beauty of being an older student is that you appreciate your teachers more and search them out from your own interest, rather than to fill a school requirement."

Reiterating the question of which was most effective, I expected Dorothy to say institutional learning to be most necessary, but she said, "Both are needed, and formal education is more and more effective. The ergonomics [involved in playing one's instrument] are now considered an important part of education. What is being taught is less traditional than in the past. Institutions are much more communicative and interactive, and teachers address the students' individual needs. In good situations, it can be quite personalized and efficient. On the other hand, as a musician you need to spend much of your life as a practitioner to develop your own voice—your own presence; I think learning by doing. You need a nice mix."

Paula Kimper is a little more critical of schools. "You can't *not* learn as you go. You have to use someone else's experience to help you teach yourself. I think everyone has to be self-taught. As far as learning institutions, I was a little disillusioned. I was put off by the whole academic approach to music, and that is why I never went to get an advanced degree. It meant writing twelve-tone music in the way they wanted you to do it; they want you to be innovative, but that is the opposite of being innovative. That's not what I want. What I hear is melodies, and I really love song forms and music that is much more accessible than what they were trying to teach. They were trying to be as inaccessible as possible. So I left that, and I've never gone back to any kind of academic thing."

No Formal Music Education

Oscar Brown Jr. said that his family "forced it on you. I wanted to play drums, but it was too loud. I did not grow up in a musical family. My sister studied ballet and piano but never became professional at either; that is just what they did for girls. I wanted to be a piano player, but I did not have dexterity in my right hand, so I escaped that."

Olu Dara, who had some training in his youth, does not see the big deal about education because it does not determine talent: "Anybody can play on the bandstand with formal education. Anyone [with formal education] from any country can play in any band, but you can't just bring them into genres such as Gospel, funk, rhythm and blues. They might be able to read music, but do they play the sound and feeling that the genre demands? Avant-garde was the music being respected at a time in my life. All you had to do was play on one record and end up in the history books whether you could play or not. I saw a lot of scams going on. I'd see a guy pick up the horn one day, then the next day end up in a magazine. [He laughs.] I saw it happen. In Europe, they'd become stars, or many guys made records. It was very European—you had to read, you had to have paper, even in avant-garde. Avant-garde was 'anti-groove'—a lot of musicians would cringe if you played in a groove—it was free music. So it was free, but if you listened, all you heard was a clump of notes, screams, and stuff. It became loud and boisterous. I had to relearn how to play my trumpet after I did a stint with that music.

It just wore me out. My lips had been distorted, and I had almost forgotten how to play my own style of music by doing that. Playing bebop and avant-garde, I had to change the way I thought. I was a natural bebop player, though. A lot of musicians couldn't play background. If it wasn't written out, they could not play riffs, but when it came time to make up a riff, put harmony to it, a lot of guys could not do it."

Ruth Brown said, "I had no formal training, and I can't read music. I could sing anything I heard. My music teacher in high school, Ora Lee Churchill, told me, 'You're gonna regret that one of these days.' Sometimes when I went into the studio to record, the arranger would bring lead sheets. In the beginning, you did not have to worry about it; they'd send you a demo, and you would learn from the record. Now all of the arrangements have a sheet for vocal line, but I still can't read it; I hear it. I'm not sure that young people are really learning music now. They can make a star out of the mixing board. Anyone can sound like they are singing. In those days, that was impossible. One thing that was important was all of the *great* singers—Ella, Sarah, Carmen, Dinah—played piano. I didn't do any of that. Dizzy Gillespie said, 'Ruth could hear a rat peeing in cotton because she can hear it.' That is what I depended on. I can hear chord changes. That is why most of my musicians stayed with me."

As Jeff Clayton concluded, "The A-team continues to learn, whether it is in a formal setting, on the bandstand, or a combination of both." He wryly suggested that the B-team tends to have more formal education than the A-team because they spent a lot of time in school, rather than working professionally.

4 Is There Such a Thing as Too Much Practice?

"*No*," says Edwin Hawkins, there is never "too much; practice makes perfect." That is a general rule, and one that Edwin prescribes for himself, but in general, as musicians grow, they practice less. I have learned from musicians how important practice is in their early development. As their work increases, their practice usually takes a different form. The more one works, the less time or need one has to practice. Almost all of the musicians spent hours practicing as they were learning. If possible, for musicians starting out, especially children, it is good to be able to find some kind of balance. If one becomes consumed with practice and has no practical application, practice becomes counterproductive. In many cases, during young musicians' formative years, the downside of intense practice is that they miss out on some social skills that come from interaction with others. Eric Reed noticed how his social skills were adversely affected by his practicing: "That's very true. I suffered from that, starting with high school. I didn't have an opportunity to develop all facets of my personality; most of my life consisted of people patting me on the back and saying, 'You are really great; no one plays like you at sixteen,' and I was believing my own press. I didn't have enough people, as my friend Wren T. Brown would say, holding me to a system of checks and balances."

Bobby Sanabria spent much of his youth engrossed in study: "I had talent, and I could imitate with my hands what the players were doing . . . I guess you can [practice too much]; it can be all-consuming. To be a musician, you have to have a well-rounded life. You don't get balance at the beginning. I lacked a lot of social skills when I got to Berklee College; I had never been out of New York City." Those who love their instruments are never *forced* to practice; they *prefer* to practice rather than go out and play with other children.

The How and What of Practicing

Ron Carter, Kenny Washington, and Billy Taylor agree: The key to practice is knowing *what* to practice. Says Kenny, "I still practice, but most important is to know *how* to practice. You have to have a regimen. When I was a kid, all I wanted to do was practice. Nowadays, my students tend to be older, in high school, and/or in college. There are other things [affecting them] than when I was coming up. They have lives. All I had to do was get good grades and practice."

A musician told me about the time he was sharing a house with another musician who played the same instrument as he did; they had two different approaches to practice. He told me that he spent all day perfecting his tone by playing long notes, whereas the other ran up and down his horn all day, noodling. The one who worked on his speed never got a good sound. It is up to each musician to determine what he wants to get out of his instrument. Jeff Clayton said that when musicians focus more on speed, they are "being unaware. That is playing stuff on automatic pilot and not being aware of how the notes interact with the music, and the person is using them as etudes, as studies, as *exercise*. That is the worst word to use in music. No music is an exercise . . . in futility. Everything we play has musical content if you give it content. In reality, when you are playing, you are playing what you intend to play; you are not exercising. When you practice the wrong way, it won't make you aware. As Dick Gregory said, 'Christopher Columbus did not discover America; it's like discovering your Cadillac with *you* in it; he discovered a continent of Indians.'"

One musician says that too much practice is an attribute of the B-team: "Isn't it deep how the B-team claims they always practice—but never get better? And if they've got all this time to practice, then that must mean they don't work that much—it's really rather an odd contradiction."

Or, as Eric Reed says, "All practice and no play makes Jack a dull musician."

Kenny Barron did not hesitate when he answered the question as it applied to him: "In my case, *no!* I don't think that I practiced enough. I wish I'd have practiced more so I'd be a better musician. I see some of the chops of these young people . . . but I have things that they don't have, like experience, so I have things that I can teach them."

Paula Kimper does not see practice as a dreaded task. "You can't force yourself. To me, it's not, 'Now I have to do my work,' it's, 'Let me at it!' How you deal with personal growth—that goes hand in hand. How you make it work in daily life. Do you play your instrument every day? Somehow, not necessarily practicing, you touch it, do you have a link to it, do you hear something? Yeah, it takes one second," she laughs. "I have this practice that I call, 'giving them their fifteen minutes.' Me, or whoever the guides or spirits are, just sit at the piano and I say, 'Okay, play whatever you want.' I move my like a Ouija board, and let things come out, and it's astonishing. Then I go to work and write tunes."

Joe Grushecky had the challenge of fronting a band and the problem of rehearsing in his home. He had to find ways to work around his nine-to-five work schedule. As a unit, rehearsing and practice was essential to their success. "We'd rehearse every night when I'd come home after work; we were religious about it, every night for five nights a week. We would practice from seven to ten o'clock; after ten, in deference to our neighbors, we would stop. Then we would go to bars and check out people and try to get them to hire us, try to observe people and try to learn our craft. We did that for a while."

The Effect of Work on Practice

Richard Smallwood does "not practice like I should. I only get to write or play in church or in a concert. The church is one of the best training grounds on how to play. You play songs you never heard. You can start in one key that does not exist or in between keys. I don't practice around the house or when I write." Dorothy Lawson and Jeff Clayton use their students to force them to practice. The demands of marriage and family have forced Dorothy to find creative ways or times to do her work: "I practice when I have something I cannot play without practice, but I rely on teaching to keep me up. I have private students, and I teach at Mannes College," she says. Like Dorothy, Eric Reed practices when needed: "These days, I only have time to practice for specific concerns: One, if I am presented with a new tune that has some difficult technical or harmonic passages, I will work on that until I get it up to a level I am satisfied with; or, two, if I am trying to figure out different ways of playing through a tune, I try to come up with alternate or different changes that will get me through the tune from beginning to end."

Ron Carter practices "one day a week, just to kind of make sure that that thing still works." His response to the "too much practice" question is, "It depends what you practice. If you don't have the right item to practice, of course, you're wasting your time. But I think in your earlier years, practice is critical to learning skill on your instrument." Gerald Cannon agrees: "I do not practice as much as I used to. I try to practice a couple hours a day, but I don't have time to do it. What I practice is scales, chord changes. At this point, I practice to keep my hands in shape, to keep my calluses up, and to stay familiar with the fingerboard. Sometimes when I am onto something that I want to develop, I will have to practice. I used to have a schedule, but I don't anymore." Jeff Clayton, like Dorothy, calls students when he wants to really get in some major practice session. He will call students and schedule four-hour practice sessions, which forces him to work alongside of them. This is valuable for both of them as he is forced to be better than they are and they try to reach his level. Billy Taylor had to deal with the effect of having a stroke, which forced him to practice again. It was remarkable to see how well he played when he resumed his performance. "Yes, I still practice. Since my stroke a few years ago I practice more now than I have in the years since I was a kid. I'd practice long and hard. My mother had to run me out of the house. I have told my students that when I was their age, I used to practice eight to ten hours a day."

Singers

Vocalists have a different challenge, given that they carry their instrument with them. When, how, and in Ruth Brown's case, *if* they practice might seem a bit difficult. Ruth Brown, by her own admission, says, "*Never!* I'm a funny singer; I don't even sing around the house. I don't rehearse in the shower. Once in a while, I'll turn on a record, and I'll hear that arrangement and sing all day." Allan Harris does practice, although he spent more time on it when he was developing. "I make sure that every song I have in my show, I'm prepared. I know the lyrics, of course, I practice my inflections, what I'm gonna say. In my formative years, I practiced everywhere. Now I practice in the mirror. Finding what it is you have to say and perfecting that voice without distraction of mimicry, fanfare, etc., getting yourself mentally prepared for what you say as an individual, so that others see you and can see clearly what you are trying to say. No misunderstanding by the audience. It's a personal endeavor! Not many people can do it, but some people hide behind practice. Some can practice once a week and be brilliant."

Brenda Feliciano said, "I do [practice] now because I am doing more classical music. I also did a lot of experimental theater. I worked with Chico O'Farrill, first as one of his lead singers, then I did contracting for him when he was doing jingles, and I did some work on camera, did movies, I just kept on singing."

5 Survival 101: From Sideman to Leader

Not everyone can be a leader, nor should they be. To front a group requires much of a person beyond good musicianship. In the jazz world, one of the biggest hindrances to becoming a leader occurs when musicians spend most of their career as sidemen. Some believe that being an accomplished sideman causes them to automatically be taken seriously as a leader. I had a conversation with a well-respected A-team sideman of many years who was trying to make the transition from sideman to leader. He was shocked, and a bit dismayed, that doors did not open for him as he had expected. Jazz pianist John Hicks once told me that at one time he and other well known, accomplished musicians had formed a group and were looking to get booked in Joe Seigel's club, the Jazz Showcase, in Chicago. Upon hearing who the members of the ensemble were, Joe's comment was that "they are just a bunch of sidemen." John was able to overcome that perception by persevering.

The death to a leader can be harrowing for those who spend their entire careers in one band. Saxophonist Jeff Clayton talked about working on some tributes for Ray Charles a few months after Ray's death. Playing on some of these gigs were some of the members of the Ray Charles band who had been with Ray for roughly twenty years. Those guys had never put themselves in a position to have to find work. When faced with *no* work due to Ray's death, they were paralyzed at the thought of having to do it, and they did not have the wherewithal to know where or how to begin. I have talked to members of other bands in which the leader died, and most suffer the same predicament. However, those who were leading groups while working in a band stood a better chance of survival.

In the pop world, one can point to people like Luther Vandross, Teddy Pendergrass, and Martha Wash, who went from the background to lead. Luther Vandross appeared on the 1974 Diamond Dogs album, along with many other top artists of the time, including Michael Jackson. His first big break came in 1975, when he co-wrote and performed as a backup singer on David Bowie's

U.K. number-one hit "Fame." He was also a backup singer for Bette Midler, Barbra Streisand, Donna Summer, and Carly Simon. He had been singing jingles and had been the main voice of the group Change. Although the group was led by Paolo Granolio (guitar) and David Romani (bass), this was ostensibly a studio creation by producers Jacques Fred Petrus and Mauro Malavasi, who first linked to form Goody Music in 1975. With material recorded in Bologna and New York, *The Glow of Love* got the group off to a winning start, with success on the U.K. charts arriving with "Searching," with Luther Vandross as lead vocal. A subsequent hit for Change was "A Lover's Holiday." Following *Miracles* and *Sharing Your Love*, Luther embarked on a solo career. In 1981, Luther's debut album *Never Too Much* was released. Between 1982 and 1985, five albums were released, all selling over a million copies each.

During the late 1960s, Harold Melvin and the Blue Notes toured regularly with the group called the Cadillacs, whose lineup featured a drummer named Teddy Pendergrass. Harold Melvin and the Blue Notes formed in Philadelphia in 1954 under the name the Bluenotes. Prior to that incarnation, the group was known as the Charlemagnes. As the Bluenotes, they saw several lineups as members came and went, with Bernard Williams leaving to lead "The Original Blue Notes" in the mid-1960s. Harold put together a new version of the Blue Notes, featuring lead singer John Atkins. The group released several further singles for the Arctic, Checker, and Uni imprints, with the lineup changing on a regular basis.

Teddy initially joined Harold Melvin and the Blue Notes, backing the band as their drummer; however, impressed by his singing abilities, the band promoted Teddy to singing lead vocals after John Atkins left in 1970. Harold Melvin and the Blue Notes were one of the most popular Philly soul groups of the 1970s. Although ostensibly led by Melvin, Teddy Pendergrass was the most influential member of the group. They had several hits from 1972 to 1975, but they phased out after the departure of Pendergrass. The songs Teddy released as a solo artist, such as "Close the Door," "Only You," "When Somebody Loves You Back," "Life Is a Song Worth Singing," and "Turn Off the Lights" still ring in my ear and take me back in time.

Like many artists, Martha Wash has felt the vicissitudes of the music industry, from performing the unaccredited powerhouse vocals behind C + C Music Factory's classic "Gonna Make You Sweat (Everybody Dance Now)," to seeing her debut solo single "Carry On" reach the number-one spot—in her own name. She began her musical journey in the late 1970s as one-half of the disco group

Two Tons of Fun, which sang with the ever-so-outrageous Sylvester. Sylvester's high-piercing voice was heard loud and clear over the horns and guitar sounds, and there was no mistaking the voices of Two Tons of Fun, who were the perfect complement to Sylvester with their booming vocal harmonies. In the early 1980s, Two Tons of Fun transitioned to become known as the Weather Girls. As part of the Weather Girls, Martha scored a Grammy nomination for a song that was destined to become a cult classic, "It's Raining Men." Martha continued to sing with the Weather Girls until the late 1980s, when she felt that it was time to move on to the next phase of her career. From then into the early 1990s, Martha became one of the most sought-after session singers, and she found herself recording for numerous acts.

As a new era of dance music set in, she saw herself being replaced in music videos and promotional pictures by women who had a more marketable image. Her work with the house music at Black Box led to her performance on lead vocals on five of the groups' singles and put Black Box on the music map. "Everybody, Everybody," "I Don't Know Anybody Else," and "Strike It Up" were among their biggest hits. Martha had not been properly credited for her work in those groups and took them to court. Eventually, she received the recognition, but it took some years. In 1993, she took control and released her first solo CD, which produced three number-one dance singles: "Carry On," "Give It to You," and "Runaround," all three of which reached the top of the charts.

An artist must be ready, willing, and able to become a leader. It takes more than sheer ability. Kenny Washington understands the demands of being a leader and is quite comfortable with being a sideman. He has no trouble getting work for several reasons. One reason is that he is a professional who can work in varied musical situations. The job of leader can be a burden, and that is why Kenny has chosen not to lead his own bands. He said, "First, the way the business and the way folks are, I wouldn't have lasted because I'd have cussed everybody out. It is a big responsibility. It is a big enough responsibility to get myself and my drums to the airport on time and not have to worry about others getting there on time. I don't have patience. I don't have a problem being a sideman. As a drummer, in a big way I shape what the music is all about, though I'm not *the* leader. A band will only sound as good as the drummer will make the band sound. I have a big part in how the band sounds, and that is not my ego talking. I like being a sideman."

Michael Wolff sums up the sideman-mentality versus that of a leader: "Being a side man is like being a kid . . . being an artist. Being a leader is like being a parent; you are taking over. As a leader, you are taking control; you are taking the credit and taking the blame. My musicians just show up; they say, 'Hey, got my ticket?' It's a blast; it's important, but it is still my responsibility, it's my view, my direction. When you look at different [visual] artists, and they paint a bowl of fruit, they paint it differently. That is what a leader does; whether it's music we play, my compositions or not, it's filtered through me. I think being a leader, the business part of it, is a fucking nightmare . . . you could not ask a worse thing on yourself, but I'm a better leader than as a sideman. I loved doing *The Arsenio Hall Show*, but I'm not cut out for the kind of servitude, the second right-hand, right-hand 'manatude' . . . I was always a leader but I did sideman gigs. . . ."

Ron Carter said, "Don't worry about being a band leader. Don't worry about playing your tunes. There is a big library that doesn't cater to your weak points or your strong points. There are a lot of tunes in the key of D-flat, not just in the key of C. So learn other people's music. Don't be a leader so quickly. That's all ego, band leader's ego, because you are the boss and only play your tunes."

He was also very clear on what makes a good leader. He spent five years with one of the greatest incarnations of the Miles Davis Quintet, from 1963 to 1968, and he could have remained longer, yet he chose to walk away from one of the best gigs at that time. Having had the mentality of a leader, he said, "Well, I think bass players are generally leaders of the band, musically anyway. So that portion wasn't a difficult transition. I think that guys today who want to be leaders don't have enough sideman experience, number one. And they haven't been in a variety of sideman positions to see how different leaders handle situations. And the leaders of those bands probably aren't good leaders. So they have a disadvantage in all those areas. So I think it's difficult for those reasons. It's got nothing to do with the guy's ability or compassion to be a good leader. It's what his experience is leading to believe a leader is supposed to be able to handle."

When I asked him to give specifics as to *what* makes a good leader, Ron did not hesitate to articulate those qualities: "Number one, the example he sets for the sidemen. Is he on time? Is he dressed properly for the gig? Is he an amiable person? Two, has he learned the library of that particular band? Is he able to have some kind of input as to the structure of the tune or the arrangement? Three, what kind of personnel does he want to pick? Does he want to pick guys who are obstinate, just to see if he can break them, or is he looking for guys who want to make his music sound better? Is he willing to take less money to get the band working? Is he willing to cut his pay to hire better guys? Does he insist on only playing his music, and last of all, is he a good player?"

When Ron does take jobs as a sideman, he is clear about his role. "Punctuality, professionalism, my bass is always in shape to play; whether I can play it or not is another story. But it's always officially capable of being played. I was always nice to the guys in the band because that probably means as much to me as anything else, and I made an effort to learn the music before I got to work. If the guy gave me a book to look at for the gigs, I would look at it. I just wouldn't it put it on my desk, and let it get cobwebs till I have to play. I would try to learn what this guy had in mind for the bass. What do you think I could do with this part—is it a reasonable bass part? If not, can I make it feel reasonable and sound reasonable to this guy?"

By virtue of his instrument, the orchestra, David Randolph is a leader. He is not a musician in the sense that he plays the piano, or any other instrument for that matter. Giving into my naïveté, I asked David Randolph to define the job of a conductor. "Without a conductor, you would be helpless," he said. "If you ask a group of individuals to sing 'Yankee Doodle,' they would sing different tempos, different keys. The same would be with the symphony orchestra, the New York Philharmonic, they would not know when to start, how loud to play. Music does not remain in the same tempo; it speeds up, slows down. Some instruments need to be brought out. A conductor interprets. . . . A conductor's instrument is 150 singers, a seventy- to one-hundred-piece orchestra, where everyone thinks that they can do a better job than you can; humans are your instrument. A conductor needs knowledge of the music, and the ability to get what he wants in a limited amount of time. Treat singers and players with utmost love and respect and admiration. I don't believe in yelling and screaming, the old autocratic way to be." What David looks for in musician whom he hires is a "pleasant blending voice and [someone who] can read music at sight; sight reading is *important!*"

Eric Reed stated, "I'm a leader. Since I was five years old, I was gregarious and an aggressive kid. I had an out-front personality—'Hey, look at me!' And it takes one of those qualities to be a leader. If you are a shy type, chances are that you won't be a very good leader. I was always a leader even when I was with Wynton Marsalis; in my mind, I was a leader. Essentially, even as a sideman, I was a leader—some people just have leadership qualities. Some people are sidemen; they are better at it, such as bassist Paul Chambers. Also, your instrument often dictates whether you'll be successful as a leader. Not many bands are run by bass players or drummers. They are seen as accompanist instruments. More and more, you are seeing them in lead groups, but that is still not as common. Groups lead by trumpeters and singers are more common.

"Art Blakey, Max Roach, Philly Joe Jones, Carl Allen, Lonnie Plaxico, Christian McBride, you have to have a certain kind of personality to be a leader. You have to have charisma, you have to connect to the audience, you have got to get to the audience in a kind of way, you have to win the audience over and make the music. With Wynton, I understood what my role was. My way to comp was interactive; I was not the average sideman who just sat back and comped behind everybody, I was very upfront. I had just as much impact as Wynton did."

Billy Taylor was always a leader, though a good portion of his early work was as a sideman. His response to my question: "Me, always a leader? [laughs] *No!* In college, I changed my major to music in my junior year, and my dad cut me off. I paid for my last two years by playing with local bands. I was leader of the school band." I asked him if the transition to leader was hard. "Yeah, sure. When I got out of college and moved to New York City, nobody knew me. I was lucky I got a chance to play, and I had to pay dues for years. I really couldn't be a leader; I led bands, trios, quartets. I tried, but I was not really a leader until many years later, about ten years later, until I was an accompanist at Birdland. I was house piano player, so I got a chance to play with every great musician, Bird [Charlie Parker], Diz [John Birks "Dizzy" Gillespie], Miles [Davis], [John] Coltrane, everyone who came through Birdland. When I came out of there, I was ready to be a leader. I got the experience of working with people, and then I was ready to lead my own group, a trio."

His students often ask him how one can make the transition from sideman to leader. "Most people I work with now as a teacher or as a leader, I believe that they are qualified to be a leader based on my experience as a leader. I know that they have what it takes. They can be leaders, but they must realize that they have to be responsible for other people and have to be cognizant of and participate in things beyond musicianship. Now business is bad, and how do you get people to listen to you? Sometimes people have, thank goodness, Web sites, and they are doing things on their own now. When I came along, you got there by being on radio, being onstage, a featured sideman in a band, then you stepped out on your own. Now everybody wants to make a star, people want to be a star, and nobody wanted to do anything less, but not everybody has the ability to do all those things. You can be a wonderful musician and not have the inclination, the interest to be a businessman, but you have to be a businessman to be a leader."

Allan Harris lamented about the bind of vocalists: "Being a vocalist has its drawbacks in jazz especially, more so than in other genres. Most vocalists are not necessarily the leaders. Nine times out of ten, they are featured. The band can carry on without them, and usually does. Sometimes they are a hindrance to what's being said onstage. The problem with some vocalists is that they feel they need to get some musicians who are adept at what they do, and that's it. They don't do their homework and bore people to death when they come onstage. That only happens in jazz. In R&B, it's a visual thing. Being a vocalist and a leader in jazz is not the same as in other genres. As a jazz singer, you are part of a team. When you are onstage, you are a part of something that is bigger than what you are."

Andy Bey began out front: "In the beginning, I became a vocalist, but at the same time as a pianist, but I did not consider myself a singer when I was young. But the accent became more on my vocals later on. I always accompanied myself before I joined my sisters, and we became 'Andy and the Bey Sisters.' They sang as a duo while I'd play piano for them. I eventually made a record by myself when I was about twelve years old. As a singer, I worked with Horace Silver for about thirty years. I did solo gigs in piano bars, played with Howard McGhee as a singer, and as a pianist with Sonny Rollins. Thad Jones/Mel Lewis, Max Roach, William H. Fisher, who produced my first LP as an adult, all hired me to work with them. I had worked one week with Max Roach, one with Ray Brown, and one with Horace at a club in Boston that George Wein owned."

Bobby Sanabria had no intentions to be a leader. "I wanted to be the ultimate sideman. I still am in many ways, so that is why I'm such a good leader. My job is to bring their vision across musically. The problem is that there are times when I am called to bring my knowledge of Afro-Cuban music, but sometimes people who call me to work delve into *my* world as tourists, which is disrespectful, and it's counterproductive to the music, that is, if they don't listen to me and how the music should be played. I became a leader because I could not express what I wanted to express as a musician, and I was not getting experience as a sideman. It was simultaneous, as I always did both as a drummer and a percussionist. At one point, I had to turn down sideman work as a percussionist. I am one of the best [percussionists], but I feel my voice is the drum-set. Unfortunately, because my name ends in a vowel and I'm Hispanic, people tend to look at me as a percussionist, not as a legitimate jazz drummer." I asked him if this perceptual problem made it difficult to get work. He answered, "It's getting harder because of how the record industry is. Also, when you become a leader, people don't seek you out. They think you'll charge too much or won't be interested. That is unfortunate."

Edwin Hawkins was propelled into being a leader. It was not what he had planned to do, but because of the success of "Oh, Happy Day," he changed course.

Choosing between being a sideman or a leader was not really a choice for Edwin. It was: "What happened to me I always attribute to God. It was a miracle what took place. We had nothing to do with that. We did a live recording in a two-track machine. We were going to hand-sell [the record] ourselves and give the contributions back to the church. After it hit, that changed everything. We even changed the name of the group, and that took us to another level."

Kenny Barron also resisted being a leader; he did not think that he had the personality to be one. He spent many years in education at Rutgers University teaching, all the while leading different groups. Kenny said, "I never sought out work, especially in Philly. I'd play dances, parties, cabarets; jazz gigs were even better. When I moved to New York City, people called me. As a leader, that is when you have to seek work. I was blessed. I'm not an aggressive person, anyway. There were some bad times, though. I moved to New York for the music. I used to visit my brother [who lived in New York City] when I was in high school, and I loved New York. In the beginning, I did mostly sideman work. I didn't start out being a leader; that started in the 1970s. It was organic, people called me, asking me to bring in a group."

The classical world of music has different constraints in terms of musicians choosing leadership or sideman work. Dorothy Lawson points out how she was led to become a co-leader in Ethel, a group of well-established musicians in the middle of their careers who have come from different angles of the business, but are all classically trained. "The violins have lengthy backgrounds in pop and jazz and rock; the violist is an arranger and a professional from Broadway. We love playing in string quartets, but we don't like being sidemen. We do it a lot and well, but we have a group of our own, which requires a consensus. It has been six years in the making . . . I like to communicate [with the audience]. It does happen in classical where people have started their own ensembles; many quartets and groups like that are organized and held together by one person. What I am involved in now is perhaps a new spin on it, but I find it works better for people of our generation and is more of a democratic ensemble. I have preferred working in situations where I felt what I do was appreciated. That it was specifically what I do and what my personality brings to someone is why people hired me. In a way, it has kept me away from orchestral positions and situations where the premium is where one is expected to be a good soldier."

Olu Dara became a leader out of necessity. He was bored with playing jazz; he did not like avant-garde, either; he wanted to stay closer to his musical roots of Mississippi, the blues; and he wanted to do it his way: "Avant-garde music helped me to take more freedom in my music. I said, 'I'm thirty-five years old, and I'm up in it.' That is when I made my decision to stay in the music. So I formed a band, and we played in the Village. I had played with everybody.

"I was my own man; I was out there on my own. Before that, Art Blakey had asked me, he was laughing at me, he said, 'This is boring the shit out of you.' He then told me to do anything that I wanted to do, avant-garde, R&B, anything. The band at that time was Stafford James, Cedric Lawson, and Carter Jefferson. We revised his band. That was the late 1960s and early 1970s. We all quit at the same time. I told Blakey that I was going to form my own band to suit my personality. I was going to play everything so I could put all of the elements into my music instead of playing just one style of music. I'd been all over the world and heard all kinds of music.

"I formed my band in *one* day. I was asked to play a concert. I had to play thirty minutes, so I went home and thought about it. I took the song 'Nefertiti,' and I played it over and over in different rhythms. That is how I got my concept. The musicians with me now are guys I had seen in other bands and I liked them, but no one would hire them. I like them as musicians and as people. Initially, I hired guys who were well known; they all had records, except me. I hired guys who would be able to play anywhere—dances, concerts, jazz festivals, funk, world-music festivals. That's the way it is, I planned this out. I wanted to fit in anywhere. I was very popular, so I did not have to make any records. I came from the old school, real old school. I put the band together in the late 1970s and early 1980s, and we never stopped working."

Part Two On Composing and Recording

*The secret of writing a good popular
song is to make it melodically simple
and harmonically attractive.*

—JULE STYNE

6 When and How to Record

The good and bad thing about technology is that more artists are able to make recordings. There is now a glut of recordings, and they do not have, in some sense, the same impact on a musician's career as before. Of course, a recording always has value, in that it is a document of your work and an example of where you are musically at a given point. Before you record, you must ask yourself what it is you want to say. If you are interested in getting airplay, there are many things to consider. **James Browne**, co-owner of the club Sweet Rhythm, who at one time managed artists, concurs: "I think that there are too many records. Everyone thinks that they have an individual voice. Well, everyone has fingerprints, too. Unless you have something different to say, be realistic. Don't make a record to feed your ego, or you are just spending money on an expensive business card."

As the business continues to change, fewer venues for artists to showcase their work exist. Getting distribution is a challenge as distributors merge and a host of other things continue to change in the industry. Musicians must become more recording-savvy. They have to understand who, what, when, and why they are going to record. Too often artists make a recording too early in their careers, and more often than not, the recordings are not radio-friendly. The length of songs must be considered; what songs will you present? **Gary Walker**, music director and weekday morning host on WBGO, Jazz 88.3FM, gave his thoughts on this: "As it pertains to jazz music, if you are a new artist, do not make a recording of all original tunes; people need familiarity." Prior to talking to Gary, I had asked Eric Reed whether emerging artists should record standards. Eric said, "I wish, if this is the attitude of announcers—that new artist should play standards—that they get rid of it. It just puts limitations on the music, which should have no limitations. Wayne Shorter and Horace Silver both have well-documented recording of standards. Horace's first CD has standards, and Wayne's first was originals, but he did one standard. He recorded 'Mack the Knife,' 'All or Nothing at All.' Down the line, they began to establish recordings of original material."

Gary continued, "I told Eric Reed that if he wants to get more airplay, he should have two tunes that are complete tunes that swing and are two-and-a-half minutes or less in length, and he would get exponentially more airplay. The reason is that most stations have hard times—I don't mean financial—that they must adhere to on the clock. Michael Bourne, afternoon host, and I are 30 percent of the listening day, and we are always looking for time to fill up to the top of the hour to get us into the news." He continues, "Why do I play so much Charlie Parker and Fats Navarro? Because none of the [expletives] are making complete thoughts in less than three minutes because they *can't* and because the compact disc, in many cases, allows them to aimlessly wander around the creative process."

I repeated to Gary what a musician had told me, that he should keep the length of his songs to under seven minutes or he would not be played. Gary Walker responded, "That is not a hard, fast rule. But if you make songs that are complete thoughts and say something in five to six minutes, then you will get more airplay than if it is twelve to thirteen minutes long."

Years ago, I interviewed a musician for my TV show, *The Art of Jazz*, who was beginning to get some recognition in the jazz scene. She had appealed to the "smooth jazz" crowd but had been criticized by the "straight ahead" jazz community for her lack of knowledge, as well as for her recordings. Not wanting to embarrass her on the show, I queried her about this after the taping. To my surprise, she told me that she had gone to CD 101 and asked them what kind of recording she had to do to get played on their station. She said, "I'm a business-woman." When I shared the story with Gary Walker, he said, "God bless her."

Do not misunderstand, new artists do get played, but at times, it is "a problem of geography," says Gary. "It has come to the point where I get swamped with product. I can get a piano trio from someone in Oregon, but it is unlikely that they will get played because there is just not enough space. What I am trying to solve is how to give a new release as much exposure as it should get. I am in the process of shrinking the number of new releases in the bin. A new CD stays in rotation around eight weeks and sometimes longer. In commercial radio, they may keep a new release in three to four months."

When to Record

I cannot emphasize how important it is to know *when* to record. Again, you must have something to say. Making demos was essential at one time, but now, musicians make CDs that *should* be demos, but they are perceived as complete packages, and often they are not up to standard. They are poorly produced, and too often, the labels look at as if they were printed on their home computers. I have been given many of those CDs by musicians who expect to have them played on WBGO. Most often, they do not fit the format of the station, and the musicians don't seem to understand this. Nowadays it *is* possible that a more appropriate station might be willing to play these independently produced CDs. In the past, this would not have been true, but the industry is changing, with the reduction of the major-label artist stable. However, if you want to cut a deal with one of the majors, note that established record labels may require a demo, and the more professional the product, the better it reflects on you, the artist. Musicians must understand and accept the fact that, according to James Browne, "this is an industry, and an industry means commerce, which means that there are basic laws of supply and demand. So if there is no demand for your product, it does not matter how much supply there is, and the fact that you have a CD does not mean it's valuable. It becomes valuable when enough people have said, 'That touches me, and I will pay for the opportunity to hear it; otherwise, it is the audio equivalent of masturbation."

One person who understands the business of recording is tenor saxophonist Javon Jackson, who once said, "I am not only competing with Joshua Redman and the other young tenor players, I am competing with guys who are no longer alive, such as Coleman Hawkins and Lester Young," because jazz fans are still listening to the legends. In an effort to broaden his appeal beyond jazz, Jackson continues to expand his material by adding funk tunes to his most recent CDs.

Richard Smallwood had what was probably a more common experience when he was starting out and working to get a record deal. When he came along, few artists were recording on their own, most had to find a label, had to do a demo, and shop it around. His story is amusing now, but at the time, he was not laughing. "When I was in college at Howard University in Washington, D.C., I was part of the first Gospel group on the Howard campus called the Celestials. Donny Hathaway was one of the organ and keyboard players and singer, and when he left, I stepped into his place. It was all about making demos. We made a demo. Since we knew no one in the industry, we took a Greyhound bus to New York City, rented a room in a YMCA for ten dollars, got a phone book, looked up all of the record companies within walking distance, and knocked on doors. We were a bunch of college kids." One interesting thing happened on that trip to New York City. "We got to meet George Butler who was at the Blue Note, and we got to play our demo for him. He listened to what I had, and he told me that that I was ten years ahead of my time. He said, 'What you are doing, no one else is doing.' He told me, 'Keep doing what you are doing, and you're gonna make it, I *promise* you.' "

After meeting with George Butler, they "ended up at the record company that had recorded the Chilites and were let in. A man listened to our demo, took us around the company, and said that he would sign us. There were no other people in the office at that time; he claimed that they had all left for the day, but he promised that he would send us the contract in three weeks. We left to go back to school, and our friends gave us a record release party—balloons and all. My manager followed up and was told that there had been a flood, but that the man would get around to it. After a series of delays, the contract never came. A year or so had passed, and one of the acts from that label came to D.C. We went to the show and talked to the performer and told him our story. At first he did not know who we were talking about, but after our description of the man, he roared with laughter and said that the man was the janitor! It was devastating back then, but funny now. It's all part of paying dues, but you have to keep plugging away.

"It was almost ten years to the day after my meeting with George Butler, before I got my record deal. I kept making demos but never heard from people. One year I did a concert in Kentucky. The promoter later went to work with the Benson label (a Christian label) and called to see what we were up to. The label was looking for black artists to sign. The president had us come to Nashville to lay down tracks on the studio. We drove down on a Thursday, and on Monday, we handed him a tape, and he signed us on the spot. We knew nothing of attorneys, so we signed."

Olu Dara made a recording early in his career, but it was not released. It was not until he was much older that he made a record with a major label, Atlantic. "When I made my last record, I had no idea what I was gonna do. I wrote the album in one-and-a-half hours before recording. I let it happen on the spot. I like to write for the musicians I am working with at that recording session. I take my cues off how they look, the vocal qualities of the other singers I am working with. Music is a science that should be done scientifically, just like cooking. Cooking is a science; that's why some people cook better than others. They go into the kitchen and make it from scratch. Just like my concept of music, that's when the adventure and excitement begins. I don't remember my lyrics, and I change them up. I do copyright my music; the business part of it, I do."

Allan Harris believed that a musician was supposed to work hard in order to be discovered. Allan said, "It took me awhile, like most artists who are late bloomers. They think that they will be discovered and be a star. Some record producer will see you in a club, and take you to New York City or Los Angeles, and this will happen by the time you are thirty. That is what we are taught: Shut up, learn your craft, and you will be discovered; but that is not the norm. You have to put something out there that will attract the people who will want to exploit you. Those people are busy. Artists new to the game don't understand that; they just know they are good, they can sing, and they can play, so why aren't they making money? It is not a personal thing. The powers that be can love your performance and not give you a dime.

"Can they make money with what you are doing? You have to have something that will stop them for a minute. That is why I put out my first CD called *Setting the Standard*. It said, 'He had gumption to do it himself'; you can't peddle an idea or an emotion." Allan's thoughts on his second CD were telling. His introduction to MONS record label came through a personal connection. They had seen Allan at a JazzTimes convention; they sat down and talked, not knowing what they each expected. "My second CD, *What a Wonderful World*, was a gift from heaven," says Allan. "I wasn't ready; I was like a deer in the headlights! I did not know MONS would get the guys who they got (Ray Brown, Benny Green, Jeff Hamilton, John Clayton). I wasn't prepared emotionally, wasn't prepared for marketing. I wish I knew then what I know now. It would have been played more, and my name would have been out farther than it is now."

Legendary bassist Ray Brown insisted that Allan put one blues track on that CD, his reason being that Ray wanted to put his stamp on it, and, "I was introducing myself as a new artist to that crowd, and I needed to give them something to grab on to, not have a CD that was just an eclectic array of standards. That song, 'Black Coffee,' would show off Ray and propel me to where I wanted to go. The song was swinging; people were able to see that I could sing straight and I could swing." Ray Brown was responsible for introducing nineteen-year-old Jeff Clayton and his older brother, John, to Concord Records. When I asked him if he thought that he was too young to record, he replied, "No, I don't think so. A recording catapults you forward; it gives you knowledge each time. I might not have made a recording that people wanted to listen to until I got a little older; they were segments of information." It took Al Jarreau seven years of working steadily before he got his record contract. He believes that his experience was in par with other recording artists. "I left the [nine-to-five] job in 1968, and in 1975, the *I Got By* album came out. I think that 99 percent of the time, somehow, a person at a record company learns about the artist, and they begin to talk."

What to Record

The audience tastes are changing. More concept records are coming out. Ron Carter says, "Your CD has to tell a story. Yeah, I have a story, and I record the songs in the order of my story. For me, that's I how I do it. Other guys have different views and approaches. I've gone there with a story to tell; when the last song is done my story is complete, and I only hope that the company will agree to that order of songs on the final product." I noticed the absence of the liner notes on CDs, something that many old-timers like me miss most. Sitting and reading album jackets was a joy and a learning experience. I asked Ron why they have almost disappeared, and he replied, "I miss them. It's cheaper not to have them. You don't pay for a writer, and it takes less paper for the inside information. I miss those days of information listed with musicians' thoughts about the songs and their tunes and the information that's necessary to make the listener feel he was part of the session."

Songwriter **Chann Berry** talked about Mary Stallings building a record around the song of his that she recorded, "Hello Yesterday." "Mary Stallings decided to form her entire CD *Remember Love*, released by Halftone Records, around the theme of the song. Geri Allen produced it." Grammy-nominee Brenda Feliciano said that she picked tunes that "some people suggested, and I like the challenge." She was nominated for Best Classical Recording. "The repertoire I did, one piece was by Schubert. It's been done by many people, and there are many ways to do it. I say it's my Puerto Rican version of it; it's who I am. Performing this German piece written in the 1800s and dealing with a shepherd; it's very emotional. I also did, on that album, a contemporary Argentinean composer who died about ten years ago. They are the most beautiful songs that sound so simple, but are difficult."

After looking back over his recording career, Allan Harris has decided to approach his future recordings differently. "My past CDs have been such a potpourri of different things. The next set of CDs will have, like *Cross That River*, a theme. People seem to be into themes, especially with vocalists. The way the mass audience is now, an artist does not want to pull too many tricks and stops. They will bypass you for someone else. Most people want something that they can groove with." When I questioned him about his CD *Love Came: The Songs of Billy Strayhorn*, Allan said, "That was from the heart. I targeted that CD to a small audience, and I knew that I would not make a lot of money on that. I did it for the love of the music and to showcase my musicianship with some hot cats like Eric Reed, and to put myself on the map. Every artist needs one CD in their formative years that is a watershed moment for them that they can look back on."

Joe Grushecky experienced the downside of being under contract and how it adversely affected one of his recordings. Steve Popovich, a maverick for Epic Records and a native of Pittsburgh, saw Grushecky's group perform. He had worked with South Side Johnny, Meatloaf, and Ronnie Spector. Joe explains, "Steve invited us to Cleveland to meet Boz Skaggs and Ronnie Specter, pretty heady stuff for some guys coming out of the cellar of Pittsburgh. We cut demos, and we cut our first record, and he produced and signed us to Cleveland Records. We were signed in 1979. We were lucky; it only took us a year and a half to get a record deal. We were actually signed in January 1977 on the MCA label. In the five years with them, we made four records. During that time, Cleveland had been taken over by MCA Records, and about fifty or sixty acts were fired. The record company kept Tom Petty, The Who, Olivia Newton John, Elton John, and us. During the process of making the record, the company put a lot of pressure on us and told us to do what they wanted. Under pressure, we played ball with them and made the worst record we ever made called, *Cracked under Pressure*. We were scared that they'd drop us, being young and naïve. The album came and went quickly. Two or three weeks after our album came out, I'd have been better off taking the money and flushing it down the commode—I'd have gotten more satisfaction. They dropped us about three weeks after that. This was in 1984–85. Recently, I started working on a new live CD, which we cut in Europe."

What's in a Name?

Some groups are known as a collective, in which no one person's name is out front. Kenny Barron formed the group Sphere with Buster Williams, Ben Riley, and Charlie Rouse. He explained, "Sphere was a cooperative effort. It started as a result of me, Buster, and Ben talking. We had been Ron Carter's rhythm section, so we [Ben and I] got Charlie, and it felt right. Our first name idea was that we call ourselves 'Circle,' but Chick Corea had a group by that name. Not until later did we learn that 'Sphere' was Thelonious Monks' middle name."

Joe Grushecky was the main influence of each group that he was in, but he did not put his name out as the leader until later in his career. Ultimately, he decided that it was important for him to have top billing, given the many changes in band personnel and their conflicting musical ideas. Joe said, "After the MCA experience, I finally had a demo session, and I got a contract at Rounder Records, and at that time, I had wised up. When I signed with Rounder, I had the problem of what name to use for my group. I started out as Brick Alley Band, though Steve Popovich hated my name and urged me not to use it. He wanted me to put my name in front of the band, so he suggested that I change my name because it was such an ethnic mouthful for most people. Before a name was chosen, he put an announcement of our signing to MCA in *Billboard* magazine calling us Iron City Bluesbusters, but we did not want to be Bluesbusters—we wanted to go by House Rockers. Steve wanted us to put our city in front of the band because he wanted us to be identified regionally. For reasons of my being naïve and lacking in business savvy, I did not follow his advice to put my name in front. So when the band broke up, I was left with a non-sellable name because people only knew us as the Iron City House Rockers. I was just a singer, so people did not know my name as the main motivation force behind that band. It took a couple of years for me to get my name back. Before the band broke up, I started to write songs with other guys. I started using my name again, but I guess, because of the Grushecky thing being a mouthful all of my life with people stumbling over it. At one time, I had recorded a song under the name 'Joey G.,' which had been my nickname as a kid. Under that name, I was Joey G. and the Brick Alley Band, and that recording had become immensely popular in the Pittsburgh area. That music was a weird mixture of 1980s' dance music and rock 'n' roll. The executives at Rounder Records wanted my group to be called Iron City House Rockers, which I refused [to do]. Thankfully, that name was all tied up, so to compromise, we came to be known as Joe Grushecky and the House Rockers. That was a good decision; I was always a guy looking forward, looking to do new material, so this enabled me to continue to represent my first couple of records and to be proud of my work instead of turning my back on it."

The Importance of a Producer

Often I hear of musicians looking for a producer, or I hear of people who claim *to be* producing a CD, so I wanted to understand *what* a producer does. Allan Harris said that if he had to do his *Love Came: The Songs of Billy Strayhorn* CD all over again, that he would choose a producer. Billy Taylor understands the function of a producer and what happens when he produces his own recordings: "Most artists are our own worst enemy. We don't look at our own work as objectively as we would if we were being critical of someone else's work. So we need to get someone to second-guess us and make sure that we don't become self-indulgent. From time to time, I have produced myself.

"A good producer is someone who looks at what you are trying to do and thinks it through with you; two heads are better than one. You do what is best for that project. I can get hung up on certain kinds of things of what I think is right. In hindsight, I would have put something in another place or done it another way. I might not have done that had I had a good producer who would help me do that, see it another way. I have had good producers in the past who have done that."

Al Jarreau talked extensively about the need for a producer, specifically regarding his latest recording, *Accentuate the Positive*. Like Billy Taylor, he said, "Two heads are better than one. Your second head should know the first head better than the first head knows itself. Your producer should be able to see inside of you and recognize little corners of you that don't get much attention, and ask you about that and ask you if you want to address that. I had that experience with Michael Narada Walden when he convinced me to sing a song in a falsetto voice that I said I did not sing in. His reaction was, 'No, you can't deprive your audience of that part of you.' That is what a producer should see, and that is what Tommy LiPuma sees, as did Jay Graydon. Producers also bring musicians together—that is the most important thing. What Tommy did for me was to bring Christian McBride on my project for *Accentuate the Positive*. Larry Williams has been with me for years, on tour, recorded with me, and he knows me better than any pianist around. Tommy picked the other players to come on, guys he knew would work well in this genre and well in the tradition of jazz. They are guys who might have hip-hop CDs in their collection." I asked Al if it was his idea to make a jazz CD. He responded, "Not mine *or* Tommy's. I feel that it was the holy angels and God were saying, 'What's wrong with you guys? You have been at Verve for about three years, and it's one of the only jazz labels. Why don't you get in a room and talk?' God conspired against our own stupidity and got us into a room to talk."

Divine intervention seemed to work for Andy Bey: "Recording again was dictated for me. If left it up to a record company, I would not have recorded again. I did not get good offers from any of them. Someone called from Roy Brooks' house in Detroit, and he was looking to make a record. It had been twenty-two years since my previous record. Cornelius Pitts was the guy, and I thought that it was a fluke, and I was not really interested. Cornelius was serious, but he is a criminal lawyer by day. He came to New York City to meet me, and he told me to make a list of songs that I wanted to play. He was looking for someone to sing ballads. I had been experimenting in singing soft. Previously I had been considered as a belter. Another guy, Herb Jordan, had been in

Detroit—he lives in L.A. now—and he had been producing artists such as Geri Allen. Cornelius asked him if he would produce me, and that is how *Ballads, Blues, and Bey* came to be."

New to the industry when he made *Sin and Soul*, Oscar Brown Jr. had no idea who the musicians would be on that record when he got to New York City to record it. "I never had the power to pick an arranger; they'd pick him for me, and when I got to New York City, I did not know anyone or who to pick. The record company picked great musicians. Al Ham, the A&R man, had been a proficient bassist before he went to work at Columbia, and he knew how to pick the musicians."

Chann Berry, a songwriter, and I had a conversation via instant message (oh, the joy of technology!), in which we exchanged thoughts about the function of a producer and how the producer relates to the writer. Here is an excerpt of that conversation:

Sheila: Do you as a songwriter ever get a say in how anyone records your songs? Do any songwriters?

Chann: Yes, some do, but jazz is a little different. Some musicians are not great producers. Most singers I've worked with were very open.

Sheila: Why is jazz different than pop?

Chann: Improvisation and . . . jazz coloring.

Sheila: So, do wrong notes take away from a song?

Chann: At the beginning of one verse on a tune, I heard a singer go one way and pianist/producer go another, and I'm sayin', WHAT DA F—K!

Sheila: I just don't know what to say—a good producer would have made them do it right. It was up to the producer to correct that!

Chann: Artist interpretation? Maybe. Yes, you are right! They should have.

Sheila: As Benny Carter told Jeff Clayton when Jeff took license with a song Benny wrote for him: "Jeff, the writer wrote the notes for a reason." I hear singers do that all of the time and the musicians don't call them on it. They change the song by changing the notes.

Chann: YES! The note is Blue! Don't make the note Yellow! At least come close to Blue.

Sheila: This is why musicians have such problems with many singers.

Chann: Yes, listening to some singers these days makes me ill. Some musicians treat music like law. Yes, bend it, blend it, but don't *break it*!

The Musician as a Self-Producer

With today's technology and with the major labels weeding out artists who do not sell, musicians have taken more control of their artistry by starting their own record labels. They have taken advantage of the Internet as a vehicle for getting their product out. What are the things to consider? When the artist decides to self-produce, she must decide on how to distribute the product. One of the biggest obstacles to making a successful recording is the problem of getting it into the hands of the listener. In general, "in its present form, the distributor is supposed to take a finished product and get it into the various retail channels," says **David Alexander**, who was once the National Black Music Marketing Director at PolyGram/Universal Distributors. (Details on distribution to follow in chapter 16.)

7 The Art of Writing a Song

What makes a good, or even a great song? How are songs written? What are the mechanics? The terms "composer" and "songwriter" are sometimes used interchangeably. The dictionary definition of a composer is "one who or that which composes; a person who writes music." A songwriter is defined as "a person who writes the words or music, or both, for popular songs." Cy Coleman penned such great songs as "Witchcraft," "The Best Is Yet to Come," "Why Try to Change Me Now," "I'm Gonna Laugh You Out of My Life," and "It Amazes Me," among others. Many of these Coleman songs have been recorded by a host of the greatest names in music, including Frank Sinatra, Tony Bennett, Liza Minnelli, Barbra Streisand, Peggy Lee, Lena Horne, Ella Fitzgerald, and others. During an interview with host Michael Bourne, on WBGO, Jazz 88.3FM, Cy (who died about a month after the interview) said that he writes "music with lyrics that makes sense; I work on harmonics."

Several of the interviewees talked about the Great American Songbook, which tells the story of the first fifty years of American popular music. Whether the music came originally from the vaudeville stage, Tin Pan Alley, or the radio, it would end up in the movies. The songbook contains some of the best of George Gershwin, Irving Berlin, Lorenz Hart, Richard Rodgers, Oscar Hammerstein II, Cole Porter, Harold Arlen, and many more artists. Other great songwriters not included in the Great American Songbook lexicon are Lennon and McCartney, Stevie Wonder, and great jazz composers such as Thelonious Monk, Benny Golson, and Duke Ellington. Classical composer Johann Sebastian Bach is considered by many to have been one of the greatest composers in Western music. When I listened to J. S. Bach as a child, I was attracted to what I considered to be his element of swing. Even now, each time I listen to his music, I find myself patting my foot. In my opinion, his use of tension and release and forward movement is what keeps his music modern.

Of course, a specific performer or original interpretation can make a song memorable; that process is not completely dependent upon the writer's talents. When Ray Charles passed away in June 2004, several performances were held to honor him and his music. Jeff Clayton played on two of the events and commented, "Ray Charles *knew* how to pick good songs." Though he was not known for his writing, he could turn almost any song into a classic. Ray Charles was an innovative singer and pianist who combined blues and Gospel in a way that pioneered soul music and earned him the nickname given to him by Frank Sinatra, "the Genius." A partial list of his hits includes, "Hit the Road, Jack," "I Can't Stop Loving You," "Busted," "Makin' Whoopee," "I Got a Woman," "Drown in My Own Tears," "This Little Girl of Mine" (covered by the Everly Brothers), and "Let's Get Stoned," the first hit for singer/songwriter team Ashford and Simpson. His version of Hoagy Carmichael's "Georgia on My Mind" was named the Georgia state song in 1979. One of the most moving recordings was his rendition of "America the Beautiful."

Ruth Brown can also pick good songs. Often she sings songs brought to her by fellow musicians. "Frank Wess would say, 'This is a good song for you,' the musicians would come out with the arrangement, and we'd swing." She and Ray Charles were good friends, and he advised her wisely, "I won't tell nobody, but *I like you very much* because you are singing what people know, and you are singing, and people know what you are singing about!"

Ruth and Ray did not record together, and Ruth did not let him live it down that he did not ask her to record one of his hits, "Baby, It's Cold Outside." "I told Ray that I was mad at him for letting Betty Carter do that song and not me."

Ron Carter suggests that the elements essential in writing a song are "melody, changes, and form." Pianist Cedar Walton is considered to be a wonderful composer. He wrote such standards as "Bolivia," "Mode for Joe," and "Ugetsu" (written in the key of D and means "fantasy" in Japanese). Kenny Washington once said that what makes Walton's songs so good is that they are difficult for a musician, but easy for the listener. When I posed Kenny's opinion to Ron Carter, his response was, "No, Cedar writes a nice melody, and he has good arrangements of those melodies. That's what's so attractive." Ron continues, "I think everyone knows they can write. Whether they want to develop that talent by taking lessons is another story."

Ron did develop his writing skills by "taking composition lessons, arranging lessons, absolutely!" Also, he is not above asking for feedback from those whom he respects: "I don't mind going to Benny Golson and saying, 'Benny, is this arrangement okay? How's this work, or why doesn't it work?' You have three or four guys in New York who I would call up and say, 'Can you help me with this?' The problem is that most jazz players don't take composition lessons; they think they don't need them, and their compositions aren't any good."

Though not a lyricist, Ron has written some words to his songs: "I have written lyrics for a couple of my tunes, and as a matter of fact, at NJPAC [New Jersey Performing Arts Center], I did a guest star out there. The singer on the faculty, Roseanna Vitro, sang 'Little Waltz,' which I had written words to years ago. But I'm just not that committed to writing lyrics on my own. I had songs of mine have lyrics put to them. But I have never spent enough time to get my language skills as a lyricist under control to feel comfortable to do that."

Kenny Barron is also a writer who does not write lyrics. When I asked if he did so, he was quick to say, "*No*, I would not even attempt it. I don't think that I'd be good at it." On the subject of composer and writer, Kenny said, "I don't think of myself as a composer; I'm still working on it. I'm trying to write for larger ensembles. I'd like to do more of that." Several of his songs have been covered by several other musicians; about that, Kenny said, "I'm happy when others record my songs, such as 'Sunshower,' and 'Voyage.' What makes them work is that they are basically very simple. When you look at hit songs, not that mine are hits, the songs are very simple melodic lines. I don't see myself as a composer; I write tunes." On the process of writing, Kenny remarked, "I can't force the process. Sometimes all of the elements will come at once, and sometimes I get a germ, and I follow it in a direction. I can't just sit and write a song."

Billy Taylor has written extensively and has successfully married jazz and classical music. One body of work that he is most proud of is his "Suite for Jazz Piano and Orchestra," and his song, "I Wish I Knew How It Would Feel to Be Free." That song was used as the theme for the 2004 Olympics, as the music for a Coca-Cola commercial, and it served as an anthem for the civil-rights movement.

"I've written a lot of music. One of my pieces I'm proudest of was a suite that was commissioned by the Utah Symphony. It was unlikely for a black musician and the Mormons to collaborate." Maurice Abravenel had served on the National Council for the Arts with Taylor, and he set up the collaboration. Says Taylor, "This was my first; I had no previous experience writing for a symphony orchestra. I tried to use the drums and percussion section of the orchestra as a big trio, but that did not work. I knew what I wanted to hear, but it did not work. Maurice helped me with that and allowed me to pick a bass player and percussionist and put them up front, like I'd do with my trio, and it worked. It was a wonderful experience.

"Then I wrote several other pieces for symphony orchestra. What I found after writing five or six pieces is that I write in a particular format, concerto grossos, meaning that I have the trio out front of the conductor of the orchestra. We'd play the jazz part because what I wrote was jazz.

"Music for me is better when not done to a formula. What I've done is use the same approach I use in jazz, and that's to take a theme and do something with the theme, using some of the techniques that I borrow from western classical music and other borrowed from things I know about playing jazz." I asked Billy what comes first for him, the melody or the lyric. He answered, "I usually start with a melody. In many cases, I'm a melodic player, so I think of melodies. My music has been like jazz. I didn't know what was coming next."

Billy began writing at a young age, as he says, "It's funny, I wanted to write popular songs like the Great American Songbook. I wanted to write like Gershwin, the composer of my youth; the popular composers were people who impressed me. I wanted to write songs like them—pretty melodies. When I studied music, I began to see how to put together songs and what you do and what forms I wanted to use. I had written for string quartets and all kinds of things. I did it in school, but I did not do it seriously. I didn't know what I was going to do with it until much later. Even in college, I dabbled with lyrics and tried to put words and music together. When I didn't write the words for a song idea, I had a lyric in mind. I never wrote it out, but I had the idea."

I have always been curious about how they come up with song titles. Sometimes musicians will explain to the audience how the songs got their names, but others get up on the bandstand and ask the audience to help them come up with a name. David Randolph argues that titles are meaningless: "I deny the usual canard that Beethoven's Third Symphony is about Napoleon—bunk, absolute bunk. It is dedicated to Napoleon, but there is nothing of Napoleon in it. I devoted my life, in part, and my lectures, to that subject. No title means anything. The only way to understand music is through music itself."

As a composer, how the title comes to Eric Reed depends. He sometimes has the title in mind, and then forms the song to fit the title. Jeff Clayton writes lyrics for all of his songs, though no singer has ever recorded any of his songs. "Sometimes the title helps shape the song," he says.

Michael Wolff had written music for movies such as *The Tic Code*, which he and his wife Polly Draper produced together. "I write better in L.A.; it's quiet . . . I just did a film score in South Pennsylvania, a coal-mining town, a documentary. I always bring my jazz approach to it, improvisation. Scoring is like making shoes, not where I get self expression; it's like doing a job."

Chann Berry writes from a place of deep emotion: "I've been writing since I was fourteen, but it was not until I was thirty that I told anybody. I was so terrified. For me and other artists, if you tell the truth, you are talking about yourself, and sometimes you don't want people to see you as you are. I write a lot of ballads. I write out of extreme pain, hence, 'Joy and Pain.' Some of the funky stuff comes from me having fun, being happy. I'm old school; I like music of the forties and fifties. I reminisce quite a bit; I like American standards. I think that I'll continue writing. I've got something to say, and I hooked up with a great musician who plays jazz piano who sounds like Kenny Rankin. We are two old souls who have come together."

Joe Grushecky became a writer by default. Though he had always written songs, he did not hone his skills until he became dissatisfied with being a cover band. He was asked to start a band by the bass player with whom he had been working. "I used to sing and write songs. I was one of the few guys who could write songs at that time. So, I said yes." His career took many unpleasant turns, but he "kept coming back to what got him into music initially." As he says, "I tried to start going down those goofy paths, and I would then get back to what got me in the music the first place: R&B, blues, the real cool song, the gritty songs, good singers, and song writers. I had written all these great songs, but I was not playing them, so I turned my back on the music industry for a while."

Like several musicians, Joe does not have one way of writing, and on occasion he sought assistance. "It's all different, usually take a song like from our record, *American Babylon*, that I did with Bruce Springsteen, a song called "Chain Smokin'," a simple sounding song, but has tricky changes to it, and it took me months to write. And I had to stick to it, change the key. Another song, 'Labor of Love,' came about because of my wife. As she was going out the door one night after dinner, I got stuck doing the dishes, and I asked her, 'Why do I have to do these?' and she said, 'It's a labor of love.' So I quit doing the dishes and wrote the song; it was in my head. I put the time and day on it and put it in a folder so I could always remember it."

On the recommendation of his wife, Joe contacted his pal, Bruce Springsteen, in hopes that Bruce would play on a song of Joe's that he was to record on his album, *End of the Century*. This led to Bruce co-writing a song. "I got in touch with Bruce via his manager, John Landau, and he invited me to L.A. Originally, Bruce was to play guitar on one song. We ended up doing two whole songs together. He moved back east at the end of one of the sessions. I took a giant leap and handed him a piece of paper and said, 'Hey, I have these really great lyrics, but the music isn't worth anything.' He liked the lyrics; he did some music, so we co-wrote two songs together. Over two years, we completed the record, *American Babylon*, and he toured with us."

The challenge of a classical composer is illustrated by Dorothy's experience as she excitedly told me what she is writing: "I write when I have something that's coming up that I have to write for. I write on a computer, and I'm pretty fast. I tend to write a form that is bracketed by true composed stuff but has improvisation in the middle, so I'm not writing everything out. Improvisation [in classical] music is coming back now. In the baroque period, the great composers—Bach, Handel, Mozart, and others—were huge talents as improvisors. Most of their music was made up as they needed it. For example, the great violinist Carelli, a famous traveling virtuoso, once published his famous pieces. They were skeletons, sketches. It has been a anomaly, in classical music, over the last 100 years where people have tried, through sophisticated means, to subvert the natural sense of rhythm."

For Paula Kimper, writing "was a process; I heard music. So I knew I could do it. When I was a kid, my biggest fear was that I would write something down that someone else had written because I heard it. Part of my reason for going to Eastman School of Music was to learn what was out there so I would not copy." I asked her about the challenges on writing new music in opera. "It's a dance, like in jazz. The downside of attempting something new in opera is the expectation of the audience. They say they want to hear something avant-garde, but then if it's too avant-garde, they don't consider it opera. If the music is too standard, then it's not avant-garde enough. My first opera was referred to as a folk opera."

Eric Reed and I talked about his impressions of jazz musicians who record popular music. "What is pop?" I asked. He replied, "There were not many categories of music when I grew up: I define pop in two ways. There's popular music, anything not jazz or classical. Anything that sells a whole lot is popular. Then there is popular music in the white sense, like Barbra Streisand, Norah Jones, and Michael Bolton. Irving Berlin, Cole Porter is American popular song as in the Great American Songbook.

"Jazz musicians have recorded those songs of Sting, The Beatles, Stevie Wonder, and such. A great song is a great song, and it depends on how it speaks to you. A musician did an arrangement of 'One,' a Marvin Hamlisch song. I'm not a big fan of Hamlisch's music, nor was I blown away with the guy's arrangement of the song. There's nothing that says that you can't take that kind of a song, and if you have any intuition or creativity, you can make it into a masterpiece. Who knew that Ramsey Lewis would make a great hit out of 'Wade in the Water,' an old Negro spiritual? He turned it into this crossover hit. It does not matter how complex or simple the song is.

"Look at 'Oh, Happy Day'. It was a blockbuster hit and only had three basic sections: the verse, the chorus, and the tag, and just one chord/four chord. [He sings it.] The nation was just ready to embrace it. It is crossover Gospel. If you have to put it in a category—first, it had a choir, in the Gospel vein, but it had Latin, jazz, pop, soul overtones. Just because it has overtones does not make it that. If you take water and put lemon in it, it does not make it lemonade, but it is water with lemon flavor. That was the trend of the day, so 'Oh, Happy Day' marked the beginnings of what came to be called contemporary Gospel. Before that were the Gospel quartets such as the Dixie Hummingbirds, Clara Ward Singers, and Mahalia Jackson; it was such a much more narrowly defined sound. André Crouch, Reverend Hawkins, Rance Allen were in their mid-twenties—young people—and they began to use their influences like Sly and the Family Stones, The Beatles, Rolling Stones, so just by default those influences seep in."

8 The Empty-Vessel Theory

This is about how you can tap into your creativity as an artist, specifically, as a writer. However, this is not to imply that if you do not understand or agree with the theory, then you are not and cannot be a good writer. The theory describes the spiritual dimension, or what some might call being "in the zone," the feeling that some writers have when they do their best work. Ray Charles said in his 1978 autobiography, *Brother Ray*: "I was born with music inside me. That's the only explanation I know of. Music was one of my parts, like my blood. It was a force already with me when I arrived on the scene. It was a necessity for me, like food or water." Michael Jackson, too, cannot account for where his music comes from. Quoted in an article some years ago, he said, "I let nature take its course. I don't sit at the piano and think, 'I'm going to write the greatest song of all time.' It has to be given to you. I believe it's already up there before you are born, and then it drops right into your lap. It's the most spiritual thing in the world. Sometimes I feel guilty putting my name on the songs . . . because it's as if the heavens have done it already."

Jeff Clayton learned about this from the late jazz drummer, Billy Higgins, and also from Stevie Wonder. He explains, "There is a place where we can go, like a big empty vial, or a vessel, that has everything creatively that we want in it floating around. Our job, standing outside the vessel, is to make ourselves open and aware, and to educate ourselves on how to read the ideas, or the notes and rhythms that are in the vessel. When we go there, if we can identify them, we are allowed to pick them out of the air as they fly around and place them in a medium that will allow us to write them in our head or on a piece of paper and play them for others. It means that we don't own what we create; we simply, out of the universe, identify those elements that were here before we got here and will be here long after we are gone. The proof of this concept, for me, is that I write songs that are far above my musical understanding, because I made myself as aware as I could and taught myself as many things as I could about music, so when I get inside this vessel I can identify them. Some people never even make it to the vessel. It is a coveted place where music is created for those who are open and aware enough to accept the music that is being created."

I asked Jeff how this relates to actual writing for those who may not be musically trained, and he replied, "There are notes, rhythms. . . . There are two parts in writing: one, the craft, how chords fit together, where they go, the augmented, the demented, or rather, diminished, the mechanical information. Two, there is pure inspiration, which is mixed in with those notes that are floating in that vessel. The wind from the vessel is the inspiration. When you put your hands out, what sticks to your hands are the things you understand enough from being outside the vessel, learning about the music that allows you to put them together into a song. When you pull them out of the vessel, they are still in raw form; it is your ability to write and rewrite—that is the craft part. The information and inspiration is in the vessel. The things with chords that you thought would never use, or the notes you thought would never go together, work perfectly. If you know nothing about music, and you go in and see a bunch of notes, it is gibberish. The empty vessel is divine inspiration with divine information, only accessible to those who are open and aware. You dream a dream of beauty and grace, and when you feel that warm breeze across your face, then you sing—you are in the vessel. The singing that comes out of your mouth, you work hard to let your mind remember and write it all down."

I have witnessed some musicians who can sit down and write songs on command. I asked Jeff about this, and he replied, "It depends on where you write it from. Some write from knowledge only. Once you become aware that it exists, you can access it; it is difficult at first, but the more you do it, the easier it is to access it. As soon as you figure out how it feels to be creative, you can go anywhere and access the force. You will find that it comes when you are not thinking; it is a mindless awareness. When I was with Stevie Wonder, when the creativity came over him, it was so big that it would include the rest of the room and stop people from talking, and we did not know why we had stopped. That's deep."

Jeff writes music and lyrics. I asked which came first, the lyric or the melody. "When the melody and the harmony and the lyric come at the same time, it is a gift from God. That means that the song will be spiritual. It just comes to you— where did it come from? If it comes from intellect, then just try to do it again. If you can't get back to it, it was not you at all. Otherwise, if one thing comes first, it is usually the melody before the lyric."

Richard Smallwood draws from an emotion when he composes songs: "Some of my most difficult times have birthed songs. Writing music that speaks to people comes from a deep well of emotions, experiences, faith, hurt, disappointment. Those songs probably touch more people; you write from that place, it's spiritual. The essence comes from a deep place coming from your knowledge of music. It

connects to the person who hears it. I get more feedback from those songs then any other songs." He is not particularly methodical when he writes: "Sometimes I just get a melody in my head, usually I'm nowhere near a piano. I'm in a hotel, in my car—the melody will come when I'm shopping, so I have a device on my phone where I just record and develop the melody when I get home. At times, I'll hear a phrase, secular or from a sermon, that will spark the creativity in me. It comes in all different kinds of ways."

Chann Berry no longer considers himself a musician, although he used to be a drummer. He now considers himself "musical." Growing up in Newark, New Jersey, and in East Orange, New Jersey, he was surrounded by the clubs in that area. Music was always in his life. "Music kept creeping up in my life, and it still does. I still can't write [music], but I can play a little by ear on the keyboard. Then I take it to someone who really is a musician, and they finish it up for me. I can write melody and lyrics and music some. My big thing is melody and lyrics. I wrote a tune for Mary Stallings, and I wrote something for Tony Bennett called 'Hello, Yesterday.' This gift, I don't know where it came from, the song came to me so quickly. When it was written, it reeked of Frank Sinatra in the 1950s, Bennett in the 1950s. Tony did not respond at first, then I gave the song to Nancy Wilson and Mary Stallings at the same time; they both loved it, but Mary recorded it first. I wrote both the lyric and the melody."

Oscar Brown Jr., too, has a more organic approach: "My tunes just come to me in my head. They usually come with words. Words bring a melody, and it is rare when the tune brings the lyric. The lyric brings the tune. The tune does not bring the lyric for me. If I make up a tune independent of a lyric, then I have to compose the lyric to that tune, just as I would if that tune was 'Work Song,' or 'Dat Dere' or some other melody I didn't write. I don't start out with a tune, or with a word, or a phrase or idea; it does not work like that for me. I had tried writing lyrics with Duke's [Ellington] 'What Am I Here For,' but when I got serious about songwriting, I had been in the labor movement and into politics, and I had the experience in show biz, so I was at a crossroads."

Heartbreak, too, brought about some of his work. Oscar notes, "Relationships have been positive, and like I said, a girl would break my heart, and I'd wind up with a song. After my heart was mended, I'd still be getting over with that song. As life goes along, you write about all aspects of it. About the heartbreak, the blues. If you hadn't been in love, you wouldn't have had the heartbreak, and you couldn't write the blues. The same goes for 'up' songs; I wouldn't have known how to write them if I hadn't had the joy of love."

Bobby Sanabria taps into the unknown when he writes. "I hear it in my head. Sometimes it's a bass line, and it can come at the most inopportune time. I'm in the car where I have no paper or a tape recorder. It does not come back. I've lost so much that way. I wrote a piece called 'Child's Walk' for my son when he was beginning to walk. It is the rhythm of him walking; it turned into a bass line in 5/4 time, a simple melody a child would be able to sing, and added some other things that were written from memory. My son writes poetry, and I'm thinking about having him write lyrics. I've worked with a lot of poets, and I love the American Songbook. Composing is intimidating. If you write and hold it up against the incredible music that has been written through the years, like the American Songbook, it's difficult. If you look at compositions in the pop and rock world, the naïveté they have in terms of harmony works to their benefit. They have the innocence in their compositions. Sometimes having a lot of knowledge is not conducive to making something, trying to impress the musician in the audience. In college I did that, but there is a lot of beauty in simplicity. Take the blues, for example. It is simple but most soulful."

Al Jarreau talked extensively about his songwriting. As he described some of his work, I could feel his deep passion for the song and the lyric. He talked about putting words to Chick Corea's "Spain" and Joe Zawinul's "A Remark You Made": "Melody comes first. My advice to people who work with words, even many who say they have written a lyric, it may be that they have written poetry, but not necessarily a lyric. I think that 99 percent of songwriting happens with melody first, some sort of musical stuff is going on first. It is an interesting process when it begins somewhere else. Take the 23rd Psalm, for example. It existed long before music was put to it. You got an unorthodox piece of music, which makes it novel, unusual, and may be very attractive in that regard." [Jarreau sings the psalm, which gives me goose bumps.] "That is unusual writing and *powerful* because that person had to work with a poem that was already written. Because that person was so sincere, he figured out how to make the climax of the song. He wrote that in so it would be at the end of the prayer, which is the climax of the song and make everything that lead up to that moment. The poem has been there a long long time.

"I just finished a lyric for the Bach, 'Air on a G String;' it's a pretty good lyric, what *balls* I got to go straight for Bach. It took balls for someone to go and write this lyric to Chick Corea or Joe Zawinul and Weather Report, 'A Remark You Made.' I wrote lyrics for it because it was a brilliant piece of music and I wanted to perform it, and I did not want to stand in front of the audience like a horn player and just sing a melody. It took about eight months to write the lyrics. I wanted it to be relevant, and I wanted to have something to say. [He recites some of the lyric.]

"If you talk about how difficult it is for a person to make changes and write a lyric that means something; say something important if you are going to jump on someone's music that is brilliant music. Do the best you can do. If you get stuck, go to the person who wrote the music and ask if the lyric means what the song is. Joe Zawinul said to me about the song, 'It's complete as it is'—that is the first thing he said. Which meant that he did not encourage me to write a lyric on this; it is complete as it is. 'I won't stop you, and I'll share publishing when someone sings your lyric.' The song is 'A Remark You Made.' Check that out if you are curious to find who I am really deep inside. The piece of music is just brilliant." You can find his vocal version of "Something That You Said" on his CD *Tomorrow, Today*.

Paula Kimper's entry into opera was "a long process. With opera it takes so long . . . I had not had any composing experience. I could not get in as a composer, though I wanted to study that and music, in general, in fact." I asked Paula what comes first, the words or the music, and she said, "It goes both ways. I read Thorton Wilder's book *The Bridge of San Luis Rey*s and heard music when I read it. I love doing research so I researched ancient Peruvian music. That is another interest of mine, like the captivation of Venus, so I had to learn Mohawk music . . . My first opera was produced in 1998 called *Patience and Sarah*. I had read the libretto and turned it down because at that time I was not an opera composer. Later I had the inspiration and thought that it would make a good opera so I went back and read it again, and my juices said 'go.' I knew there was something there to follow, so I worked with a librettist on that one."

Allan Harris combined several musical elements when he wrote the music for "Cross That River." He, like Paula, drew from the musical elements that were relevant to the time period in which the story was based. The writing proceeded like this: "The idea came first, then the lyrics came second, then I put the melodies around the lyric. I played it first on the guitar; I heard bass, guitar, and violin. As I got to know the songs better, the other instruments came later. I listened to Leadbelly, T-Bone Walker, Charlie Pride, Allman Brothers; they influenced me a lot." When he wrote the song that he cowrote with Ray Brown, "Black Coffee Blues," the inspiration came from a cup of coffee. Ray had insisted that he have a blues song on that CD. Allan commented, "I had one night to do it; it happened over a cup of espresso, it just came to me, like 'Mule Skinner' and 'One More Notch.' I don't know where that comes from; that happens a lot when you have a creative flow. Usually those songs are the best—they come from a place inhabited in your mind. You are not writing to please an audience, not to fit a bill; it just happens to be in your psyche."

Part Three On Personal Growth

*If you have patience and knowledge,
and if you are aware of all that is
happening around you, you will
gain something unexpected.*

— ALHAJI IBRAHIM ABDULAI

9 Overcoming Success and Failure

For the purpose of this book, I view success and failure in terms of achieving goals. You may desire to be a "one-hit wonder," make a lot of money, and retire. Or you may desire to have a long, productive career, or be respected for your writing. It is a personal decision. Though there is no guarantee of success (achieving one's goals), there are things that you might do that will deter you from reaching your goals. The *Random House Dictionary of the English Language* defines "success" as "1) the favorable or prosperous termination of attempts or endeavors; 2) the attainment of wealth, position, honors, or the like; 3) a successful performance or achievement." "Failure" is defined as "1) the act or an instance of failing or proving unsuccessful; lack of success; 2) non-performance of something due, required, or expected."

The things that will aid you in achieving your goals are 1) having a positive attitude and being pleasant to everyone you meet (you never know who will be in a position to give you an opportunity!); 2) being professional, showing up on time, and being prepared; 3) learning your craft; 4) working *hard*; and 5) networking. Too many artists do not understand these fundamental principles. Javon Jackson once told me, when discussing why some marriages fail, that what women do to get their man, they must continue to do after they have gotten him. In terms of your career, you must continue doing the things that you did to achieve success, even after you get to where you want to go. How many artists achieve a high level of success, in terms of widespread recognition, and then disappear? And what about the artists who were at the pinnacle of real recognition, with all of the stars aligned in their favor, but they did not move to the next level because they refused to accept the rules of the game? They stopped working; in many cases, they just burned out. Artists like Cher (Eric Reed commented that Cher will be here long after cockroaches are extinct—she just won't go away), Chaka Kahn, Madonna, and Rod Stewart have stood the test of time by reinventing themselves. There is always someone ready and willing to take your place. Too many talented musicians have retreated and become embittered.

Keep Striving

Five-time Grammy-Award winner Al Jarreau says, "You are never *there*. It is how you think about it. You can never think that you have arrived. That is the adult, healthy way to think about it. Whether you are talking about your growth as an athlete or growth as a Buddhist monk, you should always be reaching, striving for another level. If you don't love it enough to do it for free, you might want to think of doing something else. If you love it like that, you'll find a way. I have not had a huge rip-roaring success. I'll accept the limited number of people who want to hear me do it the way I want to do it. I think that there is something valuable about what I do, and I can't help it. I'm going to do it in this particular way. At some point, I might be left with having to do it at the Holiday Inn. I started there, and I'll go back there. I didn't make much money then. The love gives you the longevity, and it gives you the courage to do it during hard times. If you love it, you constantly are finding new things in it—the new you that you are excited about being today. If you think that you've made it, you won't keep looking for the new you that will keep you excited about the craft."

When I asked Al if winning the Grammys had helped his career in any way, he replied, "Of course, it has helped, but not at the cash register. *No!* There are colleagues and peers coming to a guy, and they are saying that they appreciate what he does and give him a handshake. They are saying, this is *good* work. The Grammy and $2.00 will get you on the crosstown bus."

Grammy-nominated soprano Brenda Feliciano said, "There are some people who are incredible and are better [than myself]. I have so much to learn. Don't ever think that you are great, and you have it all there. I don't talk much about the Grammy nomination. It's nice for the recognition, [but] I think that there are other artists who deserve more than myself. It's political; it's a business. The Grammy thing is a business, and sometimes they recognize those who deserve it, but there are so many talented artists who won't get recognized or get in. It's like writing grants; there is a whole process you have to submit the album to."

Bobby Sanabria "never had success on the business on any level. Other than the fact that I received two Grammy nominations—for the CD on mainstream, *Live and on Clave* (2001), and the other for *Fifty Years of Mambo*. I was nominated for Latin Grammy, the Tropical Music category. To go to the Grammys was very enlightening because I saw how little regard the media has for jazz, and it was disappointing and disenchanting and made me more resolute in my work to get people involved. Not even Hispanic TV was interested in the music, or me. People in the media don't give two flying fucks about jazz, and it is sad because without jazz, the other music would not exist.

"I see that as a disappointment, not a failure. The nominations were a great triumph for me—I am a kid from the South Bronx—I'm a survivor. It is a nice feeling that you have received that level of recognition. If anyone tells you that Grammys are BS, they are full of shit. It was an incredible experience. My problem is not with the Grammys, but with the media. They put jazz and Latin jazz music at the bottom, and jazz is America's great art form."

Andy Bey concurs, "I never had a high level of success. The word 'purpose' has a lot to do with it. I realize that anything can fall backwards; that is not negative, it is how you label those setbacks. There are a lot of disappointments and a lot of pain. It's the purpose, me making music, what I was put here for."

To Overcome Success or Failure

Allan Harris, without hesitation, said, "Failure is hardest to move beyond. Rejection is *not* good for the soul—it's BS. Failure is a truth serum. You never get over failure; you harness it and use it as a reminder of what you have to do to move beyond to become successful. You forget successes, so people remind you of your successes, especially when you are in a slump. Failure is compounded when you have another failure. For some reason, the baggage of all other failures come with each new one. Artists think that all failures are related, but they are not linked; each has its own seed. Failure is wonderful; it's debilitating, but, yes, you can get past it. You can wallow in your lack of success, or the drive to be successful can be so great that you are able to smother that feeling of rejection. Rejection causes us to feel numb. It paralyzes a lot of people and keeps them from making that next call."

"That's all important, sure," says Billy Taylor. "Many of us don't admit failure [he laughs], regardless of if we are in pop music or in my kind of music, period. But failure has to be in your vocabulary because it's beyond your control and you are at the mercy of people (such as club owners and managers). It's difficult to handle failure, and that's one of the reasons why many people succumb to the various vices such as dope, whiskey—that was the narcotic of my generation—the reason why people lost opportunities. Many people not in the field don't realize what that does to someone. You spend your time learning to play, you know whether you can play well or not, no one has to tell you that. You know what you can do, then you go somewhere, you are asked to perform, and you shoot your best shot, and somebody writes about it and says you can't play. It happened to so many people, writers or people who hire entertainers, and artists can be very cruel. The business has always been bad; it's a matter of where you are in the business and how you are able to do what you do whether it's worse or not. There are people now who deserve to be heard. I'm interested in some of my many friends who are beboppers, who are older, the people who came up the hard way and really learned their craft and could do what they did well, but were sideman. So many people have been killed by this business because the business of music is controlled by people who don't know anything about the music or *care* about the music. How can you face that? There is no way to face it. How many people can say, if you don't let me play, I'll get a job somewhere else?"

Edwin Hawkins understands the pressures of success very well. In his twenties, his rendition of "Oh, Happy Day" became what was considered an overnight sensation, taking Gospel music to the secular world. When I asked him how he handled the pressures of success, he responded, "There are pressures. I remember very well. Like Buddha Records trying to take another song and make it into something with the magnitude of 'Oh, Happy Day.' You cannot recreate that. I believe that God did it alone. We recorded it on a two-track machine in a church; what was the likelihood of that happening again? People understood the component of a successful record, but to recreate that is a greater challenge.

"The church world, especially the black church here in the Bay area, was upset that it was played on secular radio. I heard that there was a group of ministers who had petitioned to get it off the secular radio. That was very confusing to me. They had always taught us to take the Gospel into the world, and this was being done. The reaction was very strange. When it became a hit, the Gospel DJs tried to take credit for it becoming a hit, though the secular DJs played it first."

Ruth Brown has had her share of ups and downs; her life has been a roller-coaster ride—early success, disappearance from the industry, her comeback, her illnesses, and then she came back again. Success never went to her head, and Ruth is very clear about that.

"I realized I had to survive, no matter what! I got the job in *Amen Corner*. My mother died when I was working on Broadway. I missed the bus to go to the hospital. I called to say I'd go the next day, but she died when I was on the phone talking to her. When she died, I was in such hard luck, I had to borrow a coat to go take my mother's body back to Virginia. The night we buried my mother, I heard my family talking, 'We got to take care of Ruth; Mama said to take care of Ruth because she has nobody.' My mother was my crutch, and I said, "*Oh, no*, you guys don't have to worry about *me*!!! That night, I made a decision: I'm going back and get what's *mine*, and I can stand on my own two feet. That put me right back, and I tried out for everything. That is when *Black and Blue* [a Broadway production] was going to Paris, and I went to Paris with that show. I played everywhere in Harlem that had a stage. I didn't need much. I've been through all of that—phony friends, fancy cars, big houses, bad lovers— all of that. Where I live now is a senior complex; I have my puppy, wonderful neighbors, space."

At the time of our interview, Ruth was seventy-six years old, and had just had a successful three-week run at the club Le Jazz Au Bar in New York City. Though hired for two weeks, they held her over for three. That had been her first appearance since her stroke five years earlier. Ruth was wonderful and she was invited back the following year for one month.

Ruth said, "When Mama died, I was fifty-five years old. I've survived a car accident, colon cancer, and a stroke. I lost everything in the Los Angeles earthquake, and six years ago, they told me I'd have two years to live. When I went to surgery, I prayed. Afterward, the doctor said, 'I don't understand it . . . We got all of the cancer cells, and you won't need chemotherapy nor the colostomy bag.' My spiritual side is *strong*, and I believe. I don't fear God; I respect God. I want to ask for something, that's where I go. He allows me to sit in the chair, and I've been singing those songs for many years, those songs mean different things to me now. I just got to the place where I've had to talk about things that I had never talked about.

"I was told I'd never have any children [after a major car accident in 1949]. I got pregnant when I was on the road with Charles Brown. I thought that I had a tumor, but it was a baby. That's why Dinah Washington took my place on the road. It was 1955, and my label, Atlantic, said that I was crazy to come up with that baby. I was the biggest chart singer at that time, as far as women were concerned, in the black radio. It was not easy. It took me three-and-a-half years to sing again. They told me that I never would."

When Ruth had her stroke, she "had taken Joe Williams' place at his annual concert that he gave for charity. He had died, so his wife called me. The morning after the show, I was scheduled to go to Rome, but I had the stroke, and I could not speak. This was right after I had been in the hospital for the cancer. I had therapy three times a week. I was told to listen to music, but I didn't want to; *I hated it*! I was depressed, and one day my son came in and put my music on. I told him that I didn't want to hear it. Then he took my pictures of me and people I worked with and of my singing, he put on the wall my awards and proclamations so I could see them, and he told me that I had made a mark and [that I couldn't] just sit down and die. He stopped everything he was doing to take care of me. He was with me through it all. I went to the wall many times."

I asked Ruth how she had been able to survive the industry and how she was able to stay motivated. Her answer: "My love of my children. It was my choice to stop work. I came off the road and my baby, Earl, was in my mother's arms, and he screamed when I went to hold him. So I said, '*That's it*; I'm not going anywhere else.' Only place for me to work was Mount Vernon, or in the Baby Grand [Harlem], local stuff. You got to be out there, or, out of sight, out of mind. I was out from about 1965 to 1976. I had no problems doing a nine-to-five job. I worked all my life. I'm the oldest of seven children; I've been working all of my life. When I worked in Long Island, I used my married name, Blount. I worked for Headstart, I was driving a bus, cleaning homes; I was Ruth Blount. During one Black History Month, I was cleaning a house and the radio was on, and I heard the disc jockey talking about rhythm and blues. He said, 'When they write the history of R&B, this lady's name will be right up at the top.' He started playing my music. So I said, '*Where's my money*?!' That is when I started this fight to get my royalties."

Ron Carter is very specific in his definition of success. He talks about how black Americans deal with the idea of success and failure. "I think that being able to work New York is success, given that there are many bass players to chose from. I think one of the things that Afro-Americans haven't really gotten a handle on is the psychology that goes along with success. That is to say, sometimes Afro-Americans feel that they aren't worthy of this success. So many Afro-Americans have been unsuccessful in this certain area. The reverse psychology of, you don't deserve to be successful, therefore, you will not be successful. That's the other side of the coin."

On the question of failure, I asked Ron if the word "failure" was in his vocabulary. He sighed and said, "It's not a very good word. I've missed some notes on a recording. I wouldn't call it a 'failure;' I would call it a 'miss.' Something that I could do better next time around, but I did the best I could so failure is not part of that process."

Joe Grushecky is no stranger to the ebbs and flows of being a musician. He continues to work, but chose to resume a day job. One bad year forced him to make some difficult choices. "Over two years, we completed the tour for the record *American Babylon* with Bruce Springsteen. We had worked more, traveled a lot, got to Europe for the first time. I quit my day job and worked full-time as a musician. I started working a day job in 1987; I had gotten married, had kids, and I needed the supplemental income. The last year as a full-time musician before *American Babylon*, there was a terrible winter with constant cancellations. I thought that I'd have to rob banks to support myself. So I used my teaching degree again and went back to work. I needed better health care for my son, so I took a job, and I've had the same job ten years. I work the school calendar year, summers off, and on weekends I travel. During the five years recording for MCA Records, we were touted as the best band in America. But we were never treated as rock stars, so it never went to my head. We were always working our butts off to survive. We were not very savvy and received little money and just had to work and work to survive. Some nights we'd record in the day in Cleveland, then drive to Pittsburgh to do a gig at night, then drive back to Cleveland for our first record. We'd tour in my Chevy Malibu; six of us toured in my car. We weren't living high on the hog. We were older, so we were somewhat more cynical. We knew we had a good band. We were so close to making it big, and it was such a hot band. After it fell apart, it was such a heartbreaking thing. I dealt with it by turning my back on it, and I did not want to be reminded of it."

A Matter of Perspective

"Neither success or failure are permanent," says Eric Reed. "They can be lasting or very brief. Some people keep coming back. People's careers take dips, and trends change, the economy changes. You can look at this in terms of changing seasons. Success or failure is too extreme, too definitive. Stevie Wonder and Duke Ellington will always be respected as musical geniuses in everyone's mind. Just because they stopped producing great things doesn't mean they stopped being great. Some people don't know when to stop; they don't know when they've worn out their welcome and need to go reinvent themselves and go on to something else."

For Michael Wolff, "it's a mixture. My life is so successful, I'm so lucky to have met my wife and married her. I have great kids, I did a TV show, and made enough money to afford to be a jazz musician. In that way, I am really thrilled with my life. Sometimes I'm frustrated because I feel I'm not appreciated in the jazz community for how great a jazz piano player I *think* I am, my experience and everything . . . If I get someone in the room to hear my band, me playing, if they like this kind of music, they'll love it, and that to me is success."

Olu Dara "never had a failure in music, and I never had a success that was too much for me. I've always had it just right. I never thought that I needed more of this or missed out on that. I have been enjoying the idea that I could put across a song. I've been playing for over fifty years, entertaining people on all levels. I've been fortunate that I could guide myself. I took it upon myself to guide myself, not be guided by the press, musicians, anybody. I've always fought that."

The Positive Side

My sister Michele Anderson had an experience that ended up being life-changing and could have turned out badly. I always remember what she told me after her experience: "I pulled victory out of the jaws of defeat."

Jeff Clayton says, "I don't consider failure. I consider everything information. Each time you gain information, you educate yourself. There is no failure." Oscar Brown Jr. got that early in his career when he wrote the play *Kicks and Company*. It was a major production, but in essence, it flopped and never made it to Broadway. The story goes: "Opening night was in Chicago and was a benefit for the Urban League; we packed the 5,000-seat house. Black people loved it, yet, we never got to New York City. When we opened, the critics called it 'amateur night in Dixie,' and 'pelvic choreography.' The dancing was based on the twist—we wanted to use dance that the kids were doing. But it was the dance that the black kids were doing. A couple weeks later, the dance hit in the cities."

"How did you feel?" I asked (maybe a dumb question, since he'd already told me it was a painful subject).

He laughed his big, hearty laugh and said, "In my act I used to tell the audience: 'I wrote a play that was supposed to be a big hit, but instead, it closed in four days.' Then I'd sing a little of the music from the play. Then I'd tell the audience, 'People came up to me after that flop and asked me "How do you feel?" Those are the kind of people who stop at traffic accidents and say, "*Ooh*, look at *that*!" Then I'd say, 'Yeah, but I was cool,' and perform my song, 'But I Was Cool.' I spent two years working on that thing; it was heartbreaking, but it was very educational. I found that failure in something is what you have to accept. Success can be thrust upon you and frequently is. A lot of people don't deserve it but get it anyway.

Failure was a damn good lesson to me. The whole thing was so, by the time I walked through there, I had had an education in theater, and it cost $400,000, which was a lot more money than is spent on the education of most nations. I had to pay back the 3,300 bucks of the money advanced to me. It was quite a thing to be in *Time* magazine and *Life* magazine; it was big-time. This was all in eight months from beginning to end."

Recently Oscar was given an award by the Actor's Equity. Years before, he had filed a complaint against that union with the National Labor Relations Board (NLRB). He found it ironic that given his history with it that it would award him for anything. I asked him if he had any regrets in his life. "Never, never! When Actor's Equity gave me an award for my cultural contributions in New York City, I said I was glad that I was honored to get it with Langston Hughes, Eubie Blake. They got it posthumously, but I got credit pre-posthumously." He laughed. "I said that I was surprised to get it because if it had not been for *you* people, I'd have made a greater contribution. I said, 'You all don't know that I was the one who took you to the National Labor Relations Board and charged you with collusion and racial discrimination. The NLRB told me I just had a bad union, but if that was the case, I did not have one long because you people kicked me out for taking you to the NLRB because I was a pain in the ass. But I can understand that because you don't want the "great white way" to look like the NBA.' I said that on the stage; I could not *NOT* tell them [my feelings]. They *loved* it. Then they sang a nice song called 'Joy' afterward and explained to me that they were a new generation and apologized for the older generation. I could not really understand that night because what I'm trying to do; they can't allow that to actually happen. You can't have people doing what I'm trying to do, you don't see anybody trying to do what I'm doing, setting a standard of writing that does not have to apologize to white people for anything."

Paula Kimper questioned what I meant by asking her about overcoming success: "A trick question—what do you mean? That's personal growth. You don't have the right to expect that anything good will happen. If good things happen, then you treat it as a gift; you can't think that you should get a gift every day. With opera, it takes so long. I have to put anticipation on hold while I do my work, and it takes years. I don't feel like I'm not getting anything. I don't think I've gone out of style. It's part of it to be out of it for a while then come back."

"Do you believe in failure?" I asked. She replied, "It's definition—I don't talk of failure or success. A lot of good things have happened along the way. I feel I've been confirmed in my path by the universe. I kind of had that experience after my first opera at the Lincoln Center Festival in 1998. It was a really big success. It sold out, people got standing ovations, and there was a lot of press about it. I went home in August, and nobody called me for months and months, and I thought, Isn't something supposed to happen next? It was like the feeling of, nobody is looking now. So I realized I had to make another piece, and I had to call people."

David Randolph grew from getting fired. He sees failure as "more of a dis-appointment—a learning experience." He had a job as the music specialist for the Office of War Information that ended in 1947 because the war ended. "I was without work. Someone told me that CBS radio was looking for a music anno-tator for its broadcast of the Philharmonic and its own symphony orchestra. They had an opening because the person who had the job writing scripts for all of the serious music programming for the network had gone on vacation for a year. I applied, and they had already been considering me. They gave me the job offer but told me that I'd have to give up my WNYC broadcast. After discussing this with my wife and mother, I decided not to give up WNYC. They agreed that I would not have to give it up, and gave me the job as long as I would not mention CBS. So, if the man came back after one year, I'd be out of a job. He did not come back, and I was hired permanently. They loved my work. . . . On Sunday, July 16, I was married. When I came back from lunch on July 21, I was told that I was fired. *Why?* Because a guy wanted the job, he talked to others higher up, and I was out.

"That was three days after I was married; I was making five dollars a week teaching one hour a week and conducting at a school. From that point on, I did what is known as the 'bulk-head theory.' I gave lectures, I did record reviews for magazines, I conducted four choruses at one time. It was lucky that I kept my WNYC job. I had the firmness of purpose to be ready to give up the job at CBS to keep the WNYC job for no money. I was only fired from that job."

For **John Levy**, "Success never went to my head. I knew what it took to be successful, and a lot of what happened to me was the right situation going for me, at the right place at the right time. I never put that much importance on myself. I always had the respect for everybody. That did not change me; that was just my personality. When I was married to actress Gail Fisher, I was swimming in the big leagues with all of the movie stars, but I learned then that all of that was a lot of bullshit! Everybody loves you when you are a winner. In order to be successful, you have to fail. Then you know what went wrong and what you did or didn't do to make it work at that time. There are some elements in life that come into play with artists—sometimes elements, things that happen in life that are relevant to you being a success or being a failure. I learned a lot of things along the way, and I'm still learning."

Richard Smallwood says, "You have to keep reaching for success. Success is a combination of many different things. *Failure?* I've had things that did not turn out or did not take off that inspired me and changed my life. Those things that changed my life have been the difficult areas in my personal life. That's what made me grow and mature. It toughens you and is a teaching tool. Such as deaths, I can say I've been there when I see others go through them."

Ego Check

I have always been cautioned not to believe my own press. It is easy to become consumed with one's own idea of greatness, significance, or importance. To hear the roar of a crowd can be intoxicating; to have hit records and complimentary media attention is wonderful. In the jazz community, there used to be a system of checks and balances, a weeding-out process, or gatekeepers to minimize poor musicianship. There are many stories about the famous, or infamous, "cutting sessions," in which a musician who could not play on a certain level was shouted, or escorted, off the stage and told not to return until he got his skills together. Charlie Parker did not become himself the minute he stepped on the stage. His elders, like "Big" Nick Nicholas, took Bird aside and taught him a few things. More and more young musicians hitting the scene are not given the same litmus test as their predecessors. Often they come out of school, are told that they are great, and they believe it.

Staying Up to the Challenge

Michael Wolff described what it was like for him when he began to play jazz and the flak that he took from other musicians. "I have Tourette's syndrome, and I always had a lot of tics and made noises, especially as a kid. I think that I felt like in jazz, you could be a junkie, or white, or black, and have something wrong with you, as long as you could play your ass off, you were accepted. It was harder for me to be a white jazz musician than to have Tourette's syndrome. When I'd go to the Both/And Club in San Francisco, which is where I started to get in all the time, they'd say, 'You white motherfucker, get the fuck outta here!' You know, it was a really strong scene in San Francisco in those days. There were also the nice people, but there were some jive people; then I'd go home for two or three days, and I wouldn't want to come out of my room. Then I'd just get pissed off, I'd go back, and I'd play my ass off so they'd just have to play with me, y'know? So it was kind of like trial by fire, and I respond well to challenge, so I was able to get people on my side because it showed me that the music can transcend the racism, any kind of problem you might have. Because I noticed that many of the people of the jazz world, or just the people hanging out didn't fit in with regular society, so I really liked that."

Michael has a healthy ego that reflects the A-team attitude; early on, he thought enough of himself to keep on working no matter what anybody said, but he wasn't so full of himself that he ignored the need to meet the challenge. There are several examples of musicians in all genres who had great starts, but who fizzled out because they let their good press get the best of them, and they stopped growing. I know several musicians who, at some point in time, had good careers, but their careers have headed south. Some of those guys carry their feeling of importance in the past around, and when I see them coming, I feel their ego before they even say hello. They also bore people with the stories of their glory days and bemoan the fact that they have lost their stature in the scene—that their heyday has come and gone. That approach reflects the B-team attitude. The B-team musicians will also tell me, each time I see them, what they are doing, whether I ask or not. They seem so impressed with themselves that they must share it with everyone. A-team musicians do not talk about themselves. If they share any work information, it comes out in conversation.

What the musicians interviewed in this book have in common is their lack of ego. Of course, one must have a sense of self-worth to do what they do, but they are not out of touch with who they are. I consulted the *Random House Dictionary* for a definition of "ego"; there are six. The following three are my favorites: 1) the 'I' of self or any person; a person as thinking, feeling, and willing and distinguishing itself from the selves of others and from objects of its thought; 2) self-importance; 3) self-esteem or self-image; feelings.

Humility

Being an artist is perhaps one of the most fragile professions in life. So much of what artists do depends on how accepted they are. Artists have died penniless, only to have their great work discovered after their death. Not all artists seek validation through public acceptance. Thelonious Monk said, "I say, play it your own way. Don't play what the public wants . . . You play what you want, and let the public pick up on what you are doing, even if it does take them fifteen, twenty years."

You have to believe that what you have to say is important, or entertaining, and even significant. According to Michael Wolff, "I've got a mixed ego. It is hard to judge for oneself. I have a strong ego about what I'm doing." Allan Harris confronts his ego constantly. One night he had a horrible evening, which sent him back home and made him shed. He explained that "shedding" is "finding what it is that you have to say and perfecting that voice without distraction of mimicry, fanfare, etc. It is getting yourself mentally prepared for what you say as an individual, so that others see you and can see clearly what you are trying to say. It is a personal endeavor!" Allan admits, "I'm still working on it. I had one show in particular at a club called Tatou [in New York City]. Tony Bennett was in the audience, and Sammy Cahn introduced me, and *it was terrible*! It was the most embarrassing moment I've ever had onstage. I fought Tony Bennett later that night. He had wanted me to take lessons and take my show to Luther Henderson. Luther and his wife, Billie, were in the audience on the invitation of Tony, who had put the evening together, and they wanted me to come over to their place and work on my show, and I had an attitude—*imagine that*! It was real deep. I had not yet moved to New York City, but later, when I did, we [Luther, Billie, and Allan's wife, Pat] broke bread again, and Billie told me that night was terrible; I was all over the place. After that show, I went back to Miami; I had a few years to marinate; my phone did not ring. I had to go back to the drawing board and shed a lot. Ego is a hell of an impetus, because when you see someone really good, there is a balance between their ego and their talent. You want them to have an ego and to be confident in what they are trying to say. If they are self-involved and not worried about entertaining, they are almost masturbating, and the audience is a voyeur. Pop singers can't do that because they are concerned with the visual show. But exceptional jazz singers can really let the audience watch them practice their craft. For the other 70 percent of artists, ego gets you to the stage, but if your craft and talent are not in sync with your ego, you have to drop it *when* you get to the stage so you can connect with the audience. The audience helps you out and brings you out of it."

Gerald Cannon agrees. "Part of being a musician is to have an ego. It's how you use it. We are performers and entertainers." Billy Taylor put his ego to good use when he did not win a contest that he felt sure that he could win: "I was saving money to go to New York City. Tommy Dorsey was doing some concerts around the country, and there was one in D.C. The winner would get a chance to play with Tommy. I auditioned; I wanted to earn enough money to go to New York. I had played amateur contests; I had won some in the past. This was a mixed competition; black and white people were there. I knew that I played better than most people and wondered why I didn't win. It was not because I was black. I did not impress those people—that was a new experience for me. I was playing professionally, and I thought that I was all right, and that made me mad and I said, 'You guys don't know how good I am!' I went to New York, and I said, 'I'll show you....'"

Bobby Sanabria suggests keeping one's ego in check this way: "You have to surround yourself with people who respect you as an artist. I tend not to judge anyone. Anytime my ego gets overloaded with delusions of grandeur, I just put on a record of Tito Puente or Buddy Rich. I won't tolerate disrespect! I don't fire people; they fire themselves. That includes radio people. I've done interviews with people who say they know nothing about me. I did my homework, they should do theirs, so I give them hell."

Dorothy Lawson keeps herself grounded by understanding why she is a performer: "I guess it does all come down to the question of what I'm trying to do as a musician. I am not there just to have people look at me onstage. I'm there to share emotions with people—that excites me. If I did not have the confidence to think that I could do something, then I don't know why I'd be there."

Often prodigies, like Eric Reed, can get too much attention at a young age: "There has to be some balance when you are dealing with people of extreme talent; often they are encouraged to 'express themselves,' but with no parameters or boundaries. They look down on their peers, talk to adults any way [they want]; they treat other people as if they are 'less than' because they are made to feel they are special because of their talent."

When I asked if he had behaved that way, Eric said, "*Absolutely*! My parents did not allow that, but when I was away from them, I showed my ass every chance I got. People gave me *carte blanche*; I don't really understand that dynamic. Most people tolerated my behavior when it should not have been tolerated." Eric found many ways to tune out people, but most often it was by listening to music at inopportune times. Again, Jeff Clayton observed that Eric always had an earphone in his ear. Jeff did not seem to bothered by that; he took it as Eric learning his craft, but Eric now feels differently about that behavior. "This is part of the social skills, if you are around a bunch of people, it is rude to listen to music. I wasn't interested in holding a conversation with people. I can hold my own with people; I just wasn't interested—I only wanted to listen to music. Again, I wasn't monitored. I think people did not want to get in my way or hinder my music."

The Vicissitudes of Fame

Oscar Brown Jr. knows the vicissitudes of fame. His production *Kicks and Company* was much anticipated and supported. "Mr. Kicks was a character who worked for the devil. I started on the song, then I decided it would make a good play. Later I saw some kids in jail in the South who had participated in the sit-in movement. Then I got the idea for [Mr. Kicks] to corrupt them, and it took me a couple of years to write it because I had to develop the story. I was new at it. The characters started to take over, and I had a big fight with them about where they wanted to go. Plus, I was writing songs, and I had to make them up to fit the story. The agents came around, and Joe Glasser, who had managed Louis Armstrong, booked me on the *Today Show*, and I was quite a sensation. Dave Garroway was so impressed he came to see me at the Village Vanguard, and the set he saw was me performing six to eight of the songs from *Kicks*, and he offered me two hours on the *Today Show*, the *whole* show. Woody King said they passed a *Kicks and Company* law so that would not happen again; I don't know if that is true, though. It was way ahead of its time . . . so it did not run long. My ego got deflated *so* fast by the time *Kicks and Company* was over. It was nine months from beginning to end—January to October—and I had to have a comeback. People walked away from me; it was a stinker, and they did not put it on their résumé. I did the best I could, just a whole lot of illusions, and you don't know that if you've never been there. It is not like Cinderella.

"Does not mean you can't have new illusions. I was thirty-four, I was a big boy, I had been kicked out of college, the Communist party—I was too black to be red—the U.S. army, so I *knew* how to take rejection. I'd been kicked off the air frequently when I was a broadcaster so that was no sweat. As I said before, I was always too conceited to commit suicide, so when you get that out of the way, things take care of themselves."

To Be Humble

Being pleasant to people goes a long way in the music world. In the jazz community, I have seen musicians blow opportunities because they were aloof or rude to people. Musicians have lost record contracts, even lost gigs, for being nasty. I have seen humble young men turn arrogant because they believed in the greatness of their talent too early.

Richard Smallwood does not feel that his music comes from his ego. Rather he feels that he is a privileged vessel for the inspiration, Word, and music of God. "I never have dealt with that ego, but I know that it exists. It is a privilege to do what I do—why I was picked? I don't know. It is a sacred trust God has given me. My ministry extends off the stage; it can happen in the grocery store. You have to be where people can reach you. You get tired, don't want to be bothered, I just stay home." He told the story about one of his first workshops at the Smithsonian Institute, which was quite humbling for him. "The crowd was mixed, and when it ended, a white lady who had been sitting in the audience told her neighbor sitting next to her that she had contemplated suicide that morning, but after hearing the music, it changed her life, and she realized that her life was not her own. She was inspired to learn more about God." This happened early in his career and colored how he felt about his ministry. He says, regarding working with other musicians, "I can't be all things to all people, but I can be nice to them. I love my peers; I admire all of my peers. There is room for all of us, and what they do does not diminish what I have. There are people I've worked with who had big egos. I let them know that they were no better or worse than anyone else, but they were blessed because they had the good fortune to be chosen."

While the classical world is not exempt from out-of-control egos, not every musical situation is plagued with them. Says David Randolph, "I never had that problem. Maybe the two people whom we got rid of [in his chorus] did, but we don't have the problem, as such. My rehearsals have a lot of laughter; we take the music seriously, but not ourselves."

Understand Your Role

Shy people are sometimes thought to be arrogant and aloof. Although I have not had that experience with Ron Carter, his quietness might lead one to believe that he is being arrogant or that he is an egotist. I've been fortunate to meet people of all walks of life, and I find that the more secure and the more accomplished, the more humble they are. Ron Carter says, "I'm such a shy person. I'm okay when I'm not recognized at a club and have to pay a cover—how else will musicians make money? Often they have to work for the door."

I was curious to know if he had advice for young musicians concerning their egos. Ron said, "I tell the students this story. I did a recording session where the musician was not very interesting or very good at promoting his musical ideas. I proceeded to play in a fashion I felt made the music sound better and made the arrangement give more life to the song. But then the arranger came in and said, 'I like the way you played, but I want you to play what I wrote.' So I did. I tell my students, 'No matter who you are, if someone hires you, you better be ready to do what they tell you to do.' The moral of the story is, no matter how big you are, if the guy writing the paychecks tells you that you play shitty, you just have to live with that. I had a sax player in my class who played just average, and I would get on his case all the time, and he was not doing what I asked him to do. He got a job as a reviewer for a magazine, and he bombed my own records. That's personal, but it was in print, and no one knew the background of the writer reviewing my record. Those things come along, for me, to keep my ego in check and not get blown out of the water."

Be Gracious and Generous

One of the sweetest people in jazz was Etta Jones. She would speak to everyone. My friend Barbara told me about a party that she had attended with Etta and another singer. Etta was approached by a young woman who wanted to bring her grandmother over to Etta in order to introduce her. Ever so gracious, Etta said, "No, let *me* go over and meet your grandmother." Etta received many gifts that night. The other singer sat with a sour face, expecting others to come to her. Unfortunately, they did not.

Ruth Brown understands what it is to have an ego. She has witnessed divas several times in her career, but, she says, "I never had an ego like that." At Ruth's engagement at Le Jazz Au Bar, she sat for over an hour and "held court." It was so beautiful to see Ruth bask in the glow of love and give back to those who loved her.

"Unfortunately," she says, "a lot of entertainers have the wrong disposition. They treat people like, 'Oh, you are so lucky—here I am.' I always take time to talk to people to tell them I appreciate them. What has made it easier for me now at this late age is I don't remember meeting anyone who said, 'I like Ruth Brown's singing, but I can't stand that bitch; she is evil.'

"I tell young people that this is a business. You meet the same people going down as you go up. I went into it because my voice was a gift from God."

11 Self-Assessment

One of the things that separates the A-team from the B-team is the A-team's ability to look inward and to be honest with themselves about where they are. They do not allow themselves to become victims; they analyze what works for them and what does not. One musician told me that he needed to focus more on his musicianship, another needed to change management, and others needed to work on their presentation both on and off the stage. On the other hand, B-team musicians often place blame on others for why they don't work as often as they want to. They blame misguided club owners, jealous musicians, and even radio announcers who choose not to play their music. There are countless musicians who just don't "get" that they are not good musicians, and they make themselves a nuisance to the community. "B-teamers," as they are called, complain about getting passed over for jobs that less-qualified musicians get. It is rare when they 1acknowledge that they need to do any work on themselves. One could say that they are fooling themselves. I have been approached by so many musicians who wish to perform on the jazz series that I produce, and I do not understand why they cannot see that they are not on the same level of those I hire. Many do not have recordings; they have no following, no name recognition, no working band, and limited musician skills.

I don't mean to say that everyone has to strive to be an A-teamer. If you are a musician who is happy with infrequent work, then all is well. You should just be honest with yourself about who you are, the level of your skills, your ambitions, how hard you want to work, and how you define success for yourself.

James Browne talked about the state of the music business today. One of the keys to success is to have the proper perspective—you have to do the work involved to stay in the game. "When businesses get into trouble, like Sony, General Motors, Apple, etc., they downsize. Some people understand that the operation can no longer support the people, and that is what needs to happen in jazz. Three-quarters of them need to go away. Not just in jazz music, but in all music and what poses for culture, there is no quality control. Lockjaw [Davis] and those guys had realistic expectations. If you are fourteen and all the stars line up in your favor, you can have an incredible career for some time. I read an article in *Fortune* magazine that addressed this. It is not about music anymore. At the first rung on the ladder, they get more recognition, then they get a clothing line, vodka commercials, etc. If you understand what you can command and are okay with that, you will do just fine. If you wonder why you are not on a cover of a magazine, don't nobody want to hear your shit, no matter how good it might be. Artists must understand what the parameters are and what they want out of it. A lot of musicians are bottom feeders; some want to be divas and won't do the work."

Browne talked about a talented musician who at one time in her career was positioned to go to a higher level of fame. She was featured in ads, got endorsements and such, but she stopped doing the work, she fired manager after manager, and she became obstinate. That behavior did not work to her advantage.

Musical Growth

In order to grow, it is necessary to confront flaws and minimize weaknesses. Al Jarreau has had to confront who he is as an artist.

" 'Will the real Al Jarreau please stand up . . . an R&B performer, popular performer, a jazzer—you can't be all three. If you try to do that, we won't play you on our radio stations that play R&B, pop, or jazz, because you have the *audacity* to say that *you* can perform in all three? *Nope*—see you later!' I have suffered from it."

I was surprised by that comment and asked him to explain. He said, "I got a Grammy as a jazz singer. I'm claimed by the jazz press, but you and I have never talked before. And I'm talking to a bunch of jazz people who have never been interested in *my ass, never*! My press typically is R&B and pop press. I've done a jazz piece here now, so they are interested, and I love it! *But,* I know they have not been interested in me before," he laughs. *Accentuate the Positive* was a Grammy nominee for a Best Jazz Vocal Album in 2004.

I was a bit confused as to why he considered his CD *Accentuate the Positive* to be his first straight-ahead CD. I had always considered *Look to the Rainbow* to be a jazz CD. After the interview, I read an article about Al in *JazzTimes* magazine. The title of the article was "Accentuate the Swing: Al Jarreau Moonlights with Jazz." The writer wrote, "Veteran stylist Al Jarreau has recorded his first straight-ahead album since 1977's *Look to the Rainbow*," so I was not alone in my perception. When I asked him why he did not consider *Look to the Rainbow* to be a jazz album, Al said, "Because it is pop and R&B tunes. The title itself, *Look to the Rainbow*, is a show tune. The performance is jazzy, which is the way I perform it all of the time. If I had more live CDs, I'd perform as a jazz horn player or piano player, sort of, to extend the song and to allow room for myself and other musicians to improvise. *But*, if you look at the titles on *Look to the Rainbow*, I can stretch the definition and say that is a jazz performance. My CDs before were emerging a singer/songwriter work. I didn't care about what genre you put them in, I was loving the pop song that would allow me to sing, 'Boogey Down,' and 'We're in This Love Together.' I needed to express myself as a writer, and that's the areas I felt most comfortable writing in. Rhythm and blues, pop-ish kinds of writing, both very important genres of music to me, and that's where I wanted to work. That's what happened in *We Got By* and *Glow*, where I was writing as an R&B and a pop singer. There was a wonderful audience for that music in that day and time. I did that kind of writing for the first ten to twelve years of my career. Pop and R&B listeners made up the majority of the audience, so I wanted to write for them, and I wanted to write sensible, sensitive stuff for them."

Allan Harris dug deep to understand why he was not initially accepted in New York City. After a great success in Miami, Istanbul, and other places, he tried his hand at New York, but with little success. "I was not well received, not by the audience. I did not know how to present myself, what to say onstage. I was too abstract; I was not directed and focused. New York was not into fanfare like Miami. It took me a few years to shed that, and the residue is still out there. I was making a good living out there [in Miami]. I saw myself drifting into the sunset. It was a challenge, and I got my butt kicked. I brought that small-town mentality to New York, thinking that that was enough. I got the starch taken out of me. I realized that I had homework to do, and I had to grow as an artist."

As an artist who writes constantly, Oscar Brown Jr. evaluates his work, be it a song or a production. "When I produce or direct a show, there is a certain point at the beginning when I wonder what in the hell made me think this would work. Then I say, what I don't like is this, so I take it out and correct other things, and it begins to look a little better. If by then, it does not look better, I need to quit."

Perception/Perspective

Andy Bey is a spiritual and contemplative person, and it comes through in his performances. He has a way of putting me in a peaceful state, and he always knows what to say when I call for a different perspective. He sees that motivation is his driving force: "Motivation, how you become motivated, and how you lose motivation, is a choice. You can make excuses and judgments; they are understandable, but if it affects you, it is about you. There are a lot of disappointments and a lot of pain. It's the purpose, me making music, what I was put here for. It can't just be about music; it's about the person dealing with the music. You must take care of all aspects of your life. I must take care of my health, my spirit, my consciousness. If I don't, then I'm not supporting the music because I'm not taking care of myself."

I asked Dorothy Lawson if she thought that the opinions of her peers had been important. "Oh, yeah. For me, my long search was to take all of those opinions to try to understand what the relationship between their responses and my own perceptions was, and to get a consistent idea of where their point of view might be coming from."

On the topic of change, Edwin Hawkins said, "I think that change is always good and can be a positive if an individual will learn from the changes that *have* to happen. We are always evolving as we learn from our experiences. Some people think that certain experiences are negative, but I don't think so at all. Maybe some years ago, I felt that way, but now I would not change any experience I've had. I would not trade my experiences in for anything today. They taught me a lot about myself."

Ron Carter knows the kind of work that he won't take, or situations he won't play. He will not do a double-bill at a club where bands go over their allotted time. "I kind of decided I don't work for certain bands who are notorious for doing that. Playing an hour-and-a-half set and you got two bands, man you got two sets a night, the last band's there till four o'clock in the morning, just because one band's ego is in the way. So I try to avoid those situations. And I avoid jam sessions and all-star bands. You play egos. They are not fun anymore, and the camaraderie is kind of false."

Redirect/Shift Gears

Sometimes one must see one's limitations and find a way to create within those boundaries. Chann Berry realized that he would not be a working musician, and so he turned to songwriting. "I thought I'd be the next Max Roach, Louis Bellson; but that was not to be. My playing went to a certain level, did not go past it. It took discipline and study, then I became interested in radio because of Frankie Crocker."

Paula Kimper attempted several musical situations before turning to opera music. "Opera is really the last genre that I entered. Everything is a kind of process . . . I got a bachelor's degree in trumpet performance; I was a trumpet player. The trumpet was loud and I could be in the band. It was kind of ego-based in a way. I moved to New York [City] in 1979 and went into pop music. I played piano, used a custom synthesizer, had my own studio; I could do it all myself. That led me into film scoring and doing music for theater. I liked opera, listened to opera broadcasts, and I was in opera in college. When they needed stage bands, I played in the orchestra."

As the music business has its ebbs and flows, musicians often find ways to adjust, or recreate themselves. Eric Reed recognizes that he must look for different outlets. "I'm not letting the current conditions dictate what I do. Jazz has been taking a nosedive, going underground for the past four to five years, but I keep my head above water by constantly redefining myself. I'm not just Eric Reed, the performer. I start to think outside the box. I have to look at my scope of skills. Conditions define what I do, not dictate what I do. Work on the performance scene is not as lucrative as it was five years ago. *All* jazz music, the money is not there, so I found many other avenues in which to be employed, in which I can keep doing my craft—teaching, workshops, more writing projects. I'm not going to go under because jazz is going under. When jazz went underground, Ron Carter remained one of the top-notch working bassists in any scene because of his talent, what he brought to the table, his professionalism."

As a sideman, Kenny Washington could have some problems working, given the reduction of venues. On possibly becoming obsolete, Kenny said, "Naw, as long as there are people who want to hear 'spangolang' jazz, I'll always work, one way or another. You might not hear about me, but I'm always doing some quality gig. Few drummers do what I do. Most of these young guys don't want to play time and think that it is too old. They can keep on thinking that, but the music always comes back! You can see that in history, it always comes back to a groove one way or another."

Music is about self-expression and sharing. Michael Wolff has direction. He said, "Jessie Jackson said at Cannonball's funeral, 'He combined science and soul,' so you think as a musician it's scientific, but it's only to express your soul. Only to be human. If they're so hung up on a bunch of chords and changes, if it's not expressing something . . . it's not lifting weights. Ultimately, I want to take people on a journey."

When Joe Grushecky hit a wall, he had to step back and assess himself and the direction he was headed in. Unlike musicians working in other genres, he has the problem of getting older to contend with: "People are saying I'm too old; it should be about the music."

Bobby Sanabria is clear about who he is as a musician: "I'm a jazz musician who happens to be Latino. The fact that I am gives me more tools in my arsenal. Had it not been for my culture, jazz would not have been born. That has yet to be acknowledged and should be noted. It affects how you play, how you live, how you travel. It affected me positively and negatively. If you have tension in your personal life, that will affect you. You might snap at people or play better on the bandstand. As you get older, you learn to turn a negative into a positive and to handle it.

"I love teaching. I'm a player who teaches, not the reverse. There are students who get to college and don't know the rudiments, and I'll teach them. We are coming into a generation of young people who are farther and farther removed from the essential reference points that they need. I was lucky. I grew up in the last golden age of radio. Kids today just know one style of music, and if they get into jazz, *by luck*, they got it in high school or had a parent who was into jazz. We have more technically gifted players, but they lack arenas to gain life experience that will give them the street knowledge that you can get by playing with older cats who will talk to you when you do something wrong. The highest compliment in jazz is, '[You] sound good.' "

 ## What Are You Sure You Don't Know?

The question in the chapter title drew the strongest reaction from each interviewee. I have no idea *how*, nor am I sure *why* I came up with the question, but what came to mind was my television interview with drummer Charli Persip. He played with Dizzy Gillespie and had learned his music before he got his chance to play with Dizzy. Gillespie seemed impressed that the young Charli knew his music so well, but after the gig, Dizzy told Charli that he had to learn "what *not* to play." I had a conversation with radio personality Michael Bourne after I wrote this chapter, and he made the following comment: "You don't limit yourself by understanding what you don't know. Realizing how much you don't know is the beginning of wisdom." Certainty is not always a good thing. As a friend of the musician Lou Watson said, "Most conclusions are the product of a lazy thought process." Good musicians are in a constant state of searching; the more they learn, the more they want to know.

Here is how some of the interviewees answered the question:

Ruth Brown

Now, *that's* a question! You don't know the next moment whether you have time to tell someone you love them. Now, I do think about death. I never worry about it, but as I see friends slipping away, I wonder, what will they say about me? I watch *Inside the Actor's Studio*; I like that question, "When you get to the pearly gates, what would you want God to say to you?" I wonder about my answer. It just came to me, every time I sing, I pray twice. My mother liked to say that God gave me my power of voice, and I made a lot of people happy. I give thanks to God every time I open my mouth.

Ron Carter

When to stop looking for the best notes . . .

Richard Smallwood

I am sure that I don't know why I was chosen to do what I do. What makes God choose certain people to do certain things? Why me? You know your weaknesses and strengths—why me?

Paula Kimper

[Much laughter] I love that! The future, I'm sure I'll never know.

Oscar Brown Jr.

[He repeats the question, slowly.] What I'm doing here, what is the good life. I've done the best I could. I'll be damned if I understand this: How can you get to the point where you plant a bomb in a grade school and plan to kill little children—what is your cause?

Olu Dara

I don't know when I'm gonna get sick, or when I'm gonna get well. I don't know when I'm gonna die, or when I'm gonna go to jail. [We both laughed.]

Michael Wolff

So much shit I don't know. I've been working on Spanish; I don't know languages. I don't know that I'm finished growing. I don't know how to play all instruments; I definitely have weaknesses. I saw in the *New York Times* about ten years ago, there aren't just musical talents, but talents within music. There is ability to hear, to repeat it, not anyone has all of them.

Kenny Washington

[He repeats the question.] The more you think you know about jazz and music, the more you *don't* know. I'm sure I don't know all music; I don't know all the history about this music. There's always more to learn.

Kenny Barron

There are lots of things that I don't know, but I don't know what they are until it hits me.

John Levy

There's a whole lot I don't know, are you kidding? I sit at the computer and find out what's going on. There is so much technology. There is so much happening; I wish I were thirty, forty years younger.

Joe Grushecky

Nothin'. I am amazed at how little I do know. I wish I was eighteen again— I knew everything. On our new record, *True Compassion*, there is a song about that called "What Gives." The older I get, the less I know.

Gerald Cannon

A lot. [He laughs.] I don't know everything.

Eric Reed

I am sure that I don't know why I fell in love with jazz at such an early age; my parents weren't avid jazz fans, and there were only three jazz records in the house—all of which came from my maternal aunt and uncle, who were both public-school teachers.

Edwin Hawkins

Hmmm . . . *The future!*

Dorothy Lawson

[She laughs.] Oh, my *God* . . . That's amazing! Wow! I'm sure I do not know what is coming, what things are gonna look like. I take the position that it is in my hands to live with the energy that might manifest the future that I would love to live into.

David Randolph

[He laughs, repeats the question.] That's a lovely question. I can make a confession; I don't know how to conduct. I'm just learning. How the hell do you get the nerve to stand up in front of the prime hall in the world and dare to conduct the most complicated works with what little you know?

Chann Berry

I'm shocked at the wonderful question; I feel like Bill O'Reilly. I have two answers. First, I don't know if black people will ever trust. Second, I don't know for sure that the devil exists. I don't know if the world will ever come to peace.

Bobby Sanabria

Women! The most fascinating thing on the planet. That includes my mother.

Billy Taylor

I'm sure I don't know enough to make things the way I'd like for them to be. I thought I was smart and had a handle on things in the cultural sense and the musical sense. I thought that if I did my job, everything would turn out okay. It does not work that way. There are some possibilities in life; as it changes, you can't have that kind of control. The closest you can do is take the thing around you and try to influence them for the better.

Andy Bey

We are never sure of *anything*! We can only live for the moment. I'm aware of consciousness. That question sounds like you fear, or a rejection. I don't fear the unknown. There is only one power. Life is a day-to-day experience.

Al Jarreau

[Sighs] Why the hell are you asking me that question? I'm sure that I don't know why you are asking me that question. It's a good question; it just requires that the questionee is willing to look at it. There is lots I don't know about this music. I learned some things onstage this summer about trusting the moment and allowing the moment to happen with fewer filters on the moment, and going with it to be the inspiration for the next moment to follow it. That's pretty important stuff for performers like me who rely on improvisation. A lot I don't know about performing yet. There is a lot I don't know about God and the big picture. I really am curious about that, and I'm not alone.

Allan Harris

Wow! There is so much. I don't completely know how to totally capture an audience for eighty minutes. I still have to rely on a few gimmicks, which I'm trying to cut loose now. I'm getting there, where I can hold their attention, but I still have to monitor them. If I see them drifting, I go into somewhere else. I'm still trying to get to that place.

Brenda Feliciano

[Silence] Oh, a whole bunch of things. What I have is instinct. Do I really know? There is always a doubt, but I will never know enough about everything. I'm still learning.

Jeff Clayton

[He repeats the question as if asking me the question.] I'm sure that I don't know everything. I am just Jeff Clayton, the sum total of my experiences; that's who I am, and I can only tell you things that I experience. I can't make up answers to things I know nothing about. I try to stay open or aware. When I don't know something about something, I tell you I don't know about that.

Part Four On Putting on a Performance

We love you madly.

— DUKE ELLINGTON

13 Preparation for a Performance

There is nothing more annoying then to go to a show and see people making up the show as they go along. I've watched musicians look at their band-mates and ask, "What do you want to do now?" The leader will call a tune that others won't know, and the band member who knows the tune will teach it on the spot to the one who doesn't know it. Sometimes I have witnessed leaders ask the audience what they want to hear. The audience does not wish to pay to see people rehearse onstage. You must be prepared before you present yourself. A-team players are always prepared with a set list, and if they present a new arrangement, they work it out *before* the gig. How one prepares varies from musician to musician. It adds stress to the leader when members of the ensemble do not learn the music before the performance. Some musicians rehearse to death, and others prefer to stay quiet do their own personal preparations. Regardless of how you prepare, it must be done. To quote Ignacy Jan Paderewski, cellist, "If I don't practice for one day, I know it; if I don't practice for two days, the critics know it; if I don't practice for three days, the audience knows it."

Practice, Practice, Practice

When I asked Jeff Clayton about what he does to prepare, he said it simply: "Do everything possible until the music is prepared. Your job is not to prepare but to do the gig properly. The A-team will keep preparing until they get to the job. The B-team sidemen, unlike the A-team sidemen, are not perfectionists. For the B-team, okay is good enough. But not for A-team, they will not let you see a bad side of a performance."

Al Jarreau learned by example. Nat King Cole and Johnny Mathis were his influences. When Al was honing his craft in San Francisco, my friend Tina told me that all of his concerts were romantic, and that if you did not have a loved one when you went to his shows, that you'd *want* to *go find one*! Al said in response, "The romantic song comes from learning how to sing ballads like Nat and Johnny.

That caused you to fall in love if you weren't, and you wanted that feeling." Another vocalist, Allan Harris, said about the need for preparation: "I make sure that every song I have in my show I'm prepared. I know the lyrics, of course, I practice my inflections, what I'm gonna say. I practiced everywhere, but that was in my formative years. I practiced in the mirror."

Oscar Brown Jr. often travels without a working band, so preparation is essential for him. "I rehearse musicians. I used to go around with one musician who would be my musical director, and we'd hire the other musicians when we got somewhere. I could never afford to hire other than a trio or a quartet. As my son grew up, he would go with me, and he taught the music to the English or whomever we were dealing with. As I started out, I had a friend called Don Leitsetz, a Swedish man; we met at Northwestern University where we were taking film class. He would talk to me about the European style of performance, like Edith Piaf and others. I listened to Kurt Weill . . ." Don introduced Oscar to the different ways European artists rehearsed for performances, and the way they prepared to talk about their music, and this became part of Oscar's style. "I warm up. I believe in practicing how I'm gonna breathe. I study how Ella Fitzgerald and Dinah Washington did it. I'm always learning. There is not too much practicing for me, but there might be for some people."

Brenda Feliciano said, "Rest and take care of your instrument, limit hanging out especially when on tour, otherwise you will get burned out, and things can happen to you. I've seen that happen. Be prepared, and know what you are going to be doing, no matter what ensemble you perform in front of. Know your music very well; learn what other have done with the material." Feliciano is not just a singer—she is the wife of famed Grammy-Award winner Cuban clarinetist Paquito D'Rivera. They often work together, and she finds it necessary to have a separate room away from him. "I am not a prima donna; [but] you need your space to get prepared. When I travel with Paquito, I get a separate bedroom and dressing room. We have to get ready, and I don't have time to take care of what he needs. I have to do my thing." This is not uncommon for husband and wife artists. I have heard of them having adjoining rooms, separate and equal.

To Rehearse or Not to Rehearse

Working bands may not require regular rehearsals unless they are working on new material, but each member must be ready for each performance. Kenny Washington has worked with pianist Bill Charlap so often, along with Peter Washington on bass, that rehearsals are not necessary. Kenny Washington says,

"If one knows the music, there is no need to rehearse." He will mentally prepare, though. He says he "gets to the venue at least twenty minutes to one-half-hour before to relax; I do not want to be rushed."

One complaint that I heard often from jazz musicians is that some really like to rehearse, while others think it's overkill. Ron Carter's opinion is, "One rehearsal before we go to work, whenever that is. I don't like to rehearse. I think it's a waste of time and effort, but you got to do it just to say hello to everybody."

"Why is it a waste of time?" I asked.

"Most of the horn players want to play their brains out in rehearsal, and they have none left for the gig. Most guys don't have the music prepared for the rehearsal. Guys don't take it seriously and don't show up on time, and it kind of gets dragged out. Rehearsal space costs fifty dollars an hour. It's pretty expensive to get a good space. I have rehearsals just to make sure we have the music and that we agree that this is the right song for this title. That the changes are correct, and just again to have a quick musical review of the eighty-nine tunes I want to cover that week."

"Do musicians get paid for rehearsals?" I ask.

"By and large, no. Jazz players don't; classical players always got paid. They make $40,000 a year, on an average. That's the low end of the scale." says Carter.

Classical conductor David Randolph confirmed what Ron said regarding classical musicians getting paid for rehearsals. "Time is the enemy. A small orchestra will cost $35,000 for rehearsal and performance. There are union rules, they get ten minutes rest per hour, so you must know what you will ask for. We rehearse for the first time on Thursday for a concert on Saturday. I get first-rate musicians."

Keep Emotions in Check

Dorothy Lawson talked openly for the first time about a bad performance experience that she had by letting a relationship interfere. "There was a recital at Juilliard. It was my first doctoral recital, and it was a disaster, and I was unprepared. I have to admit that I was going through a tumultuous and difficult relationship, and I could not see myself beyond that, and it had an impact on my judgment. It was a lesson for me to try to forgive myself for being human. What I have been able to do is try to forgive myself and recognize, in general, that what the audience receives from my music is not entirely what I intend, anyway. Even if you are in great shape and play what you wanted, the audience will take away what resonates for them, and it might not be about you. I try hard not to drag feelings of criticism or disappointment into the dealing with the audience or other musicians. They each have their own needs to deal with."

Sometimes no rehearsal can bring out the best in an artist. Michael Wolff says, "I learned from Cannonball [Adderely]. The first gig, we never practiced—the guys lived in different places. I had the records, learned every tune. Cannonball, at one point, got off the bandstand and said, 'Now listen to Michael Wolff play with himself.' I had to do a solo, and it was trial by fire. There comes a point when you study, you just have to get up and go. I don't like to be limited. I like going off the cliff and falling, I like to be in the moment and discover. The fun of it for Sonny Rollins, I learned, he'd get on the stand and play, you never knew what he was going to do. It was ear training."

When you have a simpatico musical connection and work steadily as a unit, know your craft, and are flexible, a warm-up on your instrument is usually the only thing that you might be concerned with. Olu Dara has been playing with the same guys since the late 1970s and early 1980s, so he sees no need to rehearse. He says, "I don't have to rehearse my band; if you're a musician, you don't need to rehearse. If you're over twenty-one and a black American, you *know* black music." So, there's no surprise that he does not practice, either.

14 The Dos and Don'ts of Performing

With the promise of a ride home and a great evening of music, I dragged my friend Linda, who was not a fan of jazz music, to a club to see a musician whom I love and respect. He is an A-team jazz musician who had always put on a great show each time I had seen him. I have no idea what was on his mind that night, but I knew that we were in trouble when he announced to the audience, "You look like serious jazz fans. I don't know what we are going to do, but . . ."

It was not a good night of music, and to my chagrin, Linda agreed. Her comment to me, without any provocation, was, "They sounded like they were playing music for themselves." I, too, felt the same sentiment. When I asked her if she would come out with me again to a jazz club, she said, "*No!*"

My friends Ken and Lorna had a similar experience when they went to see one of the top pop singers. A great success with other groups, she had gone on her own with equal success. It was rumored that she had a bit of a personal setback that led her to go in a different musical direction. The tickets were not cheap, but they did not mind. What they did mind was her tardiness and her attitude. She got onstage with what seemed to be a dislike for the audience, and then she gave a lackluster performance as though the audience had annoyed her. Ken and Lorna vowed to never see her again and noted that if she performed like that in every city, she would lose audiences for good.

Another performer whom I went to see, and with great anticipation, gave a lackluster performance. During the concert, she chastised the light man and bored many of us to death. Most of the people sitting in my row, in unison, began to exit. My friends and I were about to join everyone else and leave, too, but then she began to sing a familiar song, and we remained in our seats. Still, years later, when I meet people who were at that concert, we all agree that we will not see her again. At some point my friend, Sam, encouraged his friends to see her. After the show, his friends asked him what *he* had seen in her, and they, too, vowed to never pay to see her again.

Too often I sit and say to myself that if I *had* paid to get in, I would have been unhappy. Once I got the courage to tell a musician that it was a drag to watch him onstage. He would fumble with his mouthpiece, make faces, and look uninterested in what the other musicians were doing while they soloed. He admitted that his manager had told him that, as well, so I felt better. Over the years, he has worked on his stage presence, and I now enjoy his performances a great deal. There are many examples like this, where artists do not give their all. More often than not, the audience is tolerant of bad behavior from artists and will give them another chance, but as the price of tickets escalates, they will think twice about going again.

The club scene is no longer the center of entertainment, says Ron Carter. "Younger guys have other things not working in their favor. With DVDs, CDs, home movies, entertainment clubs are not so available anymore. People stay home more now; they can stay home all night. In New York City twenty years ago, people did more sets, clubs stayed opened until 4:00 A.M. and were filled with people. Now clubs are near empty by 1:00 A.M., so they are now starting early. They want to get people coming from Long Island or from a Broadway show."

As a club owner, James Browne deals with the new environment of entertainment. He, too, agrees with Ron Carter. I asked James if he sees a difference in how the artists from genre to genre perform. "It is not common to a genre. In every genre, you have people who can communicate, and those who don't. What the successful ones understand is that it has to be a universal part of what they do. The unsuccessful ones don't understand that connection with the audience. They think that if they play a thousand notes on "Green Dolphin Street," for example, or some other standard we've heard three thousand times, that they will get over. There are musicians who play for each other and that's fine, but people won't pay to come and see that. I'm in business so don't ask me to pay for it."

I finally got to see Oscar Brown Jr. in performance. I had missed several of his other dates over the years when he was in New York City, so I was excited, especially because I saw him after we had done the interview. At age seventy-eight, he was incredible. It was like watching an actor onstage performing a one-act play. His voice was great, the show was well-paced, the material was a perfect blend of new and old songs of his. He ended by performing a duo with poet Sonia Sanchez. She read a poem; he sang "Afro Blue." Oscar sang a chorus, then Sonia recited a stanza of the poem. As they went back and forth, pianist Billy Childs played the perfect complement behind the both of them. They were brilliant and moving.

Not all performers are comfortable onstage. Louis Hayes admitted that about himself. His way to circumvent that is by having another member of the band do the talking. Some performers are shy and keep talking to a minimum. For those who do believe in talking, I suggest that you find different ways to introduce your songs. There are people, like myself, who see an artist more than one time, and after awhile, the same joke told in the same way can become boring. I like the element of surprise. You do not play the same solo the same way each time; the dialogue should change, as well. From what I gathered, there are no hard-and-fast rules to putting on a performance, except that *all* musicians must find a way to connect to the audience. After all, the audience is supporting the musicians, so all of them deserve the best that you have to give. I frequent clubs and attend various performing artists' presentations, and I am always impressed with an artist who can command an audience of any age.

I have often asked musicians how they feel having to play their "hits" time and time again. The audience, more often then not, goes to a concert expecting to hear their favorite songs, but as musicians change direction, they are less inclined to want to play the same music forever. Ahmad Jamal is one of my favorite performers. Although I have seen him perform many times over the years, it was only recently that I heard him play one of his biggest hits, "Poinciana." Before he played it, he said that everyone is trying to recreate the past, but it can't be recreated. For example, while Edwin Hawkins is not expected to perform "Oh, Happy Day" at each concert in America, that is not the case elsewhere.

"I am grateful for the song. I've been told that often when Gospel groups go to Europe, they have to sing it. A group had to put it in their contract that they would sing it, though. Thank God for that!" Hawkins laughed.

How does one keep it fresh and exciting for the audience and not disappoint them by not playing their hit(s)? Musicians must consider this question, as well as their appearance. In jazz, how one looks onstage is a priority. Bobby Sanabria, Billy Taylor, and Ron Carter all quoted one of the great drummers and leaders in jazz, Art Blakey, who said, "They see you before they hear you."

Conductor David Randolph said that he would love to not have to wear the tuxedo, but a musician must have a certain persona that the audience can relate or aspire to. Musicians have always had an impact on fashion. Cab Calloway with his zoot suits; Dizzy Gillespie, Thelonious Monk with their berets and sunglasses. Miles Davis went from suits, to tie-die, to pants that resembled fighter attire. We cannot overlook Janis Joplin, Jimi Hendrix, or The Beatles, the psychedelic generation of Bootsy Collins, George Clinton, and, lest we forget, the gowns of the women and the outfits of the Motown performers, or the current fashions that rappers bring to the hip-hop generation.

Below are some guidelines to consider when you perform. Some items may seem obvious, even common sense, but as I say, "If common sense were common, more people would have it."

1. *Don't be drunk or high.*

2. *Be sensitive; get to know your audience. Feel their energy.*

3. *Be prepared; know the songs. (Yes . . . I have seen singers forget the lyrics and musicians forget the changes.)*

4. *Regarding demeanor, look like you want to be onstage. Stand up straight.*

5. *Respect your fellow musicians. Encourage them during their solos.*

6. *Cultivate an image; dress appropriately.*

7. *Don't bore the audience with long or meaningless solos.*

8. *Don't talk down to the audience.*

Make Your Show Interesting

Al Jarreau is great at making that connection. He walks onstage full of love, energy, and charm; he knows how to draw the audience to him. I've yet to see him in a small club setting, but from all accounts, he is as adept in the small setting, as in a large hall like Carnegie Hall, where I saw him last. He says, "You gotta do a show that gives variety, and the last song should be a cleansing of the palette—like sherbet before the next delicious piece of music. That is how I put a set together onstage."

As a performer, Allan Harris works all the time in all kinds of venues. He also wrote "Cross That River," which he continues to alter and fine tune. I have seen several incarnations, and the show gets better and better. "The audience helps you out and brings you out of it," he declares.

Harris's list of dos?

"Number one: Study the audience before you go onstage. One must be in sync with what is going on outside. You are not just showing off your craft; you are an entertainer. You have to make them feel comfortable. Once you have them, you can take them anywhere you want to go. I did twenty shows with the late comedian Alan King, and he'd write down notes on what I had to do. For example, don't say, 'How yawl doin'?' Get out, sing, have a theme. Make sure the band is on the same page as you; be in sync. Number two: Do not do anything you are not comfortable with; it will always bite you in the butt. Alan scratched ten songs out of my repertoire, *my show*, ten songs out of twenty—he was brutal! Tony Bennett did the same thing to me; he, too, asked, 'Why are you doing this song?' *Scratch*! It was a rude awakening. By show number sixteen, I was rolling."

Eric Reed is a wonderful performer. Often I have talked to people who attended one of his shows, and they all talk about how well he connected with them. One woman told me that she felt like he was talking directly to her. He says, "I did not think about it. I have two ways of conducting sets. Sometimes I'll just write the sets out. It depends on how large the ensemble; the larger the ensemble, the more arranged the music is. I'll have a specific set list that won't change too much every night. For my trio, I'll go from tune to tune freely. I usually start with 'Stablemates,' one of my favorite songs to play. It is a good tune to warm up to; it's a mid-tempo tune, not too loud or soft; we get to work the kinks out. Then I can just go from there. It's an organically based way of developing a set list where you try to consider what was just played; tempo, key, feeling, meter, all that comes into play. Sometimes I just go from tune to tune without stopping. I can play four or five tunes without talking to the audience, but they like to hear talk. They need to hear a breadth.

"To engage the audience, I might act like I don't remember what I played, and they will shout out the tunes. A dead audience drains me to no end, which is why I always begin by telling them that it's okay to enjoy the music. Back in the day, people danced to the music; I tell them it's okay to interact with us, make some noise."

"When I play trio, I tend to do more standards," says Kenny Barron. "With the group that I'm working with now, I do more originals. I'm working with younger people who are virtuosos on their instruments, but have little experience. They challenge me! I like that energy. When you play with people with whom you are comfortable, you tend to play safe. I talk sometimes. I tend to keep it light— I'm not a jokester. The rule of thumb is to not end with a ballad, but sometimes that works. The songs should not sound too close to each other; if so, the audience and you will lose interest. Young people encourage you to take a chance. It is important to have a certain look and look presentable. One does not have to wear a suit and tie like Ron Carter."

For a sideman, how one is on the bandstand is important. Kenny Washington has to think about his drum solos. I remind him that I often hear how people hate drum solos, and he replies, "I always think about the melody. I learned that from Max Roach. The drummer must know the tune, the form, like everyone else in the bandstand. Also, dynamics. The worst drum solos are where guys play at one level and loud and long. That's why people don't dig drum solos. Most people can get into jazz, but the problem is nowadays the stuff is sad. Folks go hear people who are sad and will say apologetically, they did not understand it. Their guts tell them it is not happening, but they listen to critics who praise the music, so they think they don't understand it and put themselves down. If the music is done right, people don't have to understand it; they feel it. The real pros will be working, one way or another. Like Bill Charlap. That is a hell of a band. Audiences are not stupid. They don't have to know anything about jazz to like the music. That's the way jazz was years ago. Charlap plays the American Songbook, and he is getting younger audiences, and people come back. The sets are well paced, songs don't go on too long, so I'm curious to see what happens to the band, now that Tommy Flanagan is dead."

Though this is not Oscar Brown's problem, the first thing he said when I asked him about proper performance demeanor was, "Don't be drunk! Be well rehearsed; be well rested. If you have good material, good talent, and time, there is no reason not to have a dynamite performance."

Oscar Brown delights the audiences with many of his great tunes. "I love singing some of those songs, and the audience kind of expects it of me. I love 'Rags and Old Iron,' I just like to sing 'Signifying Monkey,' 'Work Song,' 'Dat Dere,' and, from later albums, 'The Snake,' and 'A Ladies' Man.' Max Roach and Abbey Lincoln told me that ['The Snake'] as a joke, and I always like to make songs from jokes. I always looked for ways to bring black culture forth, or to put Dusty Fletcher, one of my favorite comedians, to put his lines in a song."

I had seen many Ruth Brown performances before her stroke, but I cannot remember her being any better than when I saw her first appearance after. She brought us to our feet both times I saw her during her engagement. Ruth seemed to be a born entertainer.

"My friend Ray Charles used to say to me, 'When you sing, you got to get to a place where people can *understand* what you are saying, and they have feelings about what you are trying to say.' That's where I am. 'Soul is where you are about to say, convey the meaning of a song, and make people feel it, and make them *think* about it.' I remember that; I got that message right away."

On putting on a performance, she laments (needlessly so): "At this point, I can't stand on my feet too long, but I could try. The main reason why I sit [is because] I have to read the lyrics and it makes me feel safe. I had never sat down before in my whole years. I've seen singers do it. My friend B. B. King said at the rock 'n' roll hall of fame—it was me, Bo Diddley, Robert Lockwood, and B. B.—we had just done a concert, and all four of us was in a chair. B. B. said, 'Sit down; you deserved it, and you worked for it; sit down.' Art imitates life. I got my Tony Award for 'If I Can't Sell It, I Got to Sit Down on It.' Now I say, 'If *I'm Gonna* Sell It, I Got to Sit Down on It!" She laughed. "Since my stroke, my speech slides a little bit, and that song is right on the beat, but people accept it."

Several musicians have cautioned that a show should not end on a ballad. Ruth said, "It depends on what you can do, because one of the songs I close with is 'Love Letters.' I love that song! When I sing it, I feel like the audience sent *me* a love letter. When I close the show and do 'Smile,' because that's about *me*! I say, 'If you see someone who has lost hope, give them a hug and remember that you saw me. That's for me!" Ruth recited some of the lyrics. "I've been hearing that song ever since I was a child, but now it really means something to me."

Connect with the Audience

Once a month, WBGO, Jazz 88.3FM presents live broadcasts. Though there is a live audience to connect to, the millions of people listening to the radio should feel as if they are there. One performance that struck me was Jeff "Tain" Watts. He has been working several years, mostly as a sideman with Branford and Wynton Marsalis, but more and more he is leading his own group. I saw him lead twice. He is not one to talk much during his performance, so I was struck by how personable and funny he was with the host, Monifa Brown. The music was well paced, and I felt like I was at the venue—I felt as if he had connected with me. Performance is acting, being able to project what you want the audience to see, or feel. That show was an example of good radio.

Billy Taylor says, "Sure, I connect with the audience. I grew up in the age of show business. I was lucky enough to be around in the days when musicians could play in theaters, and I played with Slam Stewart, on Broadway with Cozy Cole, and I realized it was not about how fast and spontaneous I could be at the piano. I had to reach out and touch somebody. I saw others do this, [Art] Tatum, Dinah [Washington] do this. I see that can be done, so I had to learn *my way* of doing that. It took me a while, but I came up with something."

I observed that musicians under forty, for the most part, don't see themselves as entertainers. He said, "That is a mistake. I try to tell everybody who comes on with me, people who ask my advice, I tell them, 'You are in show business.' There are things you must do about your appearance, your demeanor; it's not just about sitting at the piano or singing."

As a conductor, David Randolph has a different relationship with the audience, given that his back is always turned to them. "I love connecting with the audience." When he is not conducting, Randolph connects with listeners by teaching music appreciation in a concert setting. There he makes comments and then has the musicians play excerpts of the music he discusses. "Even at Carnegie Hall in New York, believe me, the audience needs some explanation. There are people who think they know music; there are things they don't know. Occasionally I'll speak out, and they're offended, but believe me, they need it."

Dorothy Lawson is not a "typical" classical performer. She is very physical, and she smiles a lot; her enthusiasm is infectious. She says, "There is nothing universal about it, but it's the way I feel most authentic. I feel physical about the rhythm, and I feel most in contact when I allow that to come through. I smile because I'm so grateful that the audience is there. I really come to feel that the performers are the lucky ones who are being subsidized by the audience to actually develop the skill that it takes to do the stuff themselves. It is such a pleasure to be an artist, to be a musician." As a co-leader of the group Ethel, she has found kindred spirits: "The other thing, one of the funny things, about Ethel, we are all *very* physical and very engaged with the audience in that way. When we met, we all felt, *at last*! We all experienced being too much for other people, moving too much or talking about whatever on the other hand. We tailor ourselves to work well with other people."

Richard Smallwood says, "In performance, the connection has to be there with the audience. It is important to set up a rapport. They must feel that you are warm and open with them, not that you are oblivious to who they are or what they are doing. To get a good performance, the artist has to flow between the audience, and the artist has to be friendly, to be sensitive. I could not approach an audience in Norway the same way as a church audience on Sunday morning. My musicians are on pins and needles because they don't know where I'll go."

As with Oscar Brown Jr., I had never seen Richard Smallwood perform until after our interview. His program was wonderful. Though he told me that he does not preach during a performance, preach is what he did. Richard was electric. He sang; he played an inspirational piano medley. The music was well balanced. At one point, I felt as if I had been transplanted to a Sunday-morning service that was so moving that some of his backup singers "got happy," took off their shoes, and danced around. When I left, I felt uplifted. Richard gave it his all, and the audience loved it.

Some venues request a program ahead of time, but Richard will not send one. More often, he knows the first song he will perform and maybe the last. There are certain songs that are staples that people want to hear that he might include in the program.

Olu Dara, too, appreciates the audience. "Playing in different types of clubs helped me, and the band got stronger so I learned how to relate to all different audiences. Each audience is different; I never play my songs the same way for every audience. I'll change it completely sometimes for the audience. What I won't do is to play a rhythm that's boring. I won't play a standard; I want to play what I am, not what I have to do to fit in. Life changes, music changes, rhythms change. I feel you have a new generation coming up, often you have to be able to have something for them. I like to be contemporary with rhythms and stories. I talk to the audience and put them into my songs. If I see a friend, I might put them in. The audience is *very important*! It's not what kind of music you are playing—it's who you are playing to. People don't care about the type of music— they want the communication to be right."

Appearance/Presentation

For musicians like Pat Methany, appearance is not an issue. I have seen him perform several times, and he wears his "uniform" of jeans and a striped polo shirt. Over time, some musicians have changed their look. Chick Corea is one such musician. He now dons casual, Hawaiian-print shirts. Miles Davis went from suits to hippie-type clothes in the 1970s. One night Allan Harris left his suit at home by accident. I remember thinking that his dress was unusually casual for him, but I thought that was deliberate. Weeks later, we talked about that night, and he said that he was upset when he left his suit at home by accident, but the night was liberating for him, because he was able to relax more and be more focused on the songs and not on his "act." Unfortunately, this does not work for all musicians.

I know one jazz musician who has never worked on his appearance. For years, he wore a work shirt, casual pants, his beard scruffy, and his hair somewhat a mess, but he is a great player. In recent years, he began to wear a suit, but he still looks a bit scruffy. Because of his appearance, some leaders have stopped hiring him. Several of us talk about how we want to give him a "beauty makeover," but no one has the nerve to approach him. From time to time, he has fronted his own group and made some recordings, but he is not really considered a leader. I think the way a person presents himself is often a reflection of how he feels inside. A person who has a strong self-image will project it, no matter what he is wearing.

There is a double standard for women as performers. Men can get away with having one suit in which to perform, but a woman will be criticized for wearing the same outfit at each show. Women are expected to look glamorous, or at least have a look of distinction. I know women who do wear the same outfit over and over again; that is their choice, but I would not recommend it. No matter who the performer is, she should cultivate a "look" that suits her, and then stick to it. I was in Colorado talking to a presenter, and he mentioned that a singer had performed earlier that summer, and he could not get over the fact that she showed up dressed like the wait staff. I could not agree more; I had seen her perform. At one show, she hung above the stage a huge replica of the CD cover she was promoting. She looked glamorous, but in person, she looked ordinary, and she wore minimal makeup. Although, in truth, she is a natural beauty, her look onstage should have matched her look on that CD.

When the audience likes you, many do see your show more than once, so you should give them something to look at. What performers need to remember is that your visual presentation is part of your persona and can be a complement to your performance, at least in the mind of the audience. In the classical genre, all women who sing chorus or background must wear black, but the soloist can dress like a diva.

Bobby Sanabria, like so many jazz musicians, learned from the late, legendary drummer, Art Blakey. Art was known for picking great musicians, and many went on to lead their own bands. Wynton Marsalis played in Art's band, the Jazz Messengers.

"Don't look like shit onstage," says Bobby. "Even Janis Joplin, Jimi Hendricks had a certain style in their dress that ended up in popular culture. In jazz, that is a lost art. Presentation is very important. Especially the tradition I represent. It is a marginalized genre, and I'm struggling to see that we get the proper respect we deserve in Latin American music, in all facets. I want to make sure the music is presented with dignity, class, and respect. The guys before me had to pay serious dues for us. I like to look good onstage. I'm known for talking to the audience. I provide 'edutainment.' Most of the audiences don't know much about the music. Once you speak to the audience, they are learning, and they feel relaxed.

"I used to play too long. I was in the moment and programmed too much music in the set, but I've learned over the years. I want my sets to be like a good play and have a logical progression. There is always something spiritual. I play a spiritual song at the beginning to set the tone and separate myself from other leaders. Also, the soloists are featured in different settings, [and my sets are] not formulaic."

Ron Carter has firm opinions on looking appropriate. I had hired Ron to perform at The Newark Museum outdoors in the garden. The temperature was expected to be around one-hundred degrees. Out of concern for them, I suggested to Ron that he might not wear a suit and tie. His response: "The guys have summer suits." When I told Steve Kroon, one of the band members, what Ron had said, he laughed and told me that their suits were not as good as Ron's. Ron Carter is a great dresser both on- and offstage. "You see guys who look like those rappers with the over-long clothes and stuff. People expect a certain vibe from those people. They expect a certain format, a certain attitude, a certain character, a certain carriage. I think when you walk out there as we have been, as I've always done, wearing a suit and tie, they get a different view of what they expect. For me, it's like, I'm going to work. And I am not going to work dressed as I am right now. [Our interview was over the telephone.] Jeans, clogs, T-shirt—I wouldn't go like the way I'm dressed now to Birdland. You know when you're dressed like I am right now for work, people expect a different mentality. The bandstand is my office, and I'm going to my office to work. Up until three years ago, when the offices 'relaxed' their dressing standards on Friday, everybody wore a shirt and tie because that was the mentality of the workplace. When I worked with the Four Generations of Miles at the Blue Note with Mike Stern, George Coleman, and Jimmy Cobb, Mike Stern came to work wearing the same black jeans and black gym shoes every night. I said, 'Mike, look, we're all dressed differently; everyone is wearing a sport outfit but you. You've got to find your wife or somebody to find you a sport jacket by the weekend. By Friday and Saturday, if you don't have one, I'm not going to show up.' "

"Did you always feel this way?" I asked.

"Yeah," he said.

"So do you think the way people look reflects how they feel inside, or does one have nothing to do with the other?" I asked.

Ron said, "I think in a broad sense, one has nothing to do with the other. But I think that if you have an environment that's conducive to that style of dressing, guys get used to it. I hear guys tell me, 'Man, I don't wear suits anymore on the gigs.' Well, I can't hire those guys—I don't care how good they play—for they determine the direction of the band. I can't let one guy who's not a leader determine the direction of the group. Otherwise, I'm not a bandleader, and someone else has taken over the direction of the band. Whether it's musically, whether it's emotionally, whether it's visually, they can't work. So those guys are off my list as far as wanting to hire them for a gig, where they're visible. A record date, those things when you're not seeing them, that's okay to me. But when we're on the bandstand, I insist on a certain look, which is why I had suits made for the guys a few years ago. Why, I buy ties for the band. I just typed an e-mail out to tell the guys what we got to wear: gray suit, white shirt, blue shirt, Italian tie, stripped tie. We got to wear that; [the type of shoes] are optional," he laughed. "When we walk on the stage, we kind of stun people. Not to say those other guys can't play, but we have a traditional edge on them when we walk on the stage looking like that. And it happened more than once, man, we walk out there, and we get applause before we play one note—because people like the way we look. That's half the battle, getting their attention."

I asked Eric Reed if dressing was important for performance. "It depends," he said, "One thing that I hate when I played with Wynton was in the outside, hot festivals we'd have to wear three-piece suits. Outdoors is outdoors. Would I perform in jeans? I doubt it—I'm used to dressing up. Let me be clear: It has nothing to do with the music. It had *no* affect on music. If we were rock 'n' roll musicians, it would be expected. The audience would be insulted if we wor e tuxedos. I think the idea of wearing suits became important again in the 1980s because there was a lack of respect for jazz music. People did not give a damn about us jazz musicians—they saw us as junkies, strung out, temperamental, with a superior attitude. Music died, Fusion, Miles Davis. When Wynton came in, he made the statement that this is to be taken seriously and is dignified, classy music, great music to be respected. This is how I want to be presenting myself when I'm playing the music. What people were doing before was just trash."

Be on Time

On the dos and don'ts list of performance, Eric said, "Tardiness is never acceptable! Ninety-eight percent of the time I'm early; I learned that from Jeff Clayton. Showing up at three o'clock for a three o'clock rehearsal is late. To be early is to be on time, to be on time is to be late, and to be late is not acceptable. You are not ready to play if you show up at three o'clock and have to set up your instrument. Keeping people waiting for you sets a bad tone and is inconsiderate and impolite."

Ron Carter agreed, "Don't be late, and don't play the set too long. Especially when you have two groups (a double-bill at a club). The club has to clear out those people. And until they make that changeover, they're going to lose money. They're going to lose when bands have gone off the schedule. The income for the clubs has taken a big dip because they can't get the people in and out for the second or the third show, or the second or third band. Oh, yeah, that's a big issue."

This is also an issue in classical music. David Randolph said they "don't look kindly on lateness." Dorothy Lawson confirmed this when I asked if tardiness was not accepted: "It just won't work."

Attitude

A performer told me that his father gave him good advice about how to perform. His dad told him that if just one person showed up, he still played with the same enthusiasm for one person as though one hundred people had showed up. Hearing his dad, he asked him, What if no one shows up? Then ask for a mirror, his dad replied.

It can be very disappointing when there is a small audience. But when that happens, it is not acceptable for a performer to apologize all night that so few people are there—that shows a lack of appreciation for the people who did show up. This happens more often than it should, especially with B-team musicians. I went to a performance where a musician at each break lamented about the lack of audience to the point where he let us know that he was modifying his set. He began the program late and seemed to have no control of the show for the entire evening. His behavior put such a damper on the evening.

I had not been to a rock concert in years, but in 2004, Joe Grushecky and the House Rockers performed at The Newark Museum. It was quite a show and the audience was enthralled, including myself. Joe said, "Our band tries to do the best job we can, no matter what. We prefer to give it our all, no matter if five people or five thousand people are in the audience. One night we had a gig with five people, and we were working our asses off. The drummer was disappointed, and it showed. I went to him and told him that I'd kick his ass if he kept playing like that. As Keith Richards says, 'The best band is a band that changes every night.' The audience has a lot to do with performances. I like to pace the music, change tempos, change with dynamics. I refrain from swearing too much, treat the audience with respect. We've been around a long time and happen to have an audience. The hardest crowd for us is the twenty-five year olds. My son comes with younger kids. He plays guitar with us, and he brings a whole different thing to the table. If young kids are in the audience, that is cool. My son is sixteen."

Gerald Cannon related, "Elvin [Jones] told me, just play the music right. Everybody is trying to reinvent the wheel." He does not talk to the audience much, he says, "I don't like the microphone, but I do it. I only try to be me—no one else."

Never Let Them See You Sweat

As a performer, it is in your best interest to make the audience feel comfortable with what you are presenting. They take their cues from you. If you have confidence, they will feel confident; if you are involved and inspired, they will be, too. I will always remember a concert where a singer came out, started in the wrong key, or place, and told the band to stop and start again. The leader looked on in horror and so did the audience. Had she not stopped the band, I would not even have noticed that something was wrong.

Jeff Clayton talked about a gig that he was on that was memorable. This was a gig where musicians were put together, for that performance—an organist, drummer, vocalist, and Jeff. Unfortunately for them, the organist was a B-teamer. "The organist said, 'I only plays the alphabet, A, B, C, D, E, F, and G.' We decided to play the song in D-flat, but that is not in the alphabet. We asked the organist to start it off—oh, boy, what a mistake—so we all joined in after him, and we tried to make his wrong key right. We had two opposing keys fighting with each other. Then the leader, the singer, came in and tried to add her opinion to the other two very wrong opinions, which resulted in three opinions, three separately wrong notes."

"How did the audience respond?" I asked.

Jeff continued, "The train wreck would have been fine if the organist had laid out and said, 'You got it,' but B-teamers don't do that. They keep playing. The A-team will stop when someone sings a wrong note; the B-team will hold the note and be wrong and look like, what's the matter?! He acted as though the wrong note would get right, and I held my right note hoping that he would hear it.

"The singer came in with a note in a totally different key, and when the song ended, she did a B-team thing: She let the audience know it was wrong. She should have waved the band out, sung acappella; then she and I could have done a duo then add the organ when he heard what we were doing. Instead, she sang, 'And I don't know where I am . . .' She sang this to the audience, then she gave the organist a dirty look—I didn't want her to give *me* that look.

"The organist had the power in his hand, he had his foot on the gas pedal, then he looked at the audience, realized that *they knew* he was wrong so he took his coat and wrapped it over his head. He let them know that he *knew* he was wrong, and he knew they knew it. If you never let them know it's a mistake, they'll think it's a nice arrangement."

Brenda Feliciano knew how to correct a bad situation. "I sang in Mexico. The height and pollution got to me, and I had to ask for water onstage. Now I know why singers don't go to Mexico to sing. I got through it, and people said I was brave to sing, so I won respect of others. That had never happened to me before. You have to acclimate yourself first. You do what you have to do, no matter how large the audience."

15 Learning from Elders

I have always been intrigued by what jazz musicians have told me about what the masters passed to them about such things as conduct on and off the bandstand, on the business, and on life in general. The key to growth is to be able to identify the areas that you need to pay attention to and then seek others who can guide you to the next level. Do not be afraid to approach your idols; usually they are more than willing to assist—that is, if they believe you to be serious about where you are headed. Russell Malone had the nerve to tell Ron Carter that Ron was on his list of musicians to play with. Ron told him, "Then give me a call, and get me off your list." Men like Benny Carter helped Kenny Washington through a painful divorce by telling him, "Let go of that hate in your heart; it will kill you quicker than cancer."

The musicians in their seventies and eighties whom I interviewed had benefited from what their elders taught them. Guidance does not always come directly from people; one can read an autobiography, listen to a record, or watch a performer. I was fortunate to have people along my path to guide me. My elders challenged me to understand *who* I was/am and shatter my notion of *what I am*! As a young person, my dad guided me to choose a direction; as he told me, "If you do not make a decision, life will decide for you." Chann Berry, too, was given a life lesson by his grandfather: "My freshman year at Rutgers University, I was failing. I spent most of my time becoming musical director of the college radio station. I met [with] my grandfather, and I told him I was failing. He looked at me and said, 'You don't have any failures in life; you just found out you could not do it that way.' So, I have no failures in life, and I live by that. Music is evolving into something else, and something new will come. Hip hop is on its way out. Many of the artists are getting older and want to be calmer. They are growing. A new genre is coming. I think that we are going back to instruments and to voices that have substance."

As I entered the business of music, Johnny Garry cautioned me to "get my money up front," and he taught me how to emcee. There are too many life lessons imparted to me by my elders to list them all, and I continue to seek out their pearls of wisdom. Al Jarreau had his brothers introduce him to singers like Nat King Cole, Billy Eckstine, and Ella Fitzgerald. As he continued his study, it was hearing Jon Hendricks that took him to another level; he "learned to appreciate lyrics." Allan Harris had Tony Bennett and Alan King to send him inward to develop his craft and to deal with his ego. "Alan King taught me how to put a show together. Tony Bennett taught me how to read audiences so I would not fall on my face. And Tommy Flanagan [who spent many years as Ella Fitzgerald's pianist] taught me what I needed to do and *not* to do with my voice. *The most important* thing was for me to *slow down*! That was his biggest thing: 'Why rush?' He would purposely slow the song down; it was hard to sing slow. I noticed the reaction immediately, too, on the faces of the people who knew me and had seen me. I saw a peace of mind," said Allan.

Andy Bey, too, learned much from his family and from those around him. "Most of what I learned was from musicians." Billy Taylor came along in the "glory days of jazz." He had teachers in Washington, D.C., like Elmira Streets and Henry Grant, who was a dear friend of Duke Ellington and the person to who Duke turned to. Grant instructed Billy "in Debussy and the more contemporary-sounding music that became a part of the way I play music." Others, such as Jo Jones, Coleman Hawkins, Erroll Garner, and Teddy Wilson, who turned him on to Rich McClennahan and changed how he approached the piano keys, were instrumental in Billy's growth. When Billy was a young man, new to New York City, Jo Jones took him under his wing and let everyone know that he did not drink. Billy in fact *did* drink some, but Jo made sure that the guys would not encourage Billy to do so.

One momentous evening, Billy had been drinking, when some of his idols— Art Tatum being one—entered the club where he was playing to hear him play. Being paralyzed with fear and somewhat inebriated, he was unable to play. That was truly a life lesson for Billy.

Sometimes one learns what *not* to do from elders. Bobby Sanabria and Kenny Washington learned that lesson. According to Bobby, "I learned from a bandleader what *not* to do. I saw bandleaders make mistakes, such as paying low money, providing bad accommodations, not giving proper information of a tour, communicating poorly." Kenny Washington said, "I saw positive and negative things that I kept in the back of my head. I'd say I would not do things the way they did. Watching Benny Carter . . . if I could be half the man that Benny Carter was, I'd be doing great. And Milt Hinton, they were *real men*, not punks; they were not macho types. There was something about the way they handled themselves and their business—they were amazing. As much as I respected Betty Carter, I learned a lot from her that I would never do to anyone on the bandstand. She would embarrass musicians on the stand, the way she talked to them. I learned a lot from her about control on the drums, but a lot of stuff I went through with her was completely *unnecessary!*"

Dorothy Lawson learned the difference between a craftsperson and an artist "from André Naverra, the teacher I studied with in Vienna. One thing he said in class stuck with me. He was very methodical, and he had a careful routine that he wanted us to follow, and if he felt someone was slacking off or doing something in more free form, he would say (in French), 'Oh, yes, *you* are the artist; *I'm* just the craftsperson.' In a way, it's cynical. It is good to be reminded that doing something well is important, no matter how 'artistic' you think you are."

Michael Wolff worked with so many great musicians, such as Sonny Rollins, Cannonball Addereley, and Cal Tjader, and got the importance of passing down information. "Miles Davis is the good virus, as opposed to the bad virus. All of the people who played with him got good. He got it from whoever he played with—Dizzy, Bird. It was magic, passing down a tradition and point of view of constantly being creative and changing. Although I met Miles, I never played with him, but I played with Sonny, Cannonball. All the people who played with him, they passed it down. You can listen to records and play the music, but you got to meet them. I'm about the soul and what's underneath the music. I worked with a lot of different people, but I ask specific things like from Bill Evans. Then he let me watch him practice, sit behind him; it was sort of the harmonic approach, his touch that I loved."

Olu Dara learned, too: "You don't watch [others] to copy; you watch to see what not to do. People have to use life as a gauge of what not to do." Oscar Brown Jr. got advice that he did not follow: "I went to Ahmad Jamal and asked him how to get into show biz, and he said, go back to real estate. He told me that before he did *Live at the Pershing*. Max Roach talked about owning your own publishings."

Ruth Brown, too, had the benefit of her elders: "I knew them all. They'd tell me, as a compliment, but it was *good stuff*. Billie Holiday said, 'Find your own way'; Nat King Cole: 'Make sure people understand every line you are saying, every line you are singing. Speak clearly.'

"And, Lena Horne: 'Be classy. Look your best because people came to see you.'"

Part Five On the Business

*Show business is not the easiest thing to
get into, but if that's what you want,
you've got to stick with it. There have
been thrills and chills, and ups and
downs ever since I've been in show
business. It never stops.*

— SARAH VAUGHAN

16 Contracts: Watch Your Money

When Oscar Brown Jr. was offered his first recording contract with Columbia Records, he did not sign it. He sent it back and told them that "it looked like a clever circumvention of the thirteenth amendment." So they said, "Who needs him?" He looked around for a year then realized that Columbia was the best company to sign with. Al Ham, the A&R man, told Oscar one year later, "C'mon, it's our entry level contract; if you get a hit, they'll rewrite it."

Many entry-level artists are not as lucky as Oscar, although Richard Smallwood and Joe Grushecky were able to get good recording contracts without legal advice. Of course, Richard Smallwood is now an established artist, so he has more clout with his label: "I have a record deal, yes, I've been out here so long. My record company does not pressure me, and they want a CD every year or year and a half. That does not always happen, but they know that it will be good quality when I do one. I'm working on a project now that is so huge, it should have come out in 2003."

Ruth Brown was not one of the lucky ones to get a good contract. In her book, *Miss Rhythm: The Autobiography of Ruth Brown, Rhythm & Blues Legend*, you can read in detail the story of her twenty-two-year fight with Atlantic Records to get her royalties. She led the struggle, not just for herself, but for other artists who had been denied their money. Ruth signed with Atlantic in 1949 while she was in the hospital recovering from a car accident. At that point, the company had been in hard times but was moving up a bit. Without the advice of anyone except her manager, Ruth signed a contract that gave her an advance of $69 (years later, it was increased to $350) a side, and she was responsible for certain production costs. With all of her gold records, she could not understand why she had no money from her music.

She said, "It took me twenty-two years to get royalties. My lawyer, Howard Begle, did the work, not me. After an engagement, he brought my albums for me to sign, and I asked him where he got them. He said that he had paid dearly for them, and I told him I wasn't getting a penny for those records. I had not gotten a penny for my records in over thirty years. I told him I was not the only one who had not gotten any money." Although Ruth and the other musicians who fought for the royalties never got all of what they were owed, the music industry came up with some money. In Ruth's case, some of her settlement was used as the seed money to set up the Rhythm and Blues Foundation. "Showtime had my book for almost two years. My story was supposed to be made into a movie, but at the last minute, for some reason, someone stopped it. I believe that it was Atlantic; *I named names!* The truth was there. They still owe me money, but they claim that they can't find the papers. They say that they sent the papers to Virginia, but I have not lived there in over fifty-five years, and the house is no longer there. When it was over, I got about 20K, but when I got it, I owed everybody. No one ever taught me how to invest my money. A lot of us did the same things; we had husbands who ended up being our managers, but that did not work. Now my son Earl Swanson manages me . . ." It took almost the entire music community to get Atlantic to pay Ruth and other musicians monies they were due. Politicians who happened to be music fans—if not her fans—and other visible artists like Bonnie Raitt, rallied behind Ruth.

Change seems to have come to the industry as a whole when it came to contracts; but has it, really?

The following is a quote from an article by Maggie Farley and Chuck Philips that appeared in the *New York Times* on June 6, 2002:

❀ ❀ ❀ ❀

In 2002 Michael Jackson spoke out against Sony about his not getting royalties and of questionable accounting practices. He said that Sony was improperly requiring him to pay substantial sums of money that the company contends the singer owed for cash advances and promotion and production costs associated with his recent CD, Invincible. *Jackson said he did not owe Sony any money and has called into question the way the label had accounted for his royalty payments. "Record companies have to start treating their artists with respect, honor and financial justice," Jackson said in a statement. Industry sources said Jackson blamed Sony for the poor performance of* Invincible *and had made overtures to leave the company. Sony had not objected to Jackson departing, company sources said, because under the terms of his contract, he owed the label only a greatest-hits compilation and a box set—neither of which required new material. Sources said Jackson is free to shop for a new deal but is not off the hook for the advances he received until the sales of his albums recoup the outstanding amount.*

❊ ❊ ❊ ❊

Prince chose to legally change his name to the "the Artist" to get out of recording for Warner Brothers, and when his contract ended, he went back to being Prince. As reported by *Money* magazine:

❊ ❊ ❊ ❊

No stranger to going against the industry grain, Prince spent half of the 1990s publicly fighting to free himself from his contract with Warner Bros. Records, the label that he signed with in 1992 in a deal reportedly worth $100 million. During that time, Warner Bros. Records was owned by Time Warner Inc., which still owns CNN/Money. "If [young artists] are looking to have five albums plus a career, I would advise . . . staying free [from the music industry] and not signing any long-term restrictive contracts because, in the end, you end up owning nothing," Prince said on The Biz. Prince spent three years after his Warner Bros. deal collapsed releasing music exclusively on his independent label, NPG Records, and through his NPG Music Club Web site, which was a hit with fans long before the music download revolution. Members of the monthly subscription-based service receive new Prince songs, videos, and an hour-long radio show every month.

❊ ❊ ❊ ❊

Contracts: Artist to Label

It cannot be overstressed: Music is a business. Artists must deal with various types of contracts, including featured artists and featured sideman contracts between the artist and the record company. If the artist cannot get a deal with a record company, but makes his own album, he will need to enter into an agreement with a distributor. In addition to asking musicians, I consulted three industry people to get specifics on contracts and distribution. They are **Carl Griffin** (a producer and label executive), David Alexander (who worked at a major label in distribution), and attorney **Howard M. Nashel**. Howard said, "There is no question that when an artist gets a deal with a record company, he should see an attorney." According to Howard, artists should be aware of some of the basic clauses in the standard record company and artist contracts, including:

1. *The number of albums to be made.* Usually, the record company will insist on three to six options after the first album to record additional albums.

2. *The artist's royalty rate.* Successful artists whose previous albums sold well should get between 12 and 20 percent in royalties in connection with sales of the album. Many artists use the Harry Fox Agency as their agent to be sure that the record company is making the royalty payments required under the contract.

3. *Mechanical royalties.* If you are a composer of any of the songs to be recorded, you will be entitled to mechanical royalties in addition to artist's royalties. Record companies usually require that on "controlled compositions"—that is, those songs composed by the artist—the record company would only have to pay the composer a rate equal to 75 percent of the minimum compulsory license rate under U.S. copyright law. To make sure that the artist/composer obtains mechanical royalties, he should belong to one of the performing-rights organizations, such as ASCAP, BMI, or SESAC.

4. *Reduced royalties and royalty-free albums.* There will be reduced royalties for sales of the album outside of the United States. The artist/composer, in connection with distribution of certain albums, will not be paid any royalties. This includes albums sent to radio stations for publicity purposes.

Chann Berry has first-hand experience with the legal process as a songwriter: "I had written a song for Chaka Khan called 'Joy and Pain.' My friend Rosy Gaines had heard it and said, 'I'm gonna do this!' Years had passed, and I got a call from Rosy and Prince, and I thought, 'Yeah, right.' She told me that when she was on tour with Prince that they had recorded the song, but he tweaked it a bit and made it a little funky and cut the title to 'Pain.' He changed some of the lyrics a little and made it slower, so he became a co-writer and Miles Davis played the solo.

"This [song] came out on the soundtrack of *Living Single* when Chaka did it; Joshua Redman played on it. I get royalties from it—oh, yeah. I had to get an attorney to make sure that Prince would not try to take full credit for the song. It got straightened out. I am an ASCAP member. At that time, with that song, I had been signed a singles deal with Warner-Chapelle Music—I am still with them—as a writer, so they took care of the publishing and charted the song for me."

Both Carl Griffin and Howard Nashel discussed the options when an artist signs a record contract with a label. Says Carl: "It is illegal to have more than six options. In the old days, labels could sign an artist for ten years. Today you can't do that; you have a six-year option, which is a one-year deal with five-year options, which ties the artist for six years. Around the ninth month of the deal, we send a letter to the artist or to his attorney, where we decide to pick up the artist's second option. In the deal, we have mini-max deals; for example, we sign the artist for $20,000. The next [option] period, we would pick them up for $25,000, but based on calculations that only lawyers and dogs understand. If you hit a certain number, the maximum record fund could be $35,000. We have to make our money back and a little more. Each option will raise by $5,000 to $10,000. When you have those options in place, for example, if we had signed Grover Washington Jr.—God rest his soul—when he was looking for a new company, he would have commanded $125,000 upon signing. An artist of his caliber could command something, where the maximum at the end of a five-year deal could have been around $300,000. That's when it gets tricky. If he does not sell what he used to sell, they won't be able to make back the $300,000, then the company may not pick up his option."

Howard concurs: "Most record companies only want to tie themselves up for one album in order to see if it sells well. Since it is the record company that usually has the power in the deal, it will require that the contract also contains a clause giving the record company options for three to six additional albums." I asked Howard, "What if the artist wants out of the record deal?" He replied, "Since the artist signed a legally binding contract, he would have to try to buy out of the deal. Sometimes another record company that might be interested in the artist will help the artist do this."

On the question of royalties, I asked Carl about the validity of the artists' complaints. "What happens is that we have the right to charge the artist back for a number of things: recording, publicity, one-half of marketing and promotion. We will also charge back for tour support and other things, like a video and a listing party. So, when we do the calculations and the artist only sells a certain amount of product, we look at our statement, and we tell them that we have to charge them for those things. Sometimes the artist gets beat, but those are legitimate expenses."

Distribution

One of the biggest complaints by artists is that, when they make a record, the label has limited distribution, or none at all. Gerald Cannon almost signed a distribution contract until he read one line that would have been detrimental to him, or so he thought. He spent two weeks holding his arm so as not to sign the contract. In the end, he did not sign the contract, and he found a distributor that was better for him. David Alexander explained the types of relationships that artists can enter into. He spent several years as the National Black Music marketing director at PolyGram/Universal Distribution. He points out the downfall of the artist going directly to the distributor: "The artists will get screwed if they don't have a good attorney who is well-versed in those types of contracts, because they will put all kinds of things in the fine print where after a certain amount of time the distributor may own the product if the product doesn't sell. The artists may be signing over their rights or percentages, so artists have to be careful and have a good entertainment lawyer before signing."

Though things have changed a bit since he worked at PolyGram, the basic rules still exist. "There are many different distribution contracts, but it depends on the artist and on the deal and if you are going independent or with the majors," said David. "Generally speaking, the distribution company will sign an agreement with the artist, and in some cases will manufacture, warehouse, and be responsible for having their sales force work with retail buyers to get the product to the shelf. Other relationships exist where artists will ship burned, complete CDs, and the distributor will be responsible to fill the orders as they come in. That is, the artist deals directly with the distributor. When I worked for PolyGram, now Universal, I would sign with Mercury Records and use Mercury's Artist-and-Repertoire (A&R) people, publicist, and their facilities, so Mercury was the label, and they had an exclusive distribution with Universal.

"The product manager is the interface with the label. In its purest form, the distribution company is supposed to take a finished product and get it into the various retail channels. From that, it depends on the label, and the labels contract with the distribution company. There is no standard contract; all are very variable. Look at the biggest distribution companies today: They are BMG, Warner Worldwide, Universal, and Sony. There used to be six, now there are four. There are a lot of independent distributors; they tend to have relationships with major retailers, but they don't have as much clout."

David continued, "Musicians must understand the challenge of the retailer. If you are a Best Buy music section . . . there is a national plan-a-gram that they must follow, and the space is limited where they have to put R&B, rap, etc. If there are 3,000 releases that come out each year, you only have space for four or five hundred CDs. That is their job—to get facings so that they can get sold. One of the biggest risks between a label and the artist is the artist may get major promotion, airplay, MTV, etc. and there will be *no* CDs in the stores. The number-one reason why people walk out of a retailer empty-handed is that the record that they want to buy is physically not there. That is why the Internet and the digital revolution had helped a great deal."

Carl Griffin stressed the importance of the product being available to the consumer: "The artist has to know that the distributor can get out there. With all of the consolidations, a lot of the independents like Red, Reico, and Koch, they can get product in the store, but you won't get a lot of product in the store. Artists have to realize that most chains don't carry a whole lot of product, especially jazz. They want product that moves. Wal-Mart is so strong—they can afford to take a loss on a product, but they are interested in stocking Eminem and Britney Spears, not jazz. When distributors are talking to the store managers, they have to tell a story, like, is the artist number one on the charts? Is the artist willing to be touring, or does he/she have a powerful manager? You must keep in mind that they may take 1,000 pieces nationwide—that is not a whole lot per store—so the distributors must be on point and say where more product is needed as it sells. We are competing with so much now, so unless the artist is well-known and will be touring [they won't] have a whole lot of product in the store."

From the position of the label, Howard Nashel says, "When you represent some record labels, as I do, there is a pressing and distribution (P&D) deal. The distribution is different for Gospel than with jazz. A well-known label will do its own distribution. There are independent distributors in Gospel, for example, and the contracts are more or less standard. When you get into the money side, there are a number of issues: Who will pay for making the album? Who will pay for manufacturing the CD, and who will pay for distributing to the stores and getting airplay? There are independent distributors who distribute through a big record company's distribution channel, so the record company considers them its subcontractors so the company gets 5 percent on top of that partial deal. It is not uncommon for a distributor to charge from 15 percent to 25 or 30 percent, depending on how well known the artist is, as the well known artist will always get a better deal. Distribution deals are very important, just as artist/producer deals are important."

Independent: To Be or Not to Be?

More artists are choosing to record with independents. As the major labels merge and purge artists, there is little choice. Regarding how this affects the artistry of musicians, Carl says, "Independents are the most important thing in the industry today. They will move the industry forward, not the big companies. Big companies are looking for major artists that can move a lot of product; they are not innovative. An independent will be the one to find that next jazz great. I think in this climate, it is not smart to start a new label at all. It is too tough; it is difficult to sell product; the number's aren't there."

As a representative of an independent company, Carl is looking for artists. "I'm looking for people who can write new music. That is the foundation this business is based on—great songs. The Great American Songbook will always be the Great American Songbook, but I don't need to hear it again. Also, the most important thing is for the artist to have a following and to be touring. If the artist makes a record, but has a day gig, that will not do any good. It is important for people to see the artist. If he/she does not tour, or have a manager/agent, or have a booking agent, those are hard obstacles to overcome."

Carl was not looking for another singer when Diana Krall was brought to his attention by her then-manager, Mary Ann Topper, and her assistant, Anna Sula. They had been "calling me to go see Diana, so I went to the Blue Note on a Monday night. She was talented; I liked the way she played the piano, but we had Diane Schur at that time. Then Diana played 'Body and Soul.' That stopped me in my tracks. I looked at the audience as she was singing, and I realized that she was connecting with them. I followed her around, went to Toronto, and I watched young couples hold hands, and I knew that she was the next stylist, á la Shirley Horn." Carl signed her to GRP, her first recording in the United States.

I asked him if he prefers to get a finished CD or not. "It does not matter. If someone comes to me with a product, and it is radio-friendly and the artist is working, we can make a deal today. If I have to go out and find a producer, pick songs—it might take me thirty to forty to find the right ten songs—negotiate with lawyers, etc., I can do that. I'll do it more with a newer artist with great material than with someone who has been around. Now I look for singer/songwriters. We have exhausted those great catalogs [like] Gershwin. I don't need to hear anyone do those classic songs. They can't do it any better than it's been done before."

Like so many artists, Gerald Cannon produced his own self-titled CD. "First, I have my own record label. Established record labels are not doing much. They sign you and drop you. I'm finding that I have to use my money for things that the label would do, like publishing, radio promotion, etc. I have to do it myself. I learned from others. I used to want to be on Blue Note or Verve, but I don't care anymore. I find it more rewarding to be in control of my career, as difficult as that might be."

Billy Taylor, too, started his own record label many years ago: "I was not happy with what had been done with my music. I could not get anyone to record what I was most interested in. Actually, I had started two labels, but then I got an opportunity to record with a small label, so I stayed there. It worked out for a while; I just finally got those records back recently, so I can release them as I see fit."

Verve recording artist Al Jarreau has a different problem when he talked about his latest release, *Accentuate the Positive*. He does not have the problem of lack of distribution. I saw his CDs in Circuit City and Target. I was curious to know how the CD was selling, given that it is a straight-ahead jazz album, not what his audience is accustomed to from him. "I am not sure if that story can be told until several years from now, after I've played this material in concerts and gotten the audience's respect for it. And then we'll see how it does in stores. I'll have to filter that through what we all are depressed about, in terms of the record industry, in that people aren't buying this kind of music a lot, with some few exceptions. My audience feels less likely to go to a record store and dealing with someone with green hair and a bone in his nose. They won't want to deal with that."

The Benefits of Technology

The record industry is making attempts to deal with the financial problems associated with Internet downloading and other things. There has been much discussion over the years about the Napster issue and downloading, but the industry has found a way to counter that somewhat. Although people are now downloading songs in record numbers, they now have to buy the tunes. It seems that people would rather pay per song to get the tunes that they like than buy a CD and not like most of the songs on it.

Billy Taylor believes that musicians doing their own thing is a plus, "I did not do well with distribution; it was hard. I did not want to be in the record business. Now with the Internet and various ways to get their product out there without going through a distributor, it is more direct. You can't sell a zillion copies, but at least you get your record out more than you would by selling on the bandstand. People are wasting time by not doing their own thing."

Oscar Brown Jr. is quite happy with the development of the Internet: "Music seems to be in control of people who don't like the music and musicians. They don't want to pay them; you don't hear about them doing any endowing of anything that will create music." As far as future recordings, he said, "I'd like to put out a lot of stuff on the Internet and get the music out. The record companies don't want to put out but one or two recordings per year at the most, and I don't have that much time, so I'm in a hurry. The technology, the Internet, *is* a good thing for the industry. The most important thing in music is getting it heard; for me, nobody paid me to do this. I have 1,000 songs, and I own them all, so I can do anything I want to. I don't have to sell them; I can give them away. I'm more interested in giving the kids alternative songs to what they have been given on BET."

As Gerald Cannon discovered, now that he is self-produced, the burden of the costs fall on the artists. Allan Harris has financed some of his CDs. He is self-produced and had to handle most of the distribution for his *Love Came: The Songs of Billy Strayhorn.* "I still get requests from across the country; it is a slow burner. If I had to do it over again, I would have gotten a bigger distributor. Most of the sales come from the Internet. I did not want to spin my wheels, throwing this out there. We [he and his wife] tested the waters before it was recorded, and I was asked by producers, '*Why?*' No one wanted to take a risk on doing a Strayhorn thing. So, rather than get our feelings hurt, we did it ourselves."

Artist and Presenter

"Musicians still have to fight for money," said Billy Taylor, remembering an experience early in his career. "Sure, we all did. I had a trio on the road. I had put the gig in Rochester; I was proud of myself. I had put two gigs together; I was going to play there, then go to Chicago. The guy did not pay me in Rochester, New York. So, I called my father for money because I could not get to Chicago otherwise. He sent me the money. We had a contract. I went to the union, and the guy copped out on me and said he could not do anything for me. They were supposed to protect me. It's still the same today."

As Ray Brown told James Williams, "Always read the fine print; it is never good news." The relationship between the artist and the presenter is a delicate balance. Each must protect himself from dishonest people as much as possible. As a presenter, I learned that I must read the fine print. One year I hired someone in October to perform the following February for our Black History Month Program. She got first pick of dates, sent me her contact, and requested a deposit.

In most cases, I send out the contract and request a rider from the artist, but she insisted that she send me her contract. It was very detailed, and I did not read it closely. She requested a deposit, and though I avoid sending them, for her I did. Months later, days before we were to send the newsletter to the printer, she called to tell me that she needed to change her date. I explained that this would affect several people, and I was not certain that I could do it. After some tense conversations, I reread her contract, and she had protected herself. The way her contract was worded, regardless of how the show was cancelled, she would have been able to keep the deposit, and I would have had to hire her later that year in order to not lose our deposit. So I decided that I had no choice; plus, it would have been difficult to find a replacement. Lucky for me, I was able to move the other performers and let her have the other date, but after that experience, my supervisor told me never to hire her again, and I have paid more attention to the fine print when artists insist on sending me a contract."

Eric Reed is very specific when he sends out a contract. "I ask for everything that I want in the contract, down to the type of water that I want. I ask for salted cashews, water—no Evian—to the number of towels that I want on the stage and the numbers of bottles of water that I want on the stage." Joe Grushecky and the House Rockers were the first rock band that I booked. To my amusement, in their contract, they included a case of beer and their preference of brand. Of course, I gave them what they asked for. I've heard of other artists who request items, such as honey-baked ham and cognac.

Artists must be very clear on what they expect the presenter to provide. There are times when the presenter thinks that the in-house equipment is fine, and then finds out that it is not. Again, this is a lesson I learned at The Newark Museum. They had a Steinway Grand piano in the auditorium and a Kwai upright, but they were not in good condition. Before I was on staff, I was asked to assist the manager of public programs to hire performers. After several complaints from pianists, I stopped hiring pianists who were leaders to play on the upright piano. On occasion it was necessary to rent a grand piano, but given the added expense to the budget, we kept that to a minimum. The more it costs for rentals, the less money there is to pay the musicians, and I believe that musicians should be paid as much as possible.

Shortly after I had been hired full-time, I hired Eric Reed to perform on the grand piano in the auditorium. I had it tuned, so I thought all was well. After his performance, he told me how bad the piano was, and had I not been a friend, he might not have played on it. Because of his honesty, I was able to convince the directors to purchase new pianos. Eric talked about that experience in our interview: "Everything is negotiable; you have to be flexible. If the piano is bad . . . you never assume, as Samuel L. Jackson said, if you assume, you make an ass out of *U* and *ME*. Never assume that people know anything. Not everyone knows what you require, especially people you have never worked with." That ended up being a win-win for both Eric and The Newark Museum.

This is an example of how the artist and presenter work well together, but that is not always the case. I heard about a presenter who hired a duo, piano and guitar. When they arrived for their sound check, they discovered that the piano was in terrible condition—basically unplayable. The presenter claimed that others had played on that piano and had not complained. When it became clear that she would not be able to get another piano to the venue, they left. I was told by one of the musicians that they did go back at a later date and perform, so, in a sense, it worked out.

How to Set Your Fee (Pricing)

Learn how to price yourself. Your fee as a leader is often based on your level of experience and your stature. An A-team jazz musician called me, upset, when he found out that he was considered to be the B-team outside of the jazz community. He was asked to perform a highly visible gig that included top musicians from the Gospel and pop genres. The most that he could command was a fraction of what he suspected the others were getting paid. The bottom line is that your fee is based loosely on your ability to fill the room (the number of seats that you can sell). Jeff Clayton said, "There is no one set way or set formula to figure out your fee, but there are components that work better for one area but not others. You have to manipulate the numbers to fit your situation. For example, let's say the hall seats 100 people, you have a five-piece band, and you want to make $1,000. Find out how much money per seat that the $1,000 represents. You take into account the size of the room (the number of seats), the price per seat, subtract two thirds—the approximate cost of the hall rental and other expenses—and the money left is the profit that is available for you as a band. If they have sponsors, then your fee will not be based on ticket sales alone, but on how much the sponsors have contributed. If the sponsors are well-known companies, most likely the venue will have more money to offer. If the fee offered to you is not acceptable, you can factor in your stature: Have you performed there before? Do you have a new CD to sell? You have to look at all those things. Also, look at the standard amount of money that others have been paid for that same event.

Keep your ears to the ground—talk to other musicians to find out what they have been paid. When I'm told that other musicians on my level will accept a fee that I won't accept, then I get an idea how much others get paid."

I asked Jeff if musicians are open about their fees. He replied, "Musicians will discuss fees but tell you to keep it a secret. If it gets out that they accept low fees, they will not be able to demand a higher price down the road."

Over the years, musicians have been honest with me about what they get paid for performances. As a presenter at The Newark Museum, I have a better idea of the price structure, and it varies greatly from genre to genre and stature to stature. Once I hired a musician for a program where I had a big budget. Later that year, I hired one of the players who had been in that musician's group for that program. What I had to offer was a fraction of what I had paid the other guy. That musician could not understand why I was paying so little when he had made almost that much as a sideman earlier that year. He accepted the fee, but instead of bringing a trio or a quartet, he brought a pianist and performed a duo. Another time, a musician refused to bring in his group to the museum, because what I had to pay for the entire group was less than he made when he performed a duo with another artist at the museum earlier that year. Different events have different budgets, but in general, I realized that I should not offer less to a musician who I had previously hired for more money. On the occasions when I have done that, I explain my budget situation, and the musicians often understand. I do not have a problem if they downsize the number of members in their ensemble to accommodate the lower fee.

If you are not comfortable saying that you don't want to play a particular gig, one way to get out of it is to set your fee above what you know the person will pay. According to Jeff Clayton, "I price myself *out* of a gig if I don't want to do it." But beware—the presenter might surprise you by paying your high fee, so it might be best to just say that you are booked that day.

Another thing that leaders should consider is the amount of work they will get from the venue. For example, the presenter might offer a low fee per performance but promise steady work. Or, they might promise to hire the artist when they have a gig that pays more money down the road. If you are a leader, it is up to you to determine how much you want to pay each musician. If you surround yourself with all leaders, you will have to pay them more. Eric Reed says, "How I hire musicians depends on the job and the money that it's paying. If I have a gig paying $2,500, I might call less-experienced musicians, those who can use the work and appreciate the experience of working with me."

Look Ahead

Kenny Washington realized early in his career that he should put some money aside, "I try to. I call it my KIMYAS account: Those are the first initials of my favorite phrase [Kiss My Ass]. So, I always try to keep my KIMYAS money around. So, when shit gets funny, or the musicianship is not right, or if someone bothering me I say, "*Bye!*" Johnny Griffin taught me that I don't want to be beholden to anybody. When I'm working, I save some and spend some. I recommend that to anybody. I'm fortunate; I've always worked. I tell myself, you never know."

17 How to Promote and Present Yourself

You must get noticed, and you are your own best promoting agent. It is not enough to only be a good musician. Gary Walker talked about a session that he attended at International Association of Jazz Education (IAJE), geared towards vocalists. The speakers on the panel included Jon Hendricks and Kurt Elling. Kurt said to the room, "You know, the biggest problem facing jazz vocalist today . . ." The audience leaned in, holding their breath in anticipation; then he said, ". . . is that most of you are not any good!" Gary agrees, saying that most musicians skip a lot of the necessary steps: "If a musician is working one day a month, that does not cut it."

Perhaps you are happy with the one-day-a-month gig, but promotion is still necessary. You must have some type of biography; a high-quality photograph would help. Get to know the members of your musical community; know the industry people, such as radio announcers and club owners; join professional organizations; have an e-mail list or hire someone to get the word out about your performances. The way to create a buzz about yourself is to connect with as many people as you can.

As you progress in notoriety, the request for a package from a presenter diminishes, but a bio and a photo should still be made available. In most cases, artists have Web sites where the information is accessible, but from time to time, you might still have to send a photo if the resolution of the photo on your Web site is not high enough. Whether you promote via e-mail, via snail mail, or hire someone to handle your publicity is a personal decision.

"Now, I send people to my Web site. At this point, I don't even [have to send promotional materials] anymore; I just get calls. Initially I had to do it because venues weren't familiar with me, so they needed something in hand," Eric Reed reflected.

The burden of promotion should not fall entirely on the presenter, though some musicians think that it should. Allan Harris participated on a panel to assist vocalists in their careers. On the panel, and in the audience, were some singers who had fairly active careers. Their response to his comment about creating an e-mail list was surprising. One singer on that panel told him that it was hard work to come home and enter all of those names on a list. Another audience member who produced a show each year with her husband, told Allan that one could not expect friends to continue to pay money to see an artist, that's just not realistic. So then I ask, who should support you? The panelist who could not conceive of putting a list together also believed that club owners should promote the artist's engagement. Allan told her those days were over.

The Promotion Package

Your promotion package should include the following elements:

1. *An attractive folder* to keep everything together.

2. *A cover letter.* If you know the person to whom you are writing, include a handwritten note with the letter.

3. *A description of yourself* (a biography). It should be current and concise, with relevant professional achievements, such as where you have worked, with whom, current and past projects, recordings, awards (musical!), nominations, your working band, etc.

4. *A high-quality photograph.* A high-resolution photo is best. Consider getting professional headshots taken. A casual Polaroid or passport photo will not cut it.

5. *A CD of your work.* It can just be samples of your work, not necessarily a produced CD. The cassette tape is not really an acceptable submission medium anymore. Artists who do not know how to record an electronic file or burn a CD should ask someone for assistance. The CD should reflect your seriousness as an artist. Use a label; include the names of the tracks and any other musicians accompanying you. If you need the CD returned, be sure to inform the listener before you hand it over. Otherwise, assume that it is gone for good.

6. *Any press clippings or testimonials from people who have heard you.* Don't send everything ever written about you; no one has the time to read it all. It is best to scan your clippings and photo together to create a clean, succinct page of press. Don't send clippings that have been photocopied a thousand times. Be creative, but keep it simple!

7. *Contact information*. It should include the works: name, address, a phone number, e-mail address, Web site, etc.

I have encountered musicians who are great at self-promotion, but whose talent does not match the presentation. So, while a good press package does not indicate that you are a good musician, all musicians certainly need a promotion package at the beginning of their careers. I am astonished at times at how poorly musicians present themselves. On average, I receive about four packages per month. Sometimes there is no identification of who is playing on the recording and artists will even omit their own names. In our technologically advanced, computer-driven age, it also amazes me how often I receive handwritten cover letters or tapes and CDs with no label or a handwritten label.

Edwin Hawkins noted the downside of having limited funds to promote, but that is not an excuse to send something that is not presentable. "One of the things that is lacking in a smaller company is the money to promote. You can sell anything [that is] promoted properly, even if it is bad. If you promote it, people will buy it. We have not had a company that would put the money behind us in terms of promotion, which has not been good for me. You learn that everything you do is not always the greatest. Perhaps you would have sold better had more people known about you or heard you."

Here are three examples of "packages" that stand out for me as being unacceptable:

1. One young man approached me, seeking to play at a venue where I produce a jazz festival each year. Several people had told me that I should talk to him because he was really good and that I needed to listen to him. He was very sincere and explained to me that he was just beginning to seek work as a leader, and that he would send me something. What he sent was quite shocking. His package included two demo CDs, a photo, and a letter that did not contain anything close to proper standard letterform, or even Standard English. The typeface was a fancy serif typeface, and he ended several sentences with a smiley-face symbol (to my shock, another artist sent me a letter with the same symbol at the end of some sentences—whew!).

    As I said, he was asking me to consider him for a jazz gig, but he included some samples of hip hop that he had done, and his jazz sample was him playing to Jamey Abersol music. That alone showed that he was not close to being a professional. It would have behooved him to rent a studio with his friends and tape a live session. And he needed to consult someone on how to write a standard letter that was grammatically correct, as well. If you do not know what to do, then ask someone who knows.

2. Someone I had known for years who, I thought, was a seasoned musician dropped off a package for me. Like the previous gentleman, he threw some information in a manila envelope along with a *tape*, a handwritten cover letter, and some old newspaper articles that had been photocopied way too many times for me to even be able to read.

3. Familiarity is no excuse to be unprofessional. A long-time friend of mine discovered that he was, with no vocal experience, a singer. He had gotten validation from several noted musicians and decided that he should pursue a career. Using his own money, he produced a CD that he was proud of, and he wanted my opinion. One night he showed up at a venue where he knew I would be; he handed me a plastic bag and apologized for giving it to me that way. I did not mind. What he should have apologized for was what was *in* the bag. When I took out the contents, I discovered a CD with no label, no writing, nothing. Instead of a jewel case, or any casing, it was enclosed in bubble wrap. To make matters worse, he did not write the list of songs, nor did he write the names of the other musicians who were on the recording, Oh, yes, he did not write *his own name*, either. Months later, he called me and, I think jokingly, left me a message chastising me for not getting back to him with my feedback and for not *returning* the CD.

James Browne, owner of the club Sweet Rhythm, and I talked about artist presentations, and I asked him if he cared who approached him, the musician or her representative. "It does not matter; it is the approach itself. I can't tell you how many musicians come to me and say, 'I wanna play here; give me a gig.' That presentation is *no* presentation. You need to have a sample of your recording, bio material, news clippings, etc. This gives me an indication that you have been working, and I don't care where it comes from. Don't be sloppy. You won't believe what people give me. One night a musician gave me a CD with no cover. I ask for some degree of professionalism."

David Randolph found out the hard way that personal contact is important. While trying to gain some funds for the St. Cecelia Chorus, he looked through the grant book of the Foundation Center for foundations that would be suitable to give money to what St. Cecelia Chorus was doing. In going over the grant qualifications, he noticed the words "personal contact desirable." So he wrote letters to seventy-five foundations. "Sixty did not answer or said no. We knew no one. After ten to twelve years of inviting a man in charge of a foundation—he came to every concert—we got a $2,000 grant. That is the way it happens when you don't know anyone."

Whom to Promote to

Whom you promote to depends on what you are doing. You may want your music played on the radio, or you may just be promoting a performance, where an interview would be helpful. Perhaps flyers are all that you need to send either as snail mail or e-mail. Bobby Sanabria understands that "you need to connect with promoters and club owners."

Bobby continues, "The biggest asset one has is persistence." There are ways to be persistent and not be offensive. In the jazz community, too often I find that musicians do not listen to the radio, yet they want radio attention. They do not know the announcers or pay attention to shows that might feature the music that they play. I get notices from musicians the week of their engagements, which is too late for me to promote, because they don't seem to realize that I am on the air on Saturdays only. When I hosted a show with no horns on Sunday morning, musicians seemed shocked when I told them that I could not play their music; then they would take offense that a show without horns even existed. That is one way to ensure that I would write them off of my list of musicians to consider when I was able to play them. I've met singers who did not know that there was a show on WBGO that was dedicated to singers.

You cannot expect people to support you when you don't support yourself. I get several CDs each week that I will never listen to. There is not enough time for me to listen, but if the musician contacts me personally, I might make the time. Some of us on the air do not have time to read all of the promotional material that comes with the packages. One announcer told me that he just throws it away and keeps the CDs. He did confess that if the CD comes from a promoter he knows and respects, he will pay attention. When you send out an unsolicited CD, it is best to put the most pertinent information first."

You should also know who makes the decisions at the radio station to get your music in the library. Often stations like WBGO, Jazz 88.3FM have a music director, or a program director, to filter the music. Regardless of the station, you must make sure that your recording fits the format of the radio station. You may think that this is obvious, but not so. Know what you are sending and why you are sending it. Follow-up calls are important, too. Keep in mind that there is a thin line between being aggressive and being annoying. I asked Gary Walker, music director at WBGO, if he found that to be a problem. He replied, "I talk to a lot of artists on the phone, and the majority of them don't have a clue about their careers. They are great musicians, but they don't have a clue otherwise. I won't allow people to waste my time twice. It does not matter who contacts me regarding the artist, but I quickly find out if they know what they are talking about, I'll ask them to tell me something about the CD, such as, what tracks stand out and why."

Established artists like Richard Smallwood understand the power of radio and promotion. "You have to promote your product. I had a radio promotion tour, and I had taken a van and went up and down the East Coast and to radio stations and record stations. You have to do [that] to establish a foundation of what your project is. I don't think it's luck." When I met Al Jarreau, he was on a promotional tour for his CD, *Accentuate the Positive*, and we talked at the radio station about how important it was for him to do lots of promotion. Though not a morning person, he had to sing at an event early one morning; in other words, the need to be visible never stops.

Jeff Clayton understands how important promotion can be. In response to my question about what he does, he replied, "Everything humanly possible. That includes personal contact, handwritten notes, e-mail or personal notification, and last, flyers, but that almost does not work at all. I need a personal attachment to people who will come. Another thing, make sure that they are surrounded with people who they revere. Invite people like Quincy Jones, send a limousine and have them stand up; people will be impressed and look forward to going again. And start rumors that certain people will show up."

I do recall attending a concert of the Clayton-Hamilton Jazz Orchestra in Los Angeles, and Quincy and other famous actors attended; it was exciting for me to see them. One year the Clayton Brothers got their first gig in New York City at Sweet Basil (now Sweet Rhythm). They began their week on Halloween. The club is in Greenwich Village where a huge parade takes place. That night I mentioned to James Browne, who was the manager at the time, that they had been sounding great. He said, "They will be sounding great to no one tonight because no one comes out on Halloween." To his shock, the club was sold out. Collectively they had called every person they knew (several famous musicians, too) in New York City, and the people showed up, not just that night but for the entire week. The personal touch works wonders.

Radio is not the only medium that an artist should reach out to. There are cable TV stations in almost every city. Reach out to those stations that might feature your music. Seek out writers who highlight events if you are doing something special. Contact your high school or college if there is alumni news.

When to Promote

You are doing yourself a service if you are friendly and approachable. So much that happens in the music business is because of personal contact. Countless times I have observed musicians ignore people until they find out who they are. Don't think that this goes unnoticed, and it might be held against you down the line. It took Allan Harris some time to realize what he needed to do to be in New York. By his own admission, he was not well received when he first arrived: "I didn't go out and go to things like IAJE [International Association of Jazz Educators]; I did not network enough. *Duh . . . This is New York City*, and you have to present yourself like hanging out, interviews, promoting. I had no concept of that, and I had a clown manager." No matter what level you are at, you must be visible.

Bobby Sanabria believes that, as part of their learning process, musicians must be involved in the jazz community as a whole. "I urge young musicians to attend IAJE or any kind of presenters given by colleagues." Paula Kimper acknowledged how beneficial it was for her to meet people: "Yes, there very much is a community that's your world, your contemporaries. I know most of the living American composers; it's a small world. National Performing Arts is a group that meets in Pittsburgh—it's small. There is always competition, people who won't help you and you feel rejected by them, but there are some others who accept you."

There are times when it is *not* good to promote, for example, outside of a funeral service. I attended a funeral of a very well respected musician, which brought together prominent people from all walks of life. Outside the church was quite the jazz hang, as so many people had not seen each other in some time. Walking through the crowd was a musician, not well respected on any level, passing out flyers for a club that he was promoting.

Some musicians believe that any gathering of people is a place for them to hand out flyers. Each year the mayor of New York City hosts a party at Gracie

Mansion to promote the JVC festival. The event is very controlled. As I was going through security, a musician in front of me was insisting that she could hand out her palm cards because she had done so the previous year. The guard explained that all material had to have been cleared ahead of time, but she would not take no for an answer. Perhaps she thought that she could wear him down and get him to change his mind, but he did not. I watched as she argued her case the entire walk into the event.

This same performer sings backup in an ensemble. The leader had a showcase trying to attract investors in the project, and explained to her beforehand that she was not allowed to bring her palm cards. After the show, she commented to him that she should have brought her material. What did she *not* understand? She has been promoting her only CD for years, and I finally had to tell her to stop giving me her flyers; after all, I'm on her e-mail list. Once I went to see her perform, and in-between songs, she was asking people to sign her guest book. While, in her defense, I have to say that she has built up a decent following, but her approach to promotion may ultimately be a hindrance when she tries to move beyond her circle of loyal supporters. Again, there is a fine line between being aggressive and being annoying.

Then Versus Now

John Levy has the benefit of age to see what has and has not changed in the business. "When I came along, you almost had to book in order to get your artist to a certain stage in the business; then you turned them over to a booking agency, who at that time represented a certain class of entertainers/musicians. There were booking agencies that worked with people and helped develop their careers. That's all gone today. Now it's all about promotion. Artists need lawyers or people who promote an artist to get them in the marketplace on a certain level; these people don't necessarily have any experience about where they should play or what they should do. There is an entity for each one of these things; not one person can do it all. Even me, I was capable of booking, managing. I knew all of the places and where to play; I knew the promoters, the entrepreneurs personally, because I had been out there. You can't operate that way anymore today; you need a lawyer, a manager who you can trust and know the business, a booking agent. If you don't have all three, you are floundering on our own. Anybody who is anybody has all three."

18

The Importance of a Manager

For years I have asked musicians what the function of a manager is, why they have a manager, and how they evaluate their effectiveness. My questions have been met with mixed reactions. In many cases, especially with musicians just starting out, I find that they really want someone to help them find work. Or, upon further questioning, what I hear them saying is that they need a personal assistant or someone to negotiate salaries. The music business has changed from the time when managers seemed to have control of the direction of an artist. There are examples of managers who are legendary in some artists' careers, such as Joe Glasser, who managed Louis Armstrong; Colonel Parker, who managed Elvis Presley; and John Levy, who managed Nancy Wilson until her retirement in November 2004. These managers were able to direct those musicians' paths. How necessary is this in today's climate?

The Function of a Manager

Among the many hats James Browne has worn, at one time, he managed artists. He explained the manager's function to be "like a chauffeur; he drives the artists where they want to go. As a manager, I sit with an artist and assess if where she wants to go is realistic and feasible, then we decide on the best way to get there. Let's say, for example, that a singer wants to consistently play rooms the size of the Blue Note [in New York City] in five years. If that's what she wants to do, then she must do something that stands apart. Just singing 'Embraceable You' is not realistic." **Laura Hartmann** expanded on what James had described as the role of the manager, "A manager is to help an artist develop his career. In an ideal situation, a manager will assemble a team to achieve that. He will bring together a lawyer, a record company, a publicist, and a radio person. The artist and the manager are partners, and the manager makes sure that those parts work effectively together to create opportunities for the artist to see that her stars are on the rise."

At the time of our interview, John Levy still managed Nancy Wilson. Although he began as a bass player, most of his work life was spent as a manager. At one time, he had many of the A-list jazz musicians: Ahmad Jamal, Cannonball Adderely, DaKota Staton, George Shearing, Shirley Horn, and others. The role of manager has changed much over the years, "When I came along, most musicians thought about their craft, about playing, and not too much about the business end of it. In today's world, if you are a person like myself, you could not make it in this business world due to how things are structured now. It's no longer about music; it's business. Some of the younger musicians have gone to school for it, and music came as an afterthought. The music went out of the window a long time ago. In my day, the people who went into management came in with experience as musicians. They came from the field; they had some background. Now the people in the music business have to be very young to appeal to a younger audience, and music is something that is disposable like all things in this country. Management is not capable today . . . Nowadays they have no experience. It's about contacts and how much money they make; they don't intend to be honest with artists because they are disposable. The same is for artists, not just musicians; they develop people and develop them overnight and dispose of them overnight."

Laura Hartmann explained what the difference is between management and booking: "As a manager, I cannot legally be a booking agent, I need a license to do that. I get my artists noticed, but I am not a booking agent, I'm a manager. I am looking for a partner who cares as much about my clients as myself, so I can form a booking division. Management and booking should be under one roof and working for the same goal."

There are different types of managers: There are those who are established and those just getting started. Al Jarreau told me, "There are instances where established managers hear a group or an artist at an organized listen for the record company—if it's a demo, a CD, or hearing an artist live. That's a big part of it. I did have a manager at the early stage in my career who was busy trying to organize showcases for me. The guy was an unestablished manager. I think there are a lot of ways for artists to think about management. It has been suggested that a young, hungry guy who does not have a group of artists in his stable will work harder. You are just looking for a guy who had talent in that direction that you can recognize, and he'll represent you and find a way to those offices. Or, find a guy who has those contacts in those offices because he had other artists, but he won't have time to develop you because he is busy making money with other artists. I chose the hungry guy."

After having managers who proved unsuccessful, Allan Harris turned to his wife to manage him. There are challenges, but it has worked best for him. "A manager frees you up to create and make money. You need a business manger. There are those who can manage on their own and have a career that is flowing and creative, but many cannot handle it and get stressed out. They become recluses and bitter people. I need a manager. I like things other than performing, and I do other things. With my wife as manager, we have the same goals; she sees the same things as I. The manager has to play second fiddle to the artist, in the public. The artist runs the stable. I went through a few people who were friends who were successful in other ventures and thought they could manage an artist, but we did not see things the same way. We were at an impasse—a lot of dysfunctional stuff. A good manager sees mood swings and anticipates them and tailors stuff to that. [My wife] is dealing with a wild animal. I don't know how any manager does it who has an artist worth his salt. She gets burned out, too. We have much to deal with as man and woman. She must get something out of it. She might ask, Is this all there is? Hotels, performances, being in front of strangers? She has no stable to fall back on; it's just me."

Andy Bey has not always had a manager, although he has had people to function in that role from time to time. "Not all are good, and it is hard to say what makes a good manager. They read contracts, handle your travel, check on you in foreign places, take care of details. I had not had one in a long time. They must take a personal interest in their client, be good with details. They must have high self-esteem to stand up for the artist. I finally found the right one, and we must have a level of trust that goes both ways. My manager does some booking, but she has people to work with her doing that. The manager has to work with the booking agent; she can't sit and wait for an agent to call. She is organized, makes sure that the money is correct, and collects advances."

Do You *Need* a Manager?

The consensus of the musicians whom I interviewed about the need for a manager was simple—Some do and some don't. For the most part, jazz musicians leaned more toward a positive answer to that question. Kenny Washington believes that too many get a manager too soon, "I think managers are important if you are leading a band, because they have inside information as to where the work is. They have something inside that you as a leader don't have, if you get the right one, who is honest, who believes in you. I see a lot of guys who have managers that don't need managers, because they have not been out here enough and don't know enough."

Several musicians agree with Kenny Washington about when a manager is necessary. Kenny Barron says, "I have not always had a manager. As I got more work, yes, I got one. I'm not good at asking for a certain amount of money, and some people prefer to deal with someone other than the artist. Some managers book and manage. In California, they are bound by law to be separate. I have both, and it is money well spent. A manager is someone who you trust and is in your corner."

Michael Wolff gave a rousing vote of confidence to managers, saying that a manager is "*indispensable* . . . if you want to do music—unless you want to manage yourself. What happened to me was 'The Peter Principle;' you reach your level of incompetence. I have a wonderful manager. I did a lot of research on managers. I needed someone who would 'get' me. I can't just be a straight-ahead jazz guy. I'm a jazz musician, but I do this and I do this, but I do this weird thing, I write; I soloed with the Memphis Symphony. She got it!"

Billy Taylor agrees, but says that it is a mixed bag, "Yes, you do need a manager if you get a good one. All of my life I envied one musician, I knew him very well. Erroll Garner came to New York when I did, and he was lucky enough to get a woman who realized what he needed at that time he needed it and made him the star he became. Then he was taken over by one of the main artists' management in the world. For a guy who could not read music and was self-taught, that was wonderful. He was a phenomenal musician and had such a wonderful approach to the music in his heyday. He could reach out and touch people. It was different to do that stuff and play the piano. Someone once wrote, 'Erroll Garner is the best thing to happen to music since kissing.'

"There were some rough times to hold a trio together; I had to get gigs for myself. I've had two to three managers from time to time. John Levy was one of my managers at one time. John could not see commercial possibilities for me at that stage in his career as a manager. We were then, and are still, wonderful friends; I still love him and respect him. He is one of the best managers around. But he was not able to do what I needed to do for me at that time, so I had to do it myself. I got jobs on the radio."

Bobby Sanabria did not have a totally positive experience, though he recognizes the need of a manager: "I had a manager, and it helped, but unfortunately, the person took advantage of the situation. My story is common amongst all genres. What we have to work with is so minuscule, such as money, so when we get ripped off, it really hurts, and it is disenchanting. You do need a booking agent, someone to get work for you. When you get big enough, you do need some kind of management to take care of your affairs, but that costs money. Booking agents is most important in the jazz world, but you don't stop looking for work on your own. The main concern is the music."

Gerald Cannon leans toward Bobby's point of view on management. "This last year has been *whoa*! I tried to do it all myself, but you can't do it alone. I'm a bass player—that's what I do. You can get wrapped up in the business part, and you forget what you are supposed to be doing. The main thing is getting work done; if you can't do it, hire someone to do it."

Ron Carter replied to the question of management in this way: "I think that question deserves a two-pronged answer. Musicians have weaned themselves from being responsible for their musical actions off the bandstand. The result is, they need someone to speak on their behalf. What that has done is separate them from the business—and that is not a good thing—and from other musicians. Personal contact is eliminated. I've had dealings with guys who have me call their manager—they don't have their schedules and won't talk to me directly. A manager will take out his share of the money before he pays the musicians. I *abhor* that. You think this guy is so irresponsible that you will take your percent before he gets his pay and pays his band? You want a share of his publishing company, and you have not written any words to his songs, and you want his music part of *his* money? I *don't think* so! Managers have been allowed to take over more than they have a right to take over, because musicians have abdicated their right to be responsible for things they should be responsible for.

"Ahmad Jamal, Betty Carter, Miles Davis, etc., had agents because they had so much work and money had to be dealt with. The last manager, Jack Whitimore, had a hell of a stable. He had seven of the major acts at one time, and he'd give a club owner Miles if he agreed to take Betty two months later. No one has a stable of that type now. We all are doing are own thing now. Musicians have not stepped up to the plate to know how to bargain on their own behalf. They never sat down to figure out their worth; they have not been able to quantify their talent; they let club owners do it for them. They are stuck with what agents can get for them. I will not work for a certain amount of money."

My response to that comment was that some musicians don't know how to talk about money, or feel comfortable doing so. Ron's answer? "They are full of *shit*! They don't know what to work for, and they are embarrassed by that. The fear of under/overpricing themselves. If they don't start somewhere, then they let the managers/agents dictate their living conditions. I told my agent not to take a call from a club owner because I heard the conditions are abominable. It is a waste of time. I am not allowing the band to live in those conditions; if they can't change them, don't call anymore. If musicians don't take a stand, then the conditions won't change and we'll have shitty hotels, etc. The managers aren't doing the gigs, or staying in the hotels, they are just collecting the commission, and they go on to the next bonfire."

Olu Dara prefers to manage himself. His reply to the question about his need for a manager was, "*Never!* Only time was when I made a record for Atlantic. The manager did paperwork and managed tours. After two records, we dropped each other. I was too independent. I was getting better gigs on my own. The manager got upset that I never called, so we parted company. It's easy to manage myself. If people like you, they call you. You're already managed. The audience has to like it and ask for you." Oscar Brown Jr. is difficult to manage, but he believes that "a manager is important, but I rarely had one, and I'm not sure why. I was not personally unmanageable. I will come prepared, but the politics of my career has been a problem. The whole white supremacy thing requires that the managers don't compete at a certain level if they can help it. So, they don't want me to stand up with an Ira Gershwin."

For the most part, classical musicians do not require management. David Randolph never saw the need for a manager, "For a brief time, I had a publicity agent—useless, no point to it. He got me a little mention in the *New York Times*." For the St. Cecelia Chorus, David's wife has taken on some of the jobs that might cast her in that role as business manager. "The only paid people at St. Cecelia are myself and the pianist," says David. Dorothy Lawson did not need one personally: "I have, as an individual, never had a manager; as a quartet [Ethel], we have had one for three years. Ethel is an organization that sustains itself through great writing, management and outreach, educational opportunities. We have a board of directors and financial advisor. ICM just signed us and sent us out to bigger venues. Management provides access to a level of presenters you can't get to without them. Presenters need a short form to navigate. As an individual, I have lived by the phone."

The Cost of a Manager

I have heard several complaints from musicians about how much of their fee goes to a manager, a booking agent, and other miscellaneous costs. When they do not feel that they are getting their money's worth, they tend to use this as an excuse *not* to have a manager. Several musicians have approached me over the years asking me to manage them. They've said they would be happy to pay me the 15 percent commission. I have asked each of them, why me? And they say, because I care about them and the music. For the artist who is not working often or is difficult to book, I could not make a living on 15 percent of the average fee of $1,000. Managers have to eat, too. John Levy broke down the costs involved: "For a musician to have a decent manager who knows his salt and knows what he is doing, an artist has to pay 20 to 25 percent. The accountant gets 10 percent and the booking agency makes 10 to 15 percent, so the artist works for 50 percent of his or her salary."

"Yes, I've heard of artists who pay up to 45 percent in commissions," says Laura Hartmann. "If you have a U.S. agent, a European agent, a booking agent, and a manager. The U.S. agent will demand a portion of the fee of the European agent, though he did not book it, and I think that is wrong but one has little choice. That is why I want to grow my business to include the booking. The agency that handles classical musicians usually charges 20 percent commission—that includes the management fee and the booking agent fee as one together. If you separate that out, you end up paying the booking agent 15 percent and 10 percent to the manager, which equals 25 percent."

How to Find a Manager

This can be a little tricky. Jeff Clayton told me, "in jazz, a person can get out of jail, print up business cards, and call himself a manager; no credentials are required." James Browne and I discussed that as well, "In pop, there is only *one* level, and that is the top. You are either Britney Spears, or you work in Barnes & Noble. In rock 'n' roll, there are managers with whom I was highly suspect of their ability to *read*! Artists should look at what the person has done; they must have a track record."

Artists must do their homework. It is in your best interest to determine your needs (maybe what you need is a personal assistant). It is good to talk to people who are on the managers' roster and those who are *no longer* on their roster. Unfortunately, many people are not honest about their experience with a manager so as not to steer potential clients from them, but you should pay attention to how many people the manager loses; there might be a pattern. I urge you to talk to people who have dealt with the managers to find if the experience was positive, but again, you have to hope for honest feedback. If you choose to go with an inexperienced manager, have him start slowly and see how he handles himself before you sign a contract.

Laura Hartmann understands that well. "My biggest mistake was taking on people whom I liked personally and musically, and not realizing that I needed artists with ideas that they wanted to be developed. Some of my clients had bands, but where they saw themselves going was not clear. You have to have more than just being a great pianist, for example. They have to ask what they are going to do with that; unfortunately, you just can't do one thing, you have to branch out and do different things."

Sometimes management can only take you to a certain point. Edwin Hawkins said, "Initially my first manager was Mel Reid. He had the largest Gospel outlet and distributor of sheet music, and records on Gospel. We hired him on a suggestion of who he was in the Bay area. We did not know anybody professional in the music, so we asked him, and he did our first tour. After signing with Buddha Records, it got bigger with dates; we got more professional managers. That was not Reid's forte in the business. He knew record stores.

"Our first managers were with Grief and Garrett, out of Hollywood, who had managed Barry White, Jose Feliciano, and others. They showed us a different side of the business. It is absolutely and essential to have management. Most artists don't understand the business side of the business, unless maybe you take a course. Those people understand the business and know how to read contracts. When I started out, I knew *nothing* about the business."

As a presenter, I deal with my share of managers, and they can tip the scales of whether I will hire an artist that I don't know well. Most times, I try to avoid them until it is time to deal with the contract. Several times I have talked to artists about hiring them; they said yes and had me call their manager who then gave me the runaround, or said that they would not work for the money that I offered, or put the onus on the booking agent. Because I am friendly with many of them, this could be their way of not having to be honest with me. It has also happened that the manager or agent did not discuss the fee with the artists and allowed them to make the decision in taking the job. Two musicians told me that I should have talked to them directly, and when I reminded them that I had, they said, next time call me. However, often, there is not a next time.

Laura sees her role as the buffer between the artist and the presenter, and rightfully so. "I never take a gig for the artist without the artist accepting the fee. Sometimes I negotiate, but you have to trust your business sense and know when to play that card. You have to walk a thin line. If you go into a two thousand–seat hall and demand a $10,000 fee, you better be sure that your artist can fill the room. I'd rather haggle with the presenter over money or a bass amp than with the artist. The presenter who buys my client is also my client, because I want my client to be able to go back to them. It is a two-sided relationship that I want to develop, I want my client to focus on the music, not the stage plot."

One manager with whom I dealt twice did not understand that. Our first encounter was not positive, but after a year, I had forgotten how she was and asked to hire one of her artists again. The artist had insisted that he wanted to do the gig, and I thought that he had talked to her. Both times we haggled about money. She insisted that he would not work for the fee that I offered, and told me that he commanded twice as much. I had my doubts about that, given that I had seen that he was working at a local place where he could have not been making anywhere close to what I was offering.

One of our encounters resulted in a request from her that I would sign a confidentiality clause stating that I would not discuss that fee with anyone. Ultimately, in the end, I did not hire him either time because of her attitude. What upset me the most was when she told me that she needed to get her fee, too, hence her demand for more money. She was condescending to the point of being rude, so I thought, "Who needs him?" She, like many managers, missed the big picture. There are presenters who are not honest, but when an artist or manager meets someone who is, they can usually count on more work for their artist from that person. I get calls often from other presenters asking for my recommendation on who they should hire for events. Managers must understand this. If they only seek high-profile gigs for their artists, they are overlooking the small gigs that become a bridge when other work falls away.

My experience with managers is mixed. Some artists are bombarded by so many requests for interviews, charity work, etc., but it bothered me how often I got the runaround when I approached some artists to interview for this book. A simple "no," or "the artist is too busy," works well. Some managers did tell me that. It was a waste of my time for me to keep calling people back. Other managers I talked to directly told me to call at specific times; I did, only to get voicemail or no response at all. A few years ago, I went to an event in which publicist Terrie William spoke. Of the many important things she had to share, one statement stuck to me, she said, "It is downright *rude* not to return phone calls." I had not been good at calling people back, either, but that changed me forever. Besides, you never know when that person who you ignored or dismissed will come around again and you might need them. Yesterday's nobody might be somebody one day and an opportunity will have been missed.

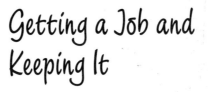

19 Getting a Job and Keeping It

Every time you get in front of an audience, you are auditioning for the next job or gig. You must present yourself as a professional. Your reputation is your calling card. You must be presentable, know how to approach people, be amenable, follow up on leads, be assertive, show that you want to work, and have a clear idea what you want to do. Jeff Clayton put it simply when I asked him how to get a gig and keep it: "Do A-team things: be prepared; be cheerful; as a sideman, don't have an opinion; dress appropriately. Believe me, if they want you, they will call you!"

Kenny Washington understood what he had to do when he began. "I was very lucky. They say you become a professional when you start getting paid. I got local gigs in Staten Island. I had an opportunity to know the great trombonist Jimmy Knepper. He was on some of those club dates, and I'd see him on the ferry. Lee Konitz needed a drummer, so Jimmy recommended me.

"I was fortunate; I had people around me who took me under their wing and recommended me. Dave Bailey [drummer and executive director of Jazzmobile for thirty-five years] was one of them. He had heard me with Walter Davis Jr., and he started recommending me to play Jazzmobile. One guy was Mike Morgenstern, who had a joint called Jazz-mania. He called me one day to play an all-star jam session, and he wanted me in the house rhythm section. It did not pay much money, but the guys on the date were Pepper Adams, 'bebop' Joe Carroll, Bill Hardiman, to name a few. Years later, a Joe Carroll record came out, and I was on it. It was from that jam session. Many musicians got my number, and Bill Hardiman called me to do a date. On the date was Walter Bishop Jr., and he got my number, and he called me."

I went to see a musician perform who had asked me to hire him at The Newark Museum. Not being familiar with his work, I attended a Jazz Vespers where he was the featured artist. The presenter gave him clear instructions as to what he was to do during the service, but he did not follow the program. After the service, his response to her was, "We got through it." He is not someone whom I would consider hiring.

It is not good to misrepresent yourself. Do not accept dates that do not suit you. Another unfortunate experience for me was when I hired two groups from a newly formed theatrical company. I was very clear with the director what I was looking for, as well as the amount of money that I had to offer. He suggested two artists whom I accepted. When I sent him the contract, he told me that one group would not do what I wanted; he had committed the performers without asking them if they would do it. He also reiterated that the fee that I offered was low for them, but he wanted to get more exposure for his company. Reluctantly, I agreed to the new terms.

The day of the event, all of the performers showed up late. They blamed it on traffic and trains, but one of the representatives told my supervisor that, given our low fee, they had not planned to get there early. The director of the company told me that they show up early when food is served. I will never hire him again and will find it difficult to give him a positive recommendation, should anyone ask me. Remember, you must always be honest. You must try to avoid what Jeff Clayton calls being "hummed out of a job." That occurs when someone inquires about you and the person being asked responds, "*Hmmmm . . .*" That can be fatal.

I have had several positive experiences, but one stands out. I was faced with the challenge to hire a rock group for a concert for The Newark Museum. Given that rock is not my area of expertise, I had several things to consider, including price and the artist's ability to sell a certain number of seats. Fortunately, I was steered in the right direction by a young co-worker, Becky. The reason for the concert was to bring attention to the Springsteen exhibit "Troubadour of the Highway." Favored artists were Clarence Clemmons and South Side Johnny.

I contacted the individual on South Side Johhny's Web site, Barry Weisblatt, who turned out to be a great resource. He listened to what our needs were, and he was very honest about who we should consider and why. He made it clear to me that we were headed in the wrong direction. Barry was patient with me and my wavering. I was amused when I would call the office and each person recognized my voice. It would have been easy for him to book the artist that we initially wanted, and he admitted that he would have made more money, but he did not feel comfortable doing that; his reputation as a new company was at stake. Barry did not over- or undersell any of the artists, and in the end, we hired the perfect group and had a great show, and the turnout was great.

Know What the Job Requires

As a club owner, James Browne often deals with the need for artists to know the requirements of a job. On weekends he has three sets. He hired a musician who did not want to perform the third set. He told her that she had been told that she was expected to sing three sets, so she agreed to sing a short third set. Midway through the third set, several people came in, but she had committed to a short set and ended. One of the patrons complained that she had done the same thing at another club, so he said, "That's it." As James pointed out, "The public does not need you. Musicians need to focus on the equivalent of the ideas put in the book, *He's Just Not That into You*." Though James does plan to bring back the singer, others who do not fulfill their obligation might not be so lucky.

Allan Harris accepts the challenge to find work that fits him. "First, don't pick a gig you can't fulfill. Don't take it only because you need it. You have to research a gig. Ask, 'Am I right for this? Should I alter what I do for it?' Some gigs you can't bend; you have to change up what you do as an artist—that goes across the board. Once you accept the engagement, you have to stick to it. What the owner buys, they want to see onstage. Or, if you are all that, they will change the gig for you, but that's rare. Do your homework; ask those who did it and were successful, and ask if they think you could do it. You got to be ready."

Billy Taylor once misunderstood what he was hired for. "There was a place on Eighth Avenue in the 1950s—the neighborhood was rough then—I went in and asked the owner, I said, you got a piano here, and he was looking for a piano player. He told me, 'I want you to play as loud and as long as you can, and when you are tired, then you stop.' I said okay, but did not take him seriously. I did not want to stop, but to slow down, then keep going. He said, 'Son, I told you, I wanted you to play loud, that boogie-woogie and stuff you played for me, and when you get tired, stop, and I'll put the juke box on.' What he wanted was for people drinking, he wanted a lot of noise, that was his thing."

I asked him how the business has changed, and how hard was it for him to get a gig. He said, "You can't do what I did before. I used to, before I could afford a trio, go to places and see where I'd want to work, and I'd ask if I could play during dinner. For example, I'd tell the owner that I'd help their business; sometimes I was surprised, they'd say yes. Everything has changed; you don't have the kind of places or kind of audiences we had. Everything has changed. There were neighborhood places, for example, on the Lower East Side. I'd play joints and had no idea how I got some of the jobs."

In terms of keeping a gig, Billy also quoted Art Blakey: "People see you before they hear you. It's up to you; where you want to go and what you want to do. Be aware of the fact that there is an audience; you have to smile; you have to make me want to listen to you play. Being serious and only playing won't get you a gig or help you keep it."

Eric Reed said, "One has to know how to play the gig and know what it requires. I start to think outside the box. I have to look at my scope of skills."

To be professional is to be responsible. To cancel is a problem, and some musicians are notorious for doing that. They double-book themselves or take a better paying gig at the last minute. I shy away from hiring people who are not leaders because a sideman, working to be a leader, might take a higher paying gig after he agreed to perform for me. This happened once, and I have yet to feel comfortable hiring that musician. As a leader, Eric Reed is often faced with this problem: "I constantly deal with that—people who double-book, people who don't take care of business. I've never done that as a sideman. If I'm gonna cancel, I give the leader enough time to find someone else. If for some reason I were to miss a flight, I would send someone else and pay that person. This is not cool, but I know A-team musicians who do it (double-book, miss flights). I believe you have a three-month period to cancel a gig, but a week before is not cool. A month before is also a drag."

Tardiness

As Eric Reed said, to be on time is to be late. I hired a musician who was notorious for being late, so I warned his manager to make sure that he got there on time. He got there, but his drummer showed up ten minutes before the show was to begin. It was unsettling to both the artist and me. Given that anything can happen on the way to the job, you should allow yourself time to arrive at the venue at least one hour ahead of the scheduled time of the rehearsal and/or the gig. In my experience, I have found, too often, that artists do not plan travel time properly, which has resulted in my having to start programs an hour later.

When I have that experience, I do not invite them back, no matter how good they are. But I have noticed that performers who are tardy are usually not very good.

"I work with young people at the Kennedy Center, and when I was at Jazzmobile, I share that with people, [don't be late] is a good message to send. People want to like entertainment," said Billy Taylor. Eric Reed says, "In the jazz world, being on time is important, but I imagine that for the Rolling Stones, timeliness is not high on their list, and that any time they show up is cool. They are expected to be late; the audience seems to expect that and would be disappointed if there was not some confusion or chaos in that world."

Approach/Attitude

How performers carry themselves before the date is important. Be professional. For example, return contracts as soon as you can; don't make the presenter hunt you down to get them. If you need a lot of attention, and constantly bother the presenter with phone or e-mailed queries, the tone of the actual event may be unpleasant. Do not call and give progress reports on how rehearsals are going and how excited you are to get the job; no one cares. When you are hired, we expect you to show up on time and get the job done. For this reason, I shy away from hiring performers who I consider to be the B-team. One experience that made me feel good was when I hired Cedar Walton, an A-team player, to perform at The Newark Museum. He sent his photo and bio right away, he followed up on what he had promised to follow up on, showed up on time for the sound check, finished before the people arrived, sat and relaxed until showtime, and gave a wonderful performance.

An artist can tarnish his reputation with a presenter due to his attitude. For example, I hired a guy to headline the jazz series at The Newark Museum. He did not send back the contract in a timely manner. I had seen him out several times, and even called his agent, but the contract never came. When I explained that he would not get paid the day of the event, his agent called me and asked me to resend the contract because the artist had lost it. Because he was the headliner, he was asked to do a radio interview. He did not seem eager to do it, and when he was on the air, the announcer said, "You will be at The Newark Museum tomorrow at what time?" The artist said, on the air, "Gee, I don't know, I was hoping that you would tell me." This made me look like a fool, as though *I* had not told him. The day of the performance, he said to me, "I did not know that an interview was a part of the gig." He had confessed on the air that he almost did not make it because he had an important studio session with a well-known producer. What struck me as odd is that musicians clamor to get radio interviews, but he did not seem to think it was important. He, too, is someone whom I would think twice about before hiring again.

Honesty is the best policy. When I consulted at The Newark Museum, I would contact the musicians, negotiate the fees, and send out the contracts. At times, the woman I worked with would insist that I hire certain musicians. One musician in particular is not one I would have hired on my own, but I followed through. In the past, she had hired him directly, but I made it clear to him that I was the conduit. I sent the contract, and then I went on a trip. Upon my return, the woman told me that the musician had called her directly and asked for more money so that he could bring another musician. There was no message on my phone that he had called me, though as a matter of protocol, she should have sent him back to me to make the request. She agreed to give him the extra money, but the night of the event, which she did not attend, he came to the gig *minus* the extra musician, but got paid the higher fee because the check had already been cut and she was not there to protest. What he should have done was to call me and let me go back to her for approval. Perhaps he thought it best to go straight to the source, but now I have her job, and I have not forgotten the experience.

A bad attitude can work against you. "Some people have chosen to be embittered and unsuccessful; not to say that one can choose to be successful. I think there are some people who are constantly retooling what they do in order to have some kind of impact on the scene. Then there are those who have dropped anchor with their idea of what the industry should be. When things do not happen to their advantage, they put everything and everyone down. I don't have any time for that; complain and see if that will get you a gig," said James Browne.

Kenny Washington told me years ago that he believed that his attitude was keeping him from work. When I asked him about that, he laughed long and hard. He replied, "Funny thing, James Williams would joke with me by saying that Lewis Nash would get the calls that they thought about calling me for. If I did not like the music, I'd say it, or they could see the look on my face. Had I wanted to, I could play anything. *If* I don't like the music, I won't do it. Nash had more patience than me, so that makes him much smarter than me. At this point in my career, I don't really care! Actually I am getting worse. I thought that when I got to be forty, I'd cool out. I'm worse because there is more nonsense out here. Now I don't care what anyone thinks of me, I'm a nice guy. When I leave this earth, what I want people to remember me for is, 'Well, I hired him for this gig, and he took care of business.' "

Some situations call for you to be assertive, just as Michael Wolff was with Cal Tjader. The day he got fired at Fantasy, Michael was walking around the halls when he spotted Cal Tjader. "I was walking around Fantasy Records, and I saw Cal, whom I recognized. I said, 'Let me introduce myself,' and I said, 'I'm Michael Wolff, and I'm ready to play in your band.' (I was cocky; I was eighteen or nineteen), and he said, 'Well, I'll be playing at El Matador in San Francisco (which was considered *the* jazz club); come sit in.' So, I went and sat in, and I worked out. So that's how I got the gig."

To have a positive attitude is essential. It worked for Gerald Cannon, who overcame a drug habit. When he returned to New York City, he had to repair his reputation. Eventually he landed a gig with Roy Hargrove: "I went after the gig with Roy. The first time, in New York, I stayed three years, and those were the most exciting years of my life—music was everywhere. We played in the subway, everywhere. I loved it! That is what is missing from the young cats—they did not have to do any of that. When I came back, it was Buddy Montgomery who brought me back. I had done gigs with Dexter Gordon, Freddie Hubbard, Art Blakey for a minute. I had been caught in the *avant-garde* side, Hamiet Bluiett and others, but I did not like it. I was bitter when I came back the third time because people did not trust me, people did not act like they knew me. I had never been high on the gig, only after, so that is what probably saved me. People think that one's life is over when you do drugs, but you never know. Roy Hargrove heard me and told me I was what he needed. . . . I've always been self-motivated. I always wanted to do this. When I got out of rehabilitation, I thought that I should put my own group together, and I found out I was good at it. I could negotiate, and I was a good leader, but you have to wait for the time to be right, and you have to have something to offer."

I have heard of musicians going behind the back of a leader to get that gig for themselves. That does not bode well for one who does that, or for the proprietor who hires that person. As I say, what is done for you can be done *to* you. Bobby Sanabria told a funny story about trying to get a gig at a club: "Max Roach saw me at a jazz club once. He was listening to the music as I was trying to get a gig at the club, and Max said to me, 'If I was in your situation, it would behoove me to patronize the establishment and buy a drink.' That was a lesson."

Persistence does not always pay off, so you must intuit when to leave people alone. James Browne says, "I have given gigs to musicians who have been consistently assertive, but there are others who can call me forever, and I won't hire them. I choose what I want to sell. You can't go to Barney's and ask them why they won't sell cornflakes. I have said to musicians that there is nothing that says, 'equal opportunity'; this is a business. I've never gone to a musician and asked, why don't you have such-and-such in your band? They would not take kindly to that."

Eric Reed summed it up when he talked about Ulysses Owens: "I still get excited listening to extremely talented young musicians. I recently worked with a drummer—Ulysses Owens—in his twenties, who had given me great hope and great exceptions. He is a beautiful person, has a beautiful attitude, he's a consummate professional, and he plays his ass off. Those types of musicians are so rare. Some musicians have horrible attitudes and act as though they are doing you a favor by playing with *you!*"

Bring an Audience

It is naïve to think that you do not have to cultivate a following. As great a musician you might be or think that you are, if you don't get people in the seats, you might not be asked back. The club owner needs to make money, period! I encounter musicians who look down on having to get people in the seats. They think that it is not their job to get the people in. I have seen musicians become incensed when the audience is limited, and they blame the proprietor. This is absurd, and, I hate to say, a B-team attitude. A relatively unknown musician came to my attention. I really enjoyed his CD, and I reached out to offer him suggestions on how he could be more noticed. He has a wonderful instrument and the potential to get a lot of recognition. Through a series of e-mails, I inquired if he had made certain contacts. His response to one of my suggestions was, "No. That's not a bad idea, although I've kind of steered away from the bring-your-own-crowd rooms."

As a businessman, James Browne takes exception to that point of view. "What I think is universal about the industry is that the music scene has changed since 9/11. It is rebuilding itself since then, and there are other changes in the last couple of years. Musicians have more of the success/failure ratio in their hands than ever before. That's the good news. The bad news is that there is more competition. There are more things vying for their attention of potential customers that they have to become more focused on what they do. You just can't only be a musician anymore; that is naïve. The fact that someone is a virtuoso does not mean anything anymore, because of the Internet and the impact of word-of-mouth marketing. I love musicians with decent-size followings that they build up themselves. They don't get played on the radio, don't get written about, but they find ways to market themselves. This has an impact on me as a businessman. I want to bring people in who bring people in. I have had the experience of sitting by myself, and the bartender and two waitresses listening to brilliant music, but we are the only ones listening. As a business person, that does not do anything for me."

You must take an active part in all aspects of your career. For more details on promotion, see chapter 17.

Be Versatile

Billy Taylor, David Randolph, and Kenny Washington used radio to bring attention to music, to themselves, and gain musical knowledge. One of Kenny Washington's teachers, Mel Lewis, told him, "If you want to be successful in this business, you have to be adaptable; you have to learn to play different styles." Olu Dara saw that firsthand: "I know some musicians who will turn down a good-paying job because it is not what they do. They'll say no because 'I only play jazz.' Some musicians are ashamed to play different kinds of music. For example, I know some musicians, drummers especially, who will turn down a job because it's a funk record or gig. They don't want to be known as a funk player or be associated with those people." During the interview, he told me that his life and his audience have not changed with the success of his famous rapper son, Nas.

Olu and I talked about a month after our interview, and he announced to me, "Things have all changed since we talked. I'm a hip hopper now! I got me a new fan base. My son and me did a song together ['Bridging the Gap'], and since then, my phone has been ringing off the hook. The whole shit changed in the last week. It feels *great*! I'm having fun; the hip-hop world has been wanting to meet me, and now I'm hanging with them; they call me Pops, I'm a lead man! Our song was groundbreaking. I'm singing the blues, and he is hip hopping off of the blues, a Muddy Waters type thing. I play instruments on the back, the harmonica, the trumpet, the guitar on it, and they have other musicians and a scratch man. We did it nouveau and oldveus." Olu laughed a big laugh.

Oscar Brown Jr. said, "Yeah, getting work the whole time—that's been the problem! I get a lot of Red, Black, and Green work. I went into schools. I was artist in residence at Howard University. I've done stuff at Chicago State, at Malcolm X College in Chicago, and later in life, I got hired at Drew University and the University of California at Riverside as a regent professor, but they did not want me to do anything. I think they regretted bringing me, and I got fired for functioning. I'd rather be out here doing it. I just did a [musical], *Great Nitty Gritty*; it [opened] twenty years ago and it got great press, but Jane Byrne had lost the election and her predecessor, Harold Washington, did not want to fund anything Jane had done."

Dorothy Lawson and Paula Kimper, too, have taken risks. I asked Dorothy what musical demands were placed on her to play with Ron Carter, and if she had to change *how* she played. She replied, "*No*, I don't have to change anything he writes, with such an empathy for the full cello sound, I think that is what he wants. Phrasing inside his music is more rhythmically propelled than a lot of classical music is. I feel tempted and provoked to explore different ways of accenting the rhythms and jazzy melodies than if I was playing classical music."

Joe Grushecky successfully carved a niche for himself in Pittsburgh by bucking the union. "I moved into the house in Pittsburgh on July 10, 1976. Pittsburgh was a very pivotal town for jazz, and a lot of show people in the forties and fifties came through. It was a real union town; the musicians' union was fairly strong so the bars were union gigs. The sets were forty minutes on and twenty minutes break, with four sets per night; that was it. One did not come out with four sets of original music. We would get to the first bar, doing our thing of a mixture of covers like John Lee Hooker, Bob Dylan, B. B. King, Lou Reed, and some obscure stuff of the day. We tried to find songwriters not known. To flesh out the night, we had gone through the top-forty list, and in the middle of the night, we looked at each other and said, 'We are the world's worst copy band,' and we were fired that night. We had no desire to do their music, and it showed; it was a terrible night.

"We figured out ways to get around this dilemma, so we decided to do one set of cool covers like blues, rhythm and blues, and one set of original material. Within a year we had more, about one hour and fifteen minutes, so we told people we would not do four sets but two one-hour sets. We broke ground here. There was one place in the city where we could play, but the guy sold the place. We got hired at this club called Decade, and the guy really loved us. This whole scene developed around us. We packed the club two nights a week."

Part Six Self-Evaluation:
Do You Have What It Takes?

This is designed to assist you in determining the areas you will need to work on if you are going to succeed as a musician. As I pointed out in the introduction, you must have a combination of technique (technology), ethics, and business savvy (administration) to make it; and all three together must equal 100 percent. Answer honestly and have some fun.

1) In past performances:
   a. I have managed to give 100 percent when I knew it was important
   b. I have always given my best when I could, but have dropped the ball on a few performances
   c. I have given more than 100 percent at just about every performance
   d. I have given an average or below average performance more than I would like to admit

2) When I perform:
   a. I always dress to impress
   b. I dress in what I am comfortable with
   c. I dress according to the venue I am playing in
   d. I wear whatever is clean

3) In the past, when a leader has asked me to fill in with a band, I:
   a. Found out what music he would be playing and learned it
   b. Waited for him to send music to me
   c. Hoped he'd ask me what I wanted to play
   d. Told him my fee and that he should call my manager

4) You're a singer and you bump into a musician you've never met, but would like to work with. You:
   a. Say, "Hey, how come you never call me for gigs?"
   b. Start talking bad about other singers
   c. Run down a list of things that you've done
   d. Tell the musician that you admire his work and let him know that you would love the chance to work with him at some point

5) When I have gone to hear musicians who I admire and would like to play with I have:
   a. Approached the leader while he's on the side of the stage and asked to sit in
   b. Suggested that he fire one of his sidemen and hire me
   c. Asked the musician whose instrument I play if he would mind if I asked the leader to sit in
   d. Sat at the bar and talked about how the sideman can't play as well as you

6) You're a young bassist and you meet Ron Carter. You:
   a. Ask him how you can get a record deal
   b. Ask him about good managers
   c. Ask him for free lessons
   d. None of the above

7) You're a musician who's been on the scene for a short time, but you're not working much. You:
   a. Figure out a way to become a better musician so people will call you
   b. Blame everybody for not calling you, coming to the conclusion that they are conspiring against you
   c. Keep waiting around for the phone to ring
   d. Complain about other players who work more than you, but don't play as well

8) You bump into a radio announcer. You:
   a. Ask, "How come I never hear my music on the radio?"
   b. Thank the DJ for playing good music
   c. Tell him you don't listen to the radio
   d. Complain about the format of the station

9) You're a female musician and you bump into Frank Foster. You:
   a. Tell him he should hire more women in his band
   b. Complain that the jazz world is sexist
   c. Decide to become such a good musician that people will have no choice but to hire you.
   d. Tell him about all of the great women musicians on the scene

10) When at a rehearsal, it is okay to:
   a. Turn your cell phone off
   b. Show up late and leave early

c. Fall asleep

d. Never take notes or make corrections, even when instructed to do so

11) In past performances as a sideman, I have:
   a. Played with my eyes closed and miss cues, etc.
   b. Done my best to support the entire band
   c. Played my parts wrong, never trying to correct it
   d. Paid attention only to my part

12) As a budding jazz musician in the learning mode (i.e., school vs. work), you will:
   a. Choose knowledge acquired via a degree or not
   b. Work a regular 9–5 job, do music on the side, and complain that you did not get your break
   c. Abandon your dream to work as a musician and become a critic
   d. None of the above

13) You made your decision to be a full time musician:
   a. You learn everything about your instrument and as much music as you can
   b. You disregard the advice of others already working on how to proceed
   c. You incorporate musical information from the past into your vision of the future to create something new
   d. You decide that your ideas are more progressive then others before you and get busy

14) You decide that you have natural talent, so you:
   a. Begin to play anywhere you can get work
   b. You take private lessons in music or your instrument
   c. Find ways to learn all that you can and seek others who can help you
   d. Find a niche and stay there and wonder why you cannot go further

15) You begin working in one genre but get asked to perform in another one. You:
   a. Say that you can't make the change and thank them for thinking of you
   b. Study the language of the other genre and apply your skills to that musical situation
   c. Accept the opportunity and force your musical idea on that situation
   d. Take the job, find you prefer that type of music and get good at it

16) You have new music to learn for a gig, so you:
    a. Spend many hours playing scales
    b. Learn the music though and through
    c. Look it over, play a little, put it down until the gig
    d. Wait until the day of the gig to practice so that the music will be fresh

17) When a member of the ensemble is taking a solo, you:
    a. Turn your back to the audience
    b. Leave the stage
    c. Listen and encourage what he is doing
    d. Go hang out at the bar until they are all finished

18) Before the gig when the audience is seated, you:
    a. Noodle at the side of the stage
    b. Confer with the musicians about the order of songs and the performance
    c. Hang out at the bar until it is time to go on
    d. Do a quick mic check

19) Your current gig does not pay well, so you:
    a. Complain to the audience how few people are there
    b. Perform as though the house was filled
    c. Delay the start time to wait for more people to come
    d. Do a short set

20) You take another gig that does not pay well, so you:
    a. Tell the audience that you are not making much money so don't expect a good show
    b. Fill the audience to show the club owner that you want to come back for more money
    c. Show up a few minutes before the gig and tell the presenter that you only show up early when you make more money and are offered food.
    d. None of the above

21) Something unforeseen has happened and you have to cancel a gig at the last minute. You:
    a. Tell the presenter that you are sorry
    b. Offer a replacement of equal stature

c. Try to work out another date

d. All of the above

22) There is a big event where you know luminaries will attend, so you:

a. Show up, stand outside, and hand out your flyers

b. Buy a ticket and attend

c. Crash the event and hit up as many people as you can to support your project

d. Stay home

23) You are beginning your career as a leader. You:

a. Seek out musicians with more experience than you and learn from them

b. Look for musicians you know you can afford who have as much knowledge and experience as you

c. You offer your music to people with whom you work as a sideman

d. Continue to seek work as a sideman to hone your craft

24) When you are hired for a performance, you:

a. Make sure that you have a contract detailing everything that you want

b. Give regular updates to the presenter on how rehearsals are going

c. Confirm that you will be there one week in advance

d. Don't bother to send back the contract until asked, then make last minute demands

25) When you see an industry person who you have not seen in a long time, you:

a. Say hello, and let him know where you have been working since you last met

b. Tell him how great you are

c. Ask him how he's been

d. Wait for him to ask you what you have been up to

26) When practicing to improve your musicianship, do you:

a. Systematically pursue an idea day after day until it becomes part of your musical vocabulary?

b. Know that too much practice will only prove to destroy your personal creative process?

c. Not finish ideas and find it hard to use under pressure at the gig?

d. Not practice at all because you consider that you are already at the top of your musical game?

27) After a performance, do you:
   a. Remember the areas that you didn't do so well and rush home to practice them?
   b. Just wait til the next night and try to play that spot better?
   c. Hear no flaws, therefore no practice or consideration is needed?
   d. Just apply effortless mastery and overcome that which you haven't played well yet?

28) When in conversation with others about your playing, do you:
   a. Tend to dominate the conversation about yourself and what you have done?
   b. Have the feeling that no one really hears what you're playing because they don't immediately give you a gig?
   c. Diplomatically, when appropriate, tell about yourself without dominating the conversation?
   d. Try to top every story being told?

29) After you record a new project, do you:
   a. Play your own music at home to yourself over and over again?
   b. Never tell anyone about your new musical project or goal until the right time?
   c. Carry it around and hand it to every industry person?
   d. Look for the best way to promote the music and your band?

30) Have you ever:
   a. Made calls to everyone you know, talked about yourself and asked for gigs?
   b. Thought to give others work as a means of getting work?
   c. Taken work from another musician or said something derogatory about that musician so that you could get the gig he or she had?
   d. Called a presenter and told him that it is time for him to hire you again?

Now add up your points:

1. $a = 2$ $b = 3$ $c = 4$ $d = 1$	16. $a = 1$ $b = 4$ $c = 3$ $d = 2$
2. $a = 4$ $b = 2$ $c = 3$ $d = 1$	17. $a = 2$ $b = 3$ $c = 4$ $d = 1$
3. $a = 4$ $b = 2$ $c = 1$ $d = 3$	18. $a = 3$ $b = 4$ $c = 2$ $d = 1$
4. $a = 2$ $b = 1$ $c = 3$ $d = 4$	19. $a = 2$ $b = 4$ $c = 3$ $d = 1$
5. $a = 3$ $b = 1$ $c = 4$ $d = 2$	20. $a = 2$ $b = 4$ $c = 3$ $d = 1$
6. $a = 1$ $b = 2$ $c = 3$ $d = 4$	21. $a = 1$ $b = 3$ $c = 2$ $d = 4$
7. $a = 4$ $b = 1$ $c = 3$ $d = 2$	22. $a = 1$ $b = 4$ $c = 2$ $d = 3$
8. $a = 3$ $b = 4$ $c = 1$ $d = 2$	23. $a = 4$ $b = 1$ $c = 2$ $d = 3$
9. $a = 2$ $b = 1$ $c = 4$ $d = 3$	24. $a = 4$ $b = 1$ $c = 3$ $d = 2$
10. $a = 4$ $b = 3$ $c = 1$ $d = 2$	25. $a = 2$ $b = 1$ $c = 4$ $d = 3$
11. $a = 1$ $b = 4$ $c = 2$ $d = 3$	26. $a = 4$ $b = 2$ $c = 1$ $d = 3$
12. $a = 4$ $b = 1$ $c = 2$ $d = 3$	27. $a = 4$ $b = 2$ $c = 1$ $d = 3$
13. $a = 3$ $b = 1$ $c = 4$ $d = 2$	28. $a = 3$ $b = 2$ $c = 4$ $d = 1$
14. $a = 2$ $b = 3$ $c = 4$ $d = 1$	29. $a = 3$ $b = 4$ $c = 1$ $d = 2$
15. $a = 1$ $b = 4$ $c = 2$ $d = 3$	30. $a = 3$ $b = 4$ $c = 2$ $d = 1$

100–120 points **A-TEAM**

Congratulations! You have what it takes to be successful. Keep working at your craft.

80–99 **B-TEAM**

Don't fret, you can reach the A-team if you desire, just look at some of your answers and see where you might want to do some work on the areas where you did not score a '4.'

79 and below **NO TEAM**

Perhaps it is time to take a good look at yourself and if you really have what it takes to succeed as a musician. If you love music you might consider finding another avenue for yourself that will be more promising. As a working musician, it's up to you whether you want to continue.

INDEX

Index

Books from Allworth Press

Allworth Press is an imprint of Allworth Communications, Inc. Selected titles are listed below.

The Quotable Musician: From Bach to Tupac
by Sheila E. Anderson (hardcover, 7 1/2 × 7 1/2, 224 pages, $19.95)

Creative Careers in Music, Second Edition
by Josquin des Pres and Mark Landsman (paperback, 6 × 9, 240 pages, $19.95)

Career Solutions for Creative People: How to Balance Artistic Goals with Career Security
by Dr. Ronda Ormont (paperback, 6 × 9, 320 pages, $19.95)

Gigging: A Practical Guide for Musicians
by Patricia Shih (paperback, 6 × 9, 256 pages, $19.95)

Rock Star 101: A Rock Star's Guide to Survival and Success in the Music Business
by Marc Ferrari (paperback, 6 × 9, 176 pages, $14.95)

Making It in the Music Business: The Business and Legal Guide for Songwriters and Performers, Third Edition
by Lee Wilson (paperback, 6 × 9, 256 pages, $19.95)

Making and Marketing Music: The Musician's Guide to Financing, Distributing, and Promoting Albums, Second Edition
by Jodi Summers (paperback, 6 × 9, 240 pages, $19.95)

The Secrets of Songwriting: Leading Songwriters Reveal How to Find Inspiration and Success
by Susan Tucker (paperback, 6 × 9, 256 pages, $19.95)

The Art of Writing Great Lyrics
by Pamela Phillips Oland (paperback, 6 × 9, 272 pages, $18.95)

The Songwriter's and Musician's Guide to Nashville, Third Edition
by Sherry Bond (paperback, 6 × 9, 256 pages, $19.95)

Please write to request our free catalog. To order by credit card, call 1-800-491-2808 or send a check or money order to Allworth Press, 10 East 23rd Street, Suite 510, New York, NY 10010. Include $5 for shipping and handling for the first book ordered and $1 for each additional book. Ten dollars plus $1 for each additional book if ordering from Canada. New York State residents must add sales tax.

To see our complete catalog on the World Wide Web, or to order online, you can find us at
www.allworth.com.